THE PEARSALL GUIDE TO SUCCESSFUL DOG TRAINING

At heart of the Pearsall training methods is a constant awareness of what we are asking of the dog. Here a class literally sees signals from the dog's point of view.

THE PEARSALL GUIDE TO SUCCESSFUL DOG TRAINING

Obedience
"from the dog's point of view"

by
MARGARET E. PEARSALL

Technical Advisor:
MILO D. PEARSALL

Third Edition
Fifth Printing—1986

HOWELL BOOK HOUSE Inc.
230 Park Avenue, New York, N. Y. 10169

Printed in U. S. A.

Library of Congress Cataloging in Publication Data
Pearsall, Margaret E
The Pearsall guide to successful dog training.

1. Dogs—Training. I. Title.
SF431.P37 1980 636.7'0887 80-16840
ISBN 0-87605-759-8

To Milo,

without whose imagination, keen and alert observation, instinctive insight into human behavior, ability to look at situations from "the dog's point of view" and a never-ending concern for our canine pals, this book and all of its ideas would never have come into being.

Milo and Margaret Pearsall and their Labrador Retriever "Tuffy" await the start of a Tracking Test

Contents

In Appreciation

I WISH to express my thanks to all who contributed toward the realization of this book—some with pictures of their trained companions, some with ideas submitted at our problem clinics or obedience instructor schools, and the friends who helped by typing the manuscript.

I particularly want to thank Mr. Ken Downs, whose talent is seen in the sketches, diagrams and "ghosted" signal pictures. Appreciation is also due the American Kennel Club for permission to include sections taken from the official "Obedience Regulations".

Some are no longer here to accept our gratitude. Without the help at home of my dear mother, Milo and I would not have been free to pursue, side by side over the years, our hobby of dog obedience training. We owe her much.

We are especially indebted to a very dear friend whose memory we shall always cherish, Eugenia Buxton Whitnel, who passed away in May 1972 before she could see her lovely photography doing a splendid job of helping tell our story. In her home city of Memphis, Tennessee, she will be long remembered for her dedication to the welfare of homeless animals.

The tremendous strides that Dick D'Ambrisi had made in his all too short months as first Obedience Director at the American Kennel Club only serve to point up how great a loss his passing means. He was not only a cherished friend, but his suggestions and encouragements are well reflected in this book.

And a word too for "Ronnie" (Ch. Jonlin's Saffron, C.D.), the Pembroke Welsh Corgi that was my dear companion for nearly seven years. It was she who first pointed up to us the importance, from the dog's point of view, of the nylon training collars, one of the greatest forward steps toward the cause for humane, logical training methods.

TO the many who have expressed their patience (and their IMpatience) waiting for this book, I hope this fulfills all expectations. This is a goal I have long wanted to reach—bringing a humane concept to the dog obedience training field, and some enlightenment to many who have not realized the importance of "the other end of the leash". The team of a dog and his own particular human working beautifully together well exemplifies the old maxim, "It takes two to make a bargain". But remember, the depth of that union is controlled and directed by the human part of the team. Let us all accept our responsibility and live up to what our dogs think of us!

—Margaret E. Pearsall

Companions

Preface

IN virtually every endeavor today, there is the aim for healthy progress—away from stagnancy or retrogression—moving ever forward. Coursing the way for this progress is a never-ending research for new theories, new methods, and new processes, and the proving of the fruits of these researches in practical application.

Especially has this been true of education. Our school systems are larger and better, teaching methods have been studied and improved, and teaching aids have been devised and utilized to make learning processes more effective and more enjoyable.

My husband and I have tried to adopt, over a period of many years, this same approach to the subject of training of dogs. When, in 1944, we started our first dog in obedience training (a five-months-old Cocker Spaniel, "Pearsall's Black Charger," trained by Milo), there was only one way to train and nobody questioned it. The theory was *"complete master dominance"*, and the tools were a heavy chain collar, a heavy lead with a big bolt snap, and plenty of muscle and voice so you could yank the lead and yell at your dog to make him do what you wanted.

It is sad to have to note that there are still many in this country who have remained in this same rut, teaching and training the same way they were taught many years ago, and never giving any consideration to how the *dog* feels.

After Milo and I got into the teaching field, with obedience training classes, challenging problems were always raising their ugly heads.

But, somehow, with imagination and ingenuity, they were generally resolved.

The success in our own classes, coupled with the many requests from other people and clubs asking advice and help, led to the writing of "Dog Obedience Training," published in September, 1958.

It was around this time that Milo was first invited to travel to help a club with their training. That trip, the first "clinic," could be written as a story in itself. But the most important thing, in regard to this "first," was that from it developed other requests for training clinics. And each clinic, in turn, proved to be fertile for yielding still more requests for them.

It has been chiefly due to the opportunity of being exposed to so many dogs, so many dog problems, so many results of poor teaching and training and lack of understanding, all over the country, that the methods and ideas contained in this book have been developed. Since retiring in March, 1963 from regular employment, still more time and study has been concentrated in this training field, including the addition of five-day Instructor Schools. Here we really get down to tearing things apart and putting them back together again, trying to analyze, diagnose and prescribe, always with the "dog's viewpoint" uppermost in our consideration.

But problems, as such, were not our primary point of attack. We realized that if some prevention treatment could be found, then problems would be minimal and both dogs and handlers would emerge as happy and natural "Companion Unions."

There was just one answer to this—earlier training, coupled with methods of teaching and showing the dogs the "right" way, with no "wrong" way habits being allowed to develop. Fortunately for us, the results of the research studies that Mr. Clarence Pfaffenberger did at Jackson Laboratory at Bar Harbor, Maine, were published about this time and made available to the public in the book *"New Knowledge of Dog Behavior."* (Howell Book House, NYC.) Then the question came, "Why not organize a program for teaching puppies and take advantage of their receptive capabilities at this age?"

The immense prospects that such a curriculum might offer was impressed upon us still further when we were privileged to visit the Guide Dog School for the Blind at San Rafael, California, on a "Puppy Testing Day," held once a week on Thursdays. We discussed our ideas for a course on Kindergarten Puppy Training (K. P. T.) and immediately received the backing of "Dear Pfaff" and also of the executive director of the school, William (Bill) Johns. After doing some re-writing, a copy of the K. P. T. Guide for Instructors was sent to each of them and both complimented us and endorsed it completely.

The Guide has been exceptionally well received, and is bringing benefit all over the country with "graduates" being unusually well behaved and adjusted pupils in Novice or Beginners classes.

Many breeders and handlers have also experienced outstanding results with showing Kindergarten trained puppies in conformation, or breed, competition at the dog shows. This same Kindergarten training constitutes the first chapter of this book on training your dog.

What better way, then, to take advantage of it, than to get your puppy out and get ready to work and play together? Let's go!

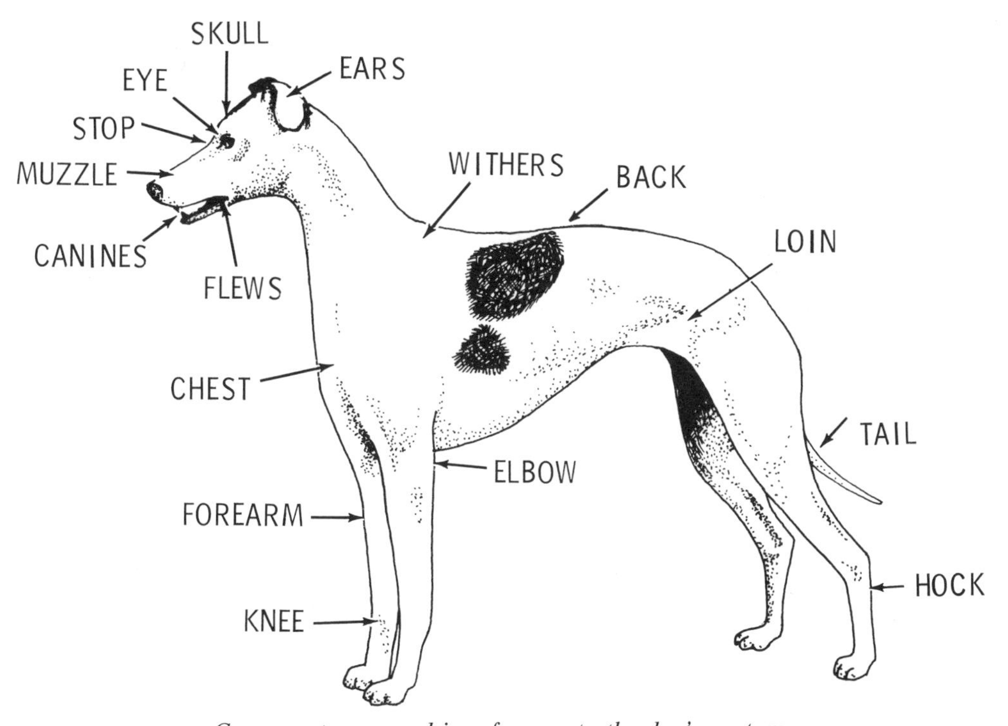

Common terms used in reference to the dog's anatomy

Group of juniors with puppies receiving instruction at dog level

K.P.T.

"KINDERGARTEN PUPPY TRAINING" is as important for our two-to-five months old puppies as is nursery school and kindergarten for our three-to-six year old children. With proper presentation, supervision and application, your puppy can learn as he grows, and with your help he will become an obedient, well-schooled, happy companion. It will be a pleasure to have him with you, at home or traveling, indoors or out.

In presenting K.P.T. as the first chapter in this training textbook, which emphasizes always the training from the "dog's point of view", we want to particularly stress the importance of socialization and guided play and activity during the most impressionable period of your canine pal's life, when he is from two to five months old. The validity of this has been proven not only in research, but in actual practise by many breeders and individual dog owners.

But one word of caution. Please do not expect your puppy, at five or six months of age, to be under the same type of control and as obedient in a formal way as a mature, trained dog. Just as in a school kindergarten for children, your teaching should take the form of *guided play,* nothing more serious than that.

Upon first acquiring your cute little (or big!) bundle of cuddly fur, you are faced with two projects immediately, to be tackled simultaneously. One of these is to choose a name for him and teach him that name; the other is to housebreak him.

Looking over their world

There are several things to consider in selecting this name, as you will be using it for the rest of his life, in play, training and general companionship. Every time you speak his name you will expect attention from him. It should be an easy name to say, yet one that does not sound similar to any of the commands you will be teaching him. It could be quite confusing to teach him the difference between "Neal" and "Heel," "Shea" and "Stay", "Lum" and "Come", "Rover" and "Over," etc. Other commands that you might be teaching are "Sit," "Stand," "Wait," "Jump," "Down," "Bring," "Hup," "Fetch," "Get It," etc. This should give you a pretty good idea of the sounds to avoid. Once you have decided upon a name, be sure you are consistent with its use all the time. Throughout the book we will be using the call name of "Buddy."

Housebreaking

As for housebreaking, we will detail only one method but it is the one that has brought us the greatest and most satisfactory success. Thus, it is the one we recommend to everyone. It also has some excellent fringe benefits along the way, as many other problems never develop if it is done correctly at the beginning. It involves the use of a collapsible wire crate, large enough to comfortably house your pal when he has grown to his full size at maturity, as this will actually serve as his bed right from the beginning, his home base, so to speak.

If you are sincere, consistent and patient, you should have excellent results within a reasonably short time. Don't expect too much from the baby as he needs a bit of aging to allow his organs to develop and and become strong. It also will be necessary to establish a regular schedule (by the *clock*) for his daily activities. In fact, don't be surprised if he sets the schedule for *you* to follow. Even though you may need to be away at work during the day, as long as you come home as early as possible and at the same time each day, the puppy will soon adjust to it.

First, select the location for the crate. If possible, place it in a room which has an outside exit that you will be using to take him out to his exercise area (always the same during the training period.) Usually the kitchen is the most practical as the floor surface offers easier cleanup in case of accidents, and it will be a rare case if none occur. It also is usually a smaller floor space than the other rooms and you will be able to keep your eye on the pup as you busy yourself around him. By the same token, your activities occupy his attention and keep him amused, as well as giving him a sense of security while you are nearby. Put the crate in a spot that is more or less out of the way, yet accessible for ease of cleaning and feeding. Cover the floor around the crate and leading to the exit door with layers of newspaper (inexpensive and easy to procure, except if you happen to get caught in the throes of a newspaper strike!)

You are now ready to introduce the new member of the family to his temporary home and his bed. If you should happen to be away at work during the day, make an all-out effort to start this training on the weekend or your days off. Let him investigate his new surroundings, smell the paper, his new bed (crate), and around the room. If he should relieve himself on the paper, don't make a big issue of it. Just pick up the papers, clean it up, disinfect and replace the soiled papers with clean ones. Introduce him to the crate, close the door, give him a toy for play and company and leave him there for a half hour or so. Offer him water, but don't wait long after he has a drink before you let him out, walking

Pup in crate in kitchen, papers on floor

Pup at kitchen door, asking "out"

toward the door and calling his name. Go outside with him and take him to his "special" area, one that will be fairly easy for you to keep clean. Remain with him until mission is accomplished; give him plenty of praise for what he has done, letting your tone of voice be happy. Then return and put him back in his crate. This crate should become his own private place, where he can sleep, eat, drink and play, as he wishes, with no curbing of his desires. It also should never be used as punishment for a mistake or act of mischief.

Give him his first supper in the crate and his water, letting him come out onto the paper as he wishes, and remove the dishes as soon as he finishes his meal. During the housebreaking period, do not allow him freedom to roam through the other rooms. Watch him for signs and actions that will give you a cue that he is ready to go out. Note how long it was following his finishing his supper. This will help you to establish the habit pattern that will work best for his particular schedule. Any time that *you* fail to get him out in time, be sure to remove the soiled paper and disinfect the spot as soon as possible. Don't scold him, though, when you're to blame and NEVER slap him with a rolled up paper or magazine to punish him. Let him know what you want by encouraging and praising him when he takes care of himself in the proper place, rather than showing your displeasure or anger when he makes a mistake. See that one or more toys are in his crate to induce him back in it when he comes back inside the house.

As his schedule gets more or less routine and he begins to realize what it's all about, start to remove his papers gradually (especially any that bear evidence of an accident), leaving the ones by the door until the very last. If you do have to leave him alone while you go to work, give him only a light meal and drink before your departure. Make sure it is early enough that he has time to take care of himself before you leave. Confine him to his crate while you are away, and also at night for his sleeping, being sure he has toys to amuse himself with. Try to set up a regular time to take him out for his last duty walk before bedtime.

Watch for indications from your pup to let you know that he wants to be let out of the crate, such as whining, crying, barking, etc. You might even start associating a command with his actions, such as "Speak!" Be sure you don't waste any time getting to him as he might be very uncomfortable and, as a general rule, no puppy is going to soil his bed if he can avoid it. Encourage him to let you know his needs, respond to his communication and you are well on your way to having housebreaking under control.

Be sure to follow the advice to remove the papers by the door at the very last and don't be in a hurry to get rid of those. Don't chance going too fast with any of this procedure as it must be geared slowly to coincide with the puppy's reaction, development physically of his ability to control his eliminations, and establishment of habit patterns. But the results can be very rewarding through understanding on your part, patience and consistency in working with him and letting him know how a little cooperation from each of you can bring much happiness to both of you.

In addition, you also will have given him a place of security where he is not banished as punishment, where he can play with his own toys, where he does not have access to any of your possessions to chew up while you're not watching, and where he will not be setting up a howl for the neighbor's ears. He also will be used to a crate in case he may, at some time in the future, have to be confined for a time at a veterinarian's or in a kennel.

Now that you and your puppy are on your way to getting to know each other, and have already accomplished some of the "nursery school" education, let us get on to Kindergarten curriculum.

About the most important thing in the beginning is for you to start to school yourself in your voice control, learning to not show your feeling in your voice, no matter what mood you are in. Maybe your wife just smashed up the car, or your husband has brought the boss home to dinner without warning, or your parents have taken away TV privileges for a week, or perhaps you've just won on your sweepstakes ticket! Just don't let it show in your voice while training.

We can generally classify the voice in four categories:

a. **Coaxing:** Used to excite the pup into doing something.

b. **Happy:** For a job well done, especially after a correction has been applied.

c. **Harsh:** *Never* to be used, even if the pup is slow to learn. *You* just might be the one to blame.

d. **Demanding:** To be used only when you are positive your pup knows what you want but refuses.

All dogs (unless physically handicapped) see and hear and have feelings, so your first concern should be from your pup's point of view. And one very good way to consider him is to form one especially important habit right now. If you smoke, *never* do it while training or playing with

Holding a puppy properly

Recommended position for hands on puppies

your Buddy. A hot ash, accidentally dropped in his eye, could cause irreparable damage.

The proper use of your hands, feet and body are next in importance for you to learn. If you want to pick up your pup, first approach him from the front so he will be able to see what you are about to do. Put one hand under his chest, between his front legs, the other over his body and under the tummy, cradling him in your arms. (See illustration.) Never grab him and lift him with the front legs, as this may have adverse affect on the proper development of the shoulder structure. He may also suffer if you lift him by the scruff of the neck. Start now, too, to teach him that your left hand is for praise and the right is associated with corrections, if and when they might be needed.

Your feet, to your pup, should never be something to fear, so be very careful where you step and how you use them when he is around you. Never, but *never,* use your feet for a correction, no matter what the situation, even though it may seem quicker and easier at the moment.

Your body can be a towering mass for your pup to fear, or, as we hope, it can be his security and something to love. In training, try to visualize everything from his point of view. Therefore, instead of bending over so that you still tower over him, it's much better to squat down and let him see you at the same level he is. There is added benefit here in that it's good for the waistline!

Be careful, too, about how you use your eyes. As crazy as it may seem to you, they can be very upsetting to your pup. Never stare at your Buddy; look over his head or to one side of him. Don't forget that your intentions are transmitted to your pup in many ways, sometimes even in ways that we cannot fathom or explain to our own satisfaction. The bond that develops between the two of you is a great fulfillment and should not be dealt with lightly.

Now that you've been given a few things to think about, let's get started with Buddy. The first order of business is a recommended list of items:

1. Plain flat or round leather collar, buckle type.
2. A piece of clothesline or similar heavy cord, about 1½ times the length of pup's body.
3. A soft, lightweight lead, 4 to 6 ft. long, with a small, lightweight snap.
4. Bright colored solid rubber balls, chosen in proportion to size of pup; gloves, toys.

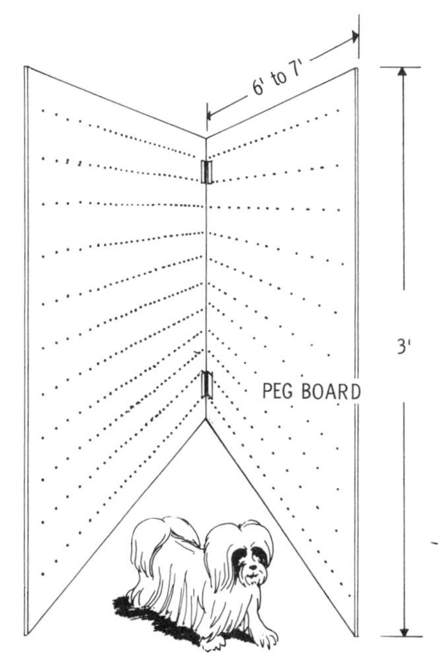

Diagram of a "V"-barrier

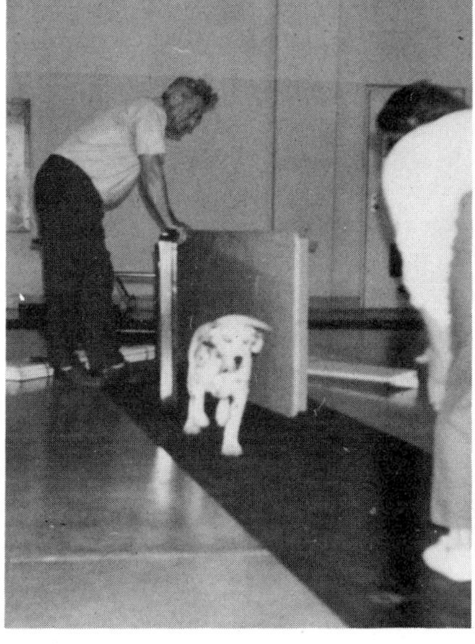
Puppy coming out of "V"-barrier

5. A "V" barrier, or material to make one (see illustration).
6. Two flat pieces of wood, small enough to fit into your hands.
7. Other noise makers, such as a bicycle horn and/or a bell, transistor pocket radio, alarm clock, etc.
8. Metal spoon with bent handle.

The collar should be just loose enough that he cannot pull his head through it. The first time you put it on him, he probably will object to it and will try to figure out some way he can get rid of this new annoyance. Just let him alone and don't give in to him or feel sorry for him, for within a short time he will accept it as something he has to wear. It should take no more than a few hours, at the most, for the new collar to become "old hat" to him. When you feel he is paying no attention to the collar and is quite used to it, you are ready for the next step in his education, that of lead breaking.

On lead control of puppy

Lead Breaking

Take a plain piece of clothesline, or something similar, making sure it is large enough in diameter to achieve the desired effect. The length of this cord should be one and one half the length of your pup's body, with no knot in it to get caught and tangled with anything. Fasten the cord to the ring of the collar and let him go on his merry way but stay where you can supervise him. This can be done either indoors or outdoors.

At first, your pup will be confused, but if you pay no attention to him you will see how quickly he learns to move around, without stepping on the cord. He probably will start by stepping on it, giving himself a jerk on the collar. He may even step on it while running, possibly throwing himself off balance and causing him to stumble. It probably will look silly but don't make the mistake of laughing at him. Just ignore him and let him figure it out for himself. Soon he will learn to avoid stepping on the cord while moving around. He will then be ready for his introduction to walking with a lead attached to the collar, and you following at the end of that lead.

The training lead should be four to six feet long, with a loop for your hand on one end and a small snap on the other to attach to the collar. There are several types available. Personally, we prefer a lightweight webbing lead and a very small spring snap, but you choose what you wish, as long as it is small and lightweight. Rest assured that the less weight there is around his neck, the less confusing this is going to be to him.

The best place to start walking on lead is outdoors, where there is plenty of room to move around. After the lead is snapped onto the collar just stand still and, in a gentle tone of voice, talk to your Buddy. He probably will just stand there and look at you, wondering what is going to happen. Squat down, praise and encourage him and he most likely will start to move. When he does, move with him, being sure the lead is always loose. If he should get the lead tangled around your legs, squat down, laugh and untangle it. Often, after a tangle like this, your pup will wait for *you* to make the next move. If such is the case, take a few steps, calling his name. If he goes with you, fine. But, if he decides to go the other way, *you go with him.*

After repeating a few sessions of this lesson, it is time to teach what a snug lead means. The easiest way is to let him get a short distance away, squat down, call his name, "Buddy, Come!" At the same time, bring him to you by gently folding and shortening the lead. When you do this the first time, don't be upset if he balks or tries to pull away. Keep him coming to you, nevertheless, using a pleasant tone of voice. You will see when he gets closer to you that he understands what you want and will come in by himself. When he does this, lavish praise and affection on him for this has been the first time you have insisted on his doing what *you* wanted, and the first time you had to follow through with a little pressure to accomplish it. Be sure, as you draw your pup to you, that you keep the lead parallel to the ground or floor, no further above it than his collar is. *Do not pull up* on his lead.

Within a day or two, you will find Buddy responding to a snug lead when you turn one way or another. When you decide to change direction, always remember to call your pup's name to let him know what you plan to do. As soon as he responds, let your voice be his praise. Form the habit, too, of always using the lead to take him outdoors and bring him back inside. He will begin to understand that his lead is part of his life, will look forward to seeing you pick it up and will associate it with the fact that you and he are about to do something together.

A little fun game can be introduced here, but it must take place indoors, or in a fenced-in area if outdoors, as your pup will be off lead for this. Perhaps he will appreciate a little diversion from his session on lead. Put him down at one end of the room or yard, praise him, and run a short distance away, clapping your hands and calling his name, getting him to chase you. Turn and face him, squat down, and praise him when he gets to you. This is not only fun and a relief from more serious exercises, it is also a foundation for his wanting to come to you when you call him.

Doors and Stairs

Working along with the lead training, it is most important that you introduce your new little companion to doors. The simplest way to start is to carry him through a few times, going out and coming back in, making sure you talk to him as you open and close the door, keeping his attention on you. The next step will be to put him on the floor, on lead and at your left side. Open the door away from you, then walk through, encouraging him to come with you. If he balks, move ahead of him, turn to face him and squat down, call him and gently make him come to you. Once you have accomplished this, the rest is easy.

Now go to the other side of the door, open it toward you and encourage him to go through the door with you. He may try to pull away but don't let him. Just ignore this and holding the lead snugly, open and close the door a few times until you see he's paying no attention to it. Then open the door all the way, walk through, not forgetting the praise when you arrive on the other side. Don't be afraid to squat down at "dog level" to give him this praise.

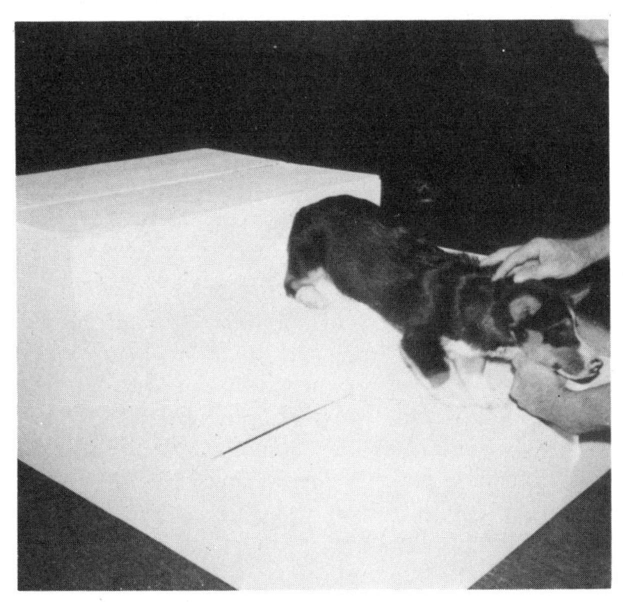

Teaching stairs to puppy, guiding with hands

Almost all homes have at least a few steps to be navigated; many of them have full length stairways. Even though you may not have any where you live, you and Buddy should be prepared to meet any situation that exists in places where you will be going together. If he should suddenly be confronted with stairs and has never met them before, it could be a really traumatic experience. A few minutes of your time now will prove to be very rewarding later.

Extremely important is the direction of approach on the introduction to the stairs. Again, try to look at the situation through Buddy's eyes, picturing the difference in what he sees when he looks *up* the stairs and what he sees when he looks *down* the stairs. In looking up, he can see only what is directly in front of him, nothing beyond. On the other hand, looking down, he has the complete picture of everything ahead of him. Therefore, start your puppy going downstairs first, preferably with only a few steps to master. Place yourself in front of him on a lower step, take hold of his collar with your left hand underneath (in front of his chest), palm up, and put the palm of your right hand on his shoulders. Very gently, apply a little pressure on the collar and coax him forward with your voice. Make him take the first step down, guiding his descent with your right hand, but don't allow him to jump. Make him *step* down. Repeat this a few times until, as you move down, he starts to come toward you. Then put the lead on, hold it in your left hand close to the collar, still being in a position to guide with your right if necessary. Keep guiding with your right hand, carrying him back to the start each time. When he can come down by himself, on a snug lead and under control with no guiding from you, he is ready to learn to go upstairs.

In starting to go up the stairs, your position is now *behind* Buddy. Place his front feet on the first step and gently raise his hindquarters with your right hand, while holding the collar with your left hand. When all four feet are on the same step, repeat the process for the next step. Keep repeating this until you can feel him responding and wanting to go up without your guidance. Then put his lead on, and reverse your own position so that you are backing up the stairs and he is in front of you. Saying "Buddy, Come!," again in a coaxing voice, and guiding him with the lead, call him up the stairs as you back up, using a little pressure on the collar if necessary. As he moves up, continue backing up and as he reaches the top, again be sure you go overboard with his praise. One of the biggest obstacles in your Buddy's training has now been overcome.

A word of caution is in order here, one that should be adhered to all through your training. When working with your pup, NEVER repeat an exercise more than three to five times. Don't risk his becoming tired or bored, thus contributing to an unpleasant association with training. There's always another day.

In addition to this, establish the habit of a play period after the lesson; that is, after an exercise has been gone through three to five times. The play period can, in reality, be something enjoyable that will be leading into an exercise to be learned in a more formal style later on. The aim here is to break the pattern before both you and Buddy become bored.

"Directed" play

For instance, take a bright colored ball (we've found a bright red to be the most attractive to puppies) and let it roll off his nose, from the top of his head. It will bounce on the floor and he will see the motion of it as it rolls away from him. It will be no time before he is chasing after it and picking it up. Don't insist on his bringing it to you, but be overjoyed if he does. Just have fun with him, even if you have to get up to go get the ball so you can repeat the exercise.

If he shouldn't seem interested at first, face him toward a wall two or three feet away. Again let the ball roll down his nose, hit the floor and roll to the wall, where it will hit and roll back toward him. This often creates more interest than when the ball just rolls away from him. Sometimes you can get even more action from the ball when you face into a corner, giving two surfaces to send the ball bouncing back.

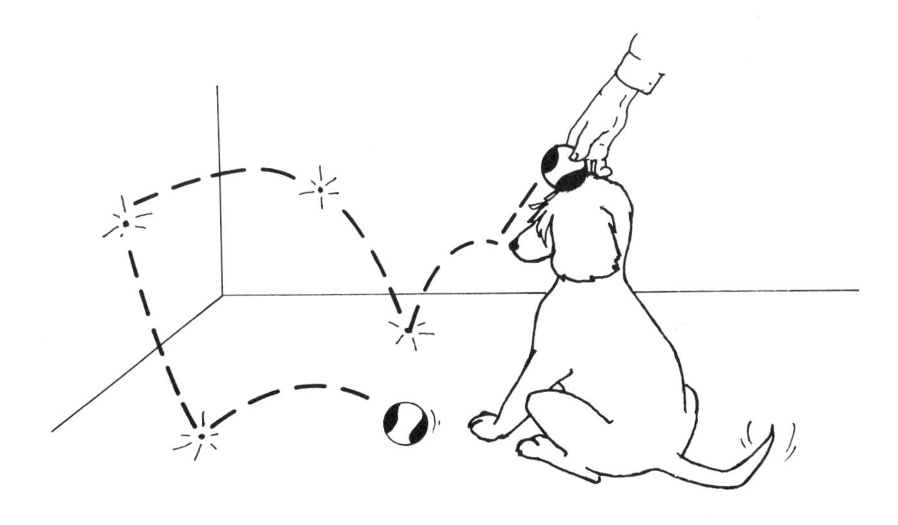

Teaching Commands

The next exercise is one designed to make the pup think for himself. You will need the "V"-shaped barrier (listed in your needed equipment) for this, as in the illustration on Page 25, or perhaps you can improvise something that will answer the purpose. It should be solid, with the opening spread just wide enough so the pup must back up before he can turn around to come out. Lower your pup into it, facing into the closed point of the "V," you standing on the outside and bending over it to let him all the way down to the floor. As his feet touch, let go of him and run back beyond the wide opening calling his name, clapping your hands, squattting down to receive him, and telling him to "Come!" It's fun to watch this, as you can almost see the wheels turning in that little head, trying to figure out just how far he has to back up before he can turn around and run free. You'll see that he catches on fast and soon he is beating you to where you were when you called him. Again, repeat no more than five times at the most. It is quite obvious, when you have done this exercise, that you have made an excellent start on the "recall," or teaching your little fellow to come to you when you call.

Let us continue on still further now and we'll see just how well your pup's brain is working and how well he can remember. You will be teaching him several commands and what each one means. You will introduce each exercise to him properly, showing him what you mean by each command. You will be teaching him four exercises without doing any walking and tiring him. These are *"Stand," "Sit," "Down,"* and you will combine the *"Stay"* command with each of the first three.

First, get yourself in a comfortable position on the floor or ground, the pup standing close in front of you, his head facing to your right, tail to your left. The lead is not on the collar now as we don't want to chance its getting wrapped around his legs. When you start working on the "Down," you will fasten it back on the collar again.

The first command will be "Stand," for here we take advantage of the natural ability and desire of a dog to *stand.* Kneeling on the floor beside him, take hold of the collar under his chin with your right hand knuckles toward the body, and gently pull forward on a level with his shoulder. At the same time, also apply a little pressure with the *back* of your left hand under his tummy, just ahead of his hind leg. Raise your left hand only high enough to make him stand on all four feet. As you are doing this, use the command "Stand, Stay." Equalize the pressure of your two hands, up with the left and forward with the right, to the degree necessary with your own pup. Repeat this until you can lower your left hand and your pup will remain standing.

Teaching STAND—first position of hands

Teaching STAND—second position of hands

Teaching SIT—first position of hands

Teaching SIT—left hand "tucking under"

Next, move your right hand (in the collar) from the front up to the top of his neck, behind his head. Apply a little pressure backward, toward the tail and at the same time, run your left hand down over his back, starting at the shoulder, continuing over the tail and down the hind legs to the hocks. The command here is "Sit, Stay" and the motion of the hands are toward each other, the right hand pulling the collar back and the left hand pushing in lightly just above the hocks, in what we like to refer to as a "tuck-in" action. Be careful that you do not let this become a judo-like chop.

While practicing these two exercises alternately, and while Buddy is standing, teach him to accept your finger in his mouth without pulling away or playing. In other words, make this a beginning of his learning to be steady when a judge wishes to examine his mouth and teeth.

A reminder, once more: Do not repeat an exercise more than three to five times before going to another one or to a play session.

In teaching the Stand and the Sit, be sure you remember to praise, using the tone of voice that will best convey your pleasure to him when he does what you want. Continue this lesson in your training sessions until he will respond to the commands with just a slight pressure on the collar with your right hand and no assistance with your left. Only when you have mastered this are you ready to teach the "Down."

In teaching the Down, first put the lead on your pup's collar. He needs to be relaxed before you can accomplish much, so start with the commands he has already learned, "Stand, Stay," "Sit, Stay." When he has settled down, is quiet and sitting (at your left, and you are down on your left knee), reach over his back with your left hand and lift his left front foot up, telling him to "Stay." Move that leg up and down (easy does it) until you feel no stiffness or tension, then let it go back to the floor. Next, with your right hand lift his right front leg and again try to get the same reaction, no tension or stiffness. Then fold up your lead in your right hand so that it comes to below his "elbow", and raise both his legs at the same time, cradling him toward you, almost as though you were teaching him to sit up.

When he is relaxed, using some pressure with your left arm or wrist (depending upon Buddy's size), tip him toward you and down so that he goes down on his right side in a relaxed position. Be sure you accompany this motion with the new command, "Down, Stay", also with praise and pleasure in your voice. But don't be too exuberant, as this will encourage him to bounce up and out of position. Once he is down, help him to remain there with just a slight pressure downward on his shoulder with your left hand, repeating the command "Stay". When you can put Buddy down, say "Stay" and remove your left hand, *and he stays,* then you are ready to practise all the exercises together, one after the other.

You may now keep the lead on for all these exercises. Try to drop the use of your left hand as soon as you can, so that all you need is your command for each one and a slight tension on the lead. When you have accomplished this, you are ready to do all of them in motion, a beginning of Heeling.

When you start this, and from now on, whenever you and Buddy are going along together and he is at your left side, you will be using the command "Heel"! Gradually he will come to associate that command with his position on your left, even though you will not be enforcing it yet in a formal way. He will learn that "Heel" means that he should be by your left side, his shoulder by your left leg. In K.P.T. we call it "controlled walking", as differentiated from the regular "heeling" you will be doing later on.

Let us get ready now to start the next big adventure, with him standing by you on your left. Call his name and give the command, "Buddy, Heel!," and start walking, making your first move with your left foot. (Your left foot will become your guide for your dog). Take no more than three or four steps, stop, and give the command "Sit!," using your left hand on the lead to help him if there should be any hesitation in his response. Don't wait to see if he *might* sit, show him it has to be done now. Call his name, tell him to Heel, take another three or four steps, give him the command "Stand, Stay" as you come to a halt. Be ready, as before, to show him what you want, if you have to.

Once again, as you start, say "Buddy, Heel!," and take three or four steps, telling him to Sit as you stop. This time, follow with a "Down" command, showing him if you have to. Be sure that *you* remember, in each step, to bestow the praise and let him know that what he has done is right, and has pleased you. Don't be afraid to repeat the "showing" part of any of the exercises if you see Buddy needs a refresher.

Before you do much practicing with your pup on the controlled walking, you should discipline your own walking habits, practicing without him if necessary. As we mentioned before, your left foot will be his guide so start to move with your left foot first. Following through with this same theory, you halt on your right foot and bring your left foot up to it. In other words, to your dog (who is right next to it), your left foot is not only the *first* in motion; it is also *last* in motion. This may not

Teaching the DOWN

1—Relaxing front legs

2—Cradled against body

3—Front feet going forward

4—Down and relaxed

make sense to you at the moment, but if you are really interested in training, both you and your pup will have to learn to work together as a unit. When you can do anything to make it easier for him, for heaven's sake, do it!

With the controlled heeling, we will keep in one direction, a large circle, leaving specific turns to be described in detail in another chapter. Controlled heeling means that you and Buddy must work together and that you need to keep his attention upon you all the time. Don't let his mind wander to something else—make your work the *most* interesting thing around him. Carry the lead, folded up, in your right hand. The left hand, palm down, should loosely hold that part of the lead going down to his collar so that no timing is lost when guiding or correction is needed. As you say "Buddy Heel!" and step forward, flip your left wrist a little on the lead, if necessary, to get him in motion. In giving any assistance with the lead, your hands should never be raised higher than your waist, and only the action of your left wrist or fingers (*not* the arm) is all that is needed. At no time should a correction with the lead be so strong that the pup's front feet are lifted off the floor.

If, while walking, your pup's attention wanders to something else, flip your wrist on the lead, say "Buddy, Heel!," with a bit more emphasis on the "Heel" this time. Don't slow down or try coaxing, as this is *controlled* walking and *control it* you must. When you come to a halt and your left foot is just about to stop its motion, give the command "Sit," applying just a slight bit of pressure on the lead with your left hand, up and backwards, as you did at the very first with your hand in the collar. Make sure the direction of motion of the lead is from the center of your pup's head toward his tail. If there should be any hesitation, let your left hand drop down and back toward the hindquarters in a motion as though you were going to "tuck him under," as a reminder. Get the sit, then praise him. Repeat this from three to five times, remembering to come in with praise and the word "Good," then give him a rest. Probably both of you will appreciate a break by now, as well as a cool drink.

Accustoming Your Dog to Noise, Other People and Other Dogs

In the next lesson, the work part will be introducing noise to your pup, but we will combine it with fun. Pick out a nice large field or fenced area to go to, one where you need not worry about your pup when you let him run free to do some exploring on his own. Take two flat pieces of wood that you can hold in your hands, but not so large that they will attract Buddy's attention. While out in the field, take his lead off and let him roam around. He probably will stay nearby at first, but pay no attention to him and soon he will take advantage of his freedom and wander away from you. However, don't get alarmed, or call him; just let him enjoy himself.

When he gets about 25 or 30 feet away, turn your back to him and slap the two pieces of wood together, lightly at first. As you repeat it, increase the sound each time. When he first hears it, he probably will look and come toward you. Pay no attention to him; don't even look toward him. Above all, don't say anything to him. Make believe you didn't even hear any noise. After you have repeated this four or five times, with each slapping of the wood blocks getting louder, you will find him looking toward the sound but paying less and less attention to it, returning almost immediately to his exploring. As you occasionally repeat the field-fun and work routine you can change to a horn or bell from a child's bicycle, a transistor pocket radio (volume can be increased gradually), and other sounds. Just be careful that none of them has a frightening effect. One ingenious K.P.T. teacher has mounted a bell and a horn on the curved head of a walking cane, a sort of two-in-one training aid. One caution—avoid using a whistle, especially if you have one of the sporting breeds and plan to train him for hunting or field trials, or if you have one of the herding breeds and plan to train him in this work.

When you have finished your lesson, put your lead back on his collar, naturally with lots of praise, and go back home for some rest for both of you. Try to plan these forays into the field in the cool of the evening when it will be much more pleasant for both of you.

The next lesson will take place in a busy shopping center, but not during a hot time in the day. Park as near the stores as you can, opening the car windows so that all the noise from the hustle and bustle of people and the traffic can be heard. Pay no particular attention to your pup; don't pet and pamper and console him. Soon his curiosity will get the better of him and you will see him watching things on his own.

Let your puppy get to hear the voices of strangers. At opportune times, as someone passes the open window of your car, stop him and ask for the correct time. (But hide your wrist watch, and don't let him hear you ask the next passerby the same question, lest he wonder about you.)

On your next trip to the shopping center, put Buddy on lead and let him get out of the car with you. Go over near one of the stores and stand around, just "watching the world go by." Again, don't make a fuss over him. If you see that he is getting a little nervous, from the loud noises and/or dogs going by, control him with the lead and speak to him in a reassuring tone. He will soon settle down and accept the disturbances as nothing to fear.

If you see a fairly clear area with few people in motion, try a little heeling. As you start to move, encourage him with your voice and be ready to reassure him any time he may need it. Look for a shopping cart outside a store, walk up to it and let Buddy smell it and explore it. If he shows any fear, let him see you touch it. You can even move it back and forth a bit to let him realize there is nothing there to hurt either of you.

After this introduction to the cart is successfully behind both of you, look for somebody who is pushing a cart along the walk. Move toward it, making sure the cart passes on *your* right side, away from your pup. After he reacts favorably to this, find another and, this time, have it pass on his side, on your left, being careful not to crowd him too close to the cart. Each time you do this, your voice should be all the praise and encouragement that he needs.

With the lesson over, you and Buddy now head back to your car. One thing you should begin to practice, making it (eventually) a continuing habit, is to stop before any traffic crossing and have your pup "Sit-Stay" or "Stand-Stay" before getting a further command to "Heel" when the traffic is clear. This habit might, someday, save his life (yours, too!). Also, it is a good idea to form the habit of making Buddy "Sit-Stay" before leaving and entering a car.

When it is playtime, try to make it as interesting and varied as you can, but don't forget that it is still a part of his training. By this time your pup should be playing with the balls, gloves, maybe even a small dumbbell, etc., carrying them and showing off, head held high and proud as punch! You can have the most fun with him if you are in a yard or a field. Toss the ball or glove a short distance so he can see it. When he gets it, call him to you with lots of enthusiasm and excitement. Never forget that "so-important" praise when he does something you've asked him to.

Each time, as you take it, toss the object just a little further away. Repeat a few times until you toss it into some taller grass where it is not obvious to him. Here you'll see your Buddy start to use his nose to find something! It is hard for us to comprehend how keen a sense of smell a puppy has from birth. Buddy started to learn your scent from the first day the two of you met. So, in play, you're teaching him to use his nose to find something you have touched.

If he should become confused at first, when he cannot see it, don't sound off at him. Call "Buddy" and run out to it, pick it up and toss it

Teaching RETRIEVE on lead

1—Going out, loose lead

2—Picking it up

3—Happy delivery, praise

again, a short distance. As he goes for it, you should return to the spot from where you first threw it into the taller grass. Call him to you, praise and encourage him, take it and let him know you're most happy with him. Repeat this two or three times more, then call it a day. You and your partner have had fun and it has also been a good training session.

Your final big lesson in Kindergarten (although it need not necessarily be done after all the others—it can be done in-between if more convenient) is that of introducing Buddy to other puppies. If a K.P.T. class is given by a reputable training club in your area, you are most fortunate and you would be wise to take advantage of it. This would be much easier than for you to try to round up a group of people who had puppies close to Buddy's age and who would be willing to meet for this purpose. Each pup of the group should be under somebody's watchful eyes, as there is most likely to be at least *one* bully in the crowd and he should be taught promptly that he should mind his manners. At this point, somebody should step in to him, administer a light slap *under the chin,* with the fingers of the open right hand, palm side up, or the snap of a thumb in the same spot, depending upon the size of the puppy. This should be all that is needed, although it might have to be repeated once or twice.

You can start the group in a small yard or a room and let all the pups loose. As they start to play and investigate each other and the new people, toss in some balls, toys, gloves, or such, for them to play with. Again, don't pamper them or worry if they start a little rough and tumble. It is much better for you to laugh and clap your hands to take their minds off being hurt or pestered by another pup. If one comes to you to be consoled, instead of picking him up, find a ball or something and toss it out to divert his attention. If he wants to stay with you, walk through the group to the other side and he most likely will stop on the way to play with the others. Don't take a chance on leaving such a group of pups alone to play by themselves, without supervision. Also, be sure all collars are off before the pups join in group play like this, to avoid any accident, as it is possible for a pup to catch a tooth or a leg in another's collar. It is also a good thing for you to remember to remove rings, bracelets and wrist watches so your pup's teeth or toenails cannot get caught in them. This group play also gives the opportunity for the pup to meet strange people, get used to new sounds and different motions.

You and Buddy have now completed a full course in Kindergarten Puppy Training and if you have really tried, we feel sure both you and he have learned a great deal and are much better off for it. If you have enjoyed it, we invite you to continue on and read and apply the training in the following chapters. If you can find an Obedience Training School with competent and well-recommended instructors, we strongly advise that you register with them and participate in their training classes, as association with other dogs can be most beneficial. You, yourself, will also receive very important instruction and help in teaching your pup more advanced work. Don't be perturbed if much of the instruction is repetition of what you have already learned, for your pup now has to learn to do these things in the presence of other dogs, other people and in a strange place. But it *will* be much easier for you and Buddy than it is for those who are not K.P.T. graduates. And above all else, keep your training fun!

A list of "Do's" for training:

Do: Teach only what you understand.
Do: Follow any correction with praise and work.
Do: Work with your pup as a team.
Do: Wear quiet, comfortable shoes when training.
Do: Wear clothing that does not interfere with your pup.
Do: Stop your training before losing your temper.
Do: Be consistent with your training, at home or in class.
Do: Keep old shoes and slippers, as toys, away from your pup.

A list of "Don'ts" for training:

Don't: Correct by slapping with a lead.
Don't: Correct by using your feet.
Don't: Correct if you are not positive your pup fully understands.
Don't: Be a show-off with your training.
Don't: Overtrain.
Don't: Repeat any exercise more than five times.

PROBLEMS IN K.P.T. TRAINING

Puppy shows no interest in playing with a ball.

Face into a clear corner of a room with your puppy, let a brightly colored ball roll off his head and down his nose, bouncing in front of him and caroming against the wall. This is a real "starter" to get him interested.

Puppy won't move with cord attached to collar.

Leave him alone in his own familiar yard, with the cord on, under your supervision. But don't let your presence be obvious to him. You might even consider observing him through a convenient window.

Puppy is afraid of grooming and of being on a table.

Begin the process of getting him used to it by first sitting down and holding your puppy in your lap, then moving him onto a chair in front of you, and then onto a table that is solid. Take it slowly, in easy stages. Be sure that the table is not wobbly, as this could make things worse.

Puppy is afraid of a crate.

Let a wire dog crate, which allows him to see everything around him, serve as his bed and his "security corner". Put some of his toys in it. A good location for the crate is a corner of your kitchen.

Puppy doesn't like to be picked up.

Perhaps he has had the unpleasant experience of someone hurting or dropping him as he was picked up. Check yourself to find out if you're doing it right. Gain his confidence before letting anyone else pick him up, and then allow it only under your supervision.

Puppy dislikes or fears collar being put on.

Put his collar on and let him go around the yard or any other familiar area on his own. Be sure you are nearby so you can observe his reaction. Praise him while you are putting it on *and* when you take it off.

Puppy does not like to be touched for the stand or sit.

Be sure you use only a plain buckled collar and get him used to just feeling your hands on him, anywhere. Make it a fun game to begin with, before you even try a controlled Stand and a Sit.

Puppy rebels at controlled walking on lead.

When you are working with him, never lean or tower *over* him. Squat down and coax him at *his* level, using a pleasant tone of voice.

Puppy lies down when he's touched.

Pick him up, carry him and put him back on his feet again. Make a temporary game of it.

Puppy acts afraid if his feet are lifted.

Again, make a game of it. Laugh as you pick up his front, the same when you lift his rear. This helps to remove his fear.

Puppy wants no part of having his feet touched.

Once more, make a game of handling his feet. If this developed from being hurt during a clipping or nail cutting, leave the clipper or nail cutter nearby and while playing, reach over once in a while and pick it up. Get him used to having it near him before you try using it again.

Puppy resents any pressure on the collar.

Be sure you use only a plain buckled collar, no slip collar. While he's sitting or standing, use a slight pressure on the collar to get him used to it gradually, accompanied by praise and a pleasant tone of voice.

Puppy trembles and tries to hide from noise.

Be careful to plan so that any noise comes from in front of him, and time it so that it occurs when he is occupied.

Puppy acts afraid when you're holding the lead.

Circle around your puppy. Your good tone of voice and the vibrations of your feet will soon convince him that there might be some fun in this game, after all, and he'll make an effort to join in your game.

Puppy tries to fight the lead when tension is felt on the collar.

Backtrack to the Stand and Sit without motion, but apply a bit more pressure on the collar as you practise it, along with an encouraging tone of voice.

Puppy is afraid of moving objects.

A helper makes it easier to take care of this situation. From a short distance away, so the puppy can watch what is going on, have the helper move a cart, a bike, a doll carriage or whatever you can come up with, then stop and leave it there. Take your puppy over to it and let him investigate it, as thoroughly as he wants to. Introduce him to it by touching it, moving it, laughing as you are going through these motions. Get him used to one moving article before you change to others.

Puppy is afraid of stairs.

Go back to the basic introduction to the stairs, working down only three or four steps at the beginning. Remember to *start him going down first* so he can see where he's going, but avoid any long stairways, as the very look of one can be frightening. This may involve your carrying him up the few steps, in order to be in position to go down, but it is worth it.

Puppy is afraid of a door opening toward him.

Repeat the practise of going through a door which opens away from him, then on returning back through it (opening toward him), pick him up and carry him through. A few times back and forth in this manner should allay his fears; then you can try it with him on his own four feet in both directions.

Puppy fights against having nails cut.

Get yourself into a comfortable sitting position and pick up your puppy, put him in your lap and over on his back, all four feet up. He will take it much better in this position. At first, make believe you're going to cut but only click the cutter so he can hear it but not feel it. Be extremely careful, whenever you do any cutting, that you do not cut into the quick, the tender part.

GROUP PROBLEMS

If you have your puppy in a Puppy Kindergarten Training class, you may have encountered some additional problems and they should be worked out with the cooperation of the instructor and other class members.

Puppy refuses to stand up, to move, to play.

Place him in the group circle with the other puppies but ignore him completely. He will soon find out he is missing out on the fun and attention and will join in on his own.

Puppy avoids men, stays near women.

Try to get a circle made up of men only, and caution them to make no sudden moves or sharp or loud noises around this puppy until the situation is improved. Vice versa if opposite situation.

Puppy bullies others in his group.

The group instructor should administer the correction for this and check it as early as possible. A correction should be given under the chin with the hand or a flip of the thumb, depending upon the size of the dog.

Puppy seems afraid of the toys in the circle.

Toss or roll the toys back and forth across the circle, paying no attention to this puppy unless he starts to get excited and shows interest in them.

Puppy stays with owner, refuses to leave.

Owner should not be a part of the circle. He should go away from it, once he has put the puppy down in it.

Puppy is afraid of noises in class.

People making up the play circle should clap hands (softly at first), laugh, reach out and touch the pups, play with them, but wait to touch this pup until he gets around to asking for it.

Puppy continually tries to leave the circle.

Return him immediately, if he manages to get through, but don't baby him.

Puppy tries to hide when left for "race recall".

When the owners leave their puppies, the one with this puppy should go only a few feet away, squat down and coax the puppy into him.

Puppy is confused with movement of other puppies.

In this case, take your puppy out in front of the others, about 10 or 15 feet, sit down on the floor with him and watch the others as they go racing by, laughing as they're passing you.

Puppy tries to climb in your lap for cuddling.

Discourage any "babying" treatment. Stand up and expect him to stand on his own four feet, too. If he starts to follow the other pups as they go by, follow along behind him quietly.

Puppy is confused when in a line with others in front of and behind him.

Put him in the center of the group so he can watch all of them. Then start moving in a small circle, gradually widening it until you rejoin the line with the others.

Basic Training

IN THIS CHAPTER on basic training there will be a good bit of repetition of what has already been covered in K.P.T. There will be more detail and emphasis however, and even for those who have gone completely through the puppy training, this repetition will be well worth the results achieved. For those who may have thought to start the training of their dogs with this chapter, we advise that it would be more practical to read the Kindergarten training material as a background for the basic training.

Once again, and we cannot emphasize this strongly enough, all through your training and when it has been completed, first and foremost in importance is your tone of voice. You are going to have to become very conscious of your voice and be able to do a little self analysis on this. Practise until you have made a habit of giving commands as your dog would like to hear them. Above all, strive to be natural. One note of caution here: use a little discretion about where you decide to do your practising. Otherwise a neighbor might get panicky and call for the men with the white coats to come over and pick you up! Once this dog training gets to you, you can get into such a state of concentration that you're oblivious to everybody and everything within sight or earshot of you.

As mentioned in the first chapter, there are tones of voice to cultivate and tones of voice to avoid. Try to get used to using a normal tone that Buddy is accustomed to hearing around the house, adding a happy ring to it for your praising, and a bit more authority to it for your commands.

Let him know you mean business when you demand something from him, but don't let any harsh correction or punishing tone creep into your voice. A coaxing or pleading voice will not get the desired response, will not encourage respect and obedience; nor will you get anywhere with a sharp, cross voice, as this can convey just as much unpleasantness as physical punishment. You want your Buddy as a companion and, still more important, *he* wants *you* as one. Don't let your emotions show in your voice (other than what is required when you're working with him) and don't try to fake anything with him. He will be able to see through you every time, so why bother trying to fool him? It proves to be wasted time and energy. Also, an unusually loud command is unnecessary, as a dog's normal hearing is so acute that it is one of his outstanding attributes.

If a more severe tone of voice should be needed as a correction, clip your words off as you say them, to get more immediate attention. In doing this, be careful you do not accompany this with glaring or staring at your dog. Remember this all through training: *Whenever you are facing your dog, always look above his head or a bit to his side, never at his eyes.*

Right now we want to have you become familiar with commands you will be using, teaching your dog different exercises as you go along through the basic part of his education and on into the more advanced phases. Always use your dog's name for attention, then follow with a command that you want him to carry out. Some of these are *"Heel," "Sit," "Stand," "Down," "Stay," "Wait"* and *"Come."* Another word we would like to have you get in the habit of using is not a command but is extremely important in your training. This is the word *"Good!"* for it is so easy to inject your feelings and pleasure into it and let Buddy know you are happy with his performance.

As you are teaching and practising the exercises as presented in this beginning of your training, expect obedience but *not* to the point of a perfect precision performance. You should, however, have a controlled execution of your commands. Do not allow bad habits to develop that will be necessary to break later on. It is always so much better to make good habits the rule, rather than have to correct bad ones and train all over again.

For your first exercises and your practise sessions, we are asking you to work without your dog. You should be familiar with the commands and timing and be able to "make your feet track" before you try to work with your dog. Let's avoid one confused handler plus one confused dog at the outset.

Heeling

Footwork is so important to your dog that we will go into it in as minute detail as we can. Your dog works next to your feet and learns to take cues from them, so if you are not consistent with your footwork you can easily throw him off. Learn to *work with him, not against him.* You will find a large mirror is a wonderful help for you. Place it so you can walk toward it and watch your feet. We might suggest that you locate it at floor level, against a wall, easy for you to approach and watch yourself, checking to find out if you are right (or wrong!).

As you start the heeling, your first step is most important! Remember, throughout your training, your left foot and leg are going to be your dog's guide. As you take that first step (normal size) with your *left* foot, call your dog's name and give command, as "Buddy, Heel!" Walk as normally as you can, making sure you are going in a straight line. Some people are heavy-footed on one side or the other and may veer left or right. Check in your mirror. If you have this trouble, pick out some point dead-ahead in front of you and school yourself to walk toward it. Conquer this now, *before* you start to work with your dog.

If you should happen to be a very heavily built person, especially if much of that weight is in the thighs, or if you have a crippling handicap that makes it difficult for you to take that first step directly forward and you find you are throwing your foot to the left, in front of your dog, then concentrate on trying to put your foot slightly to the right on that first step. This will help your dog to keep right with you from the start, instead of lagging and catching up later.

Another thing you should become conscious of, especially if you have a short or low dog, is the type of walking (or in running, as in the fast pace taken up later) step that you take. This is one case where you may have to develop *new* habits and make them look normal to others. Once again, try to look at your footwork from the dog's viewpoint. How do you think he feels, all the way down there, near the floor, if your heels are coming right up in his face? Would you really blame him if he lagged behind or heeled wide? What to do? This is simple, but it may be somewhat difficult to change your walking habit. You are going to have to learn to walk as nearly flat-footed as possible, keeping your heels down.

Now that we have you moving forward, we are going to have to teach you how to halt. Bear in mind that, just as your starting and your moving should be natural and normal, so should your stopping. Don't try to be a show-off and expect your dog to make a breath-taking stop with you.

It is not fair to him and it puts an undesirable stamp on you. Nor does it look any better to take several little mincing steps as you come into a halt. Try to develop habits that will help your dog to know just what you are going to do. Remembering that the perfect Heel position is your dog's shoulder by your *left* leg and headed in the same direction as you, using your left leg as the guide, stop on your right foot and bring the left foot up to it, the left being the *last* in motion. Imagine your dog by your side and what would happen if you stopped the opposite way. If you halted on your left, with the right foot still moving, he would also still be moving, thinking you were still in motion. This would bring him into a delayed halt, causing a forging or a crooked sit, or both.

All of these details are *most* important for all those planning to continue training and to prepare themselves and their dogs for competition in Obedience classes at dog shows and matches. Many times an exhibitor loses points on crooked sits and poor heeling and it comes as a shock to them if they are told it was their own fault, not their dog's. Even a seasoned exhibitor would do well to check his basic footwork to see if he can improve his dog's performance by improving himself.

The about turn is one of the most difficult things to teach as there is no set pattern to follow. Your mirror, again, will be a very important aid when you practise this. You want to make your turn in such a way that your dog is able to keep up by your side with no lagging. You also want to avoid the military type of turn which leaves one foot back as you reverse direction and forces your dog to wait for it to be moved before he can travel around your body, resulting in his hanging back and lagging. If you have been drilled in military service, it will be even more difficult for you, as you must break this habit and form a new one to use when working with your dog.

And believe us, in this case, the new habit will pay off. Again, see it as your dog would see it. Check yourself and see how you are placing your feet and if your heels are staying close to the floor, especially with the little dogs. A lot of these things will probably seem very awkward to you at first but practise and concentration will soon perfect them to such a stage that they will be the normal thing for you to do. Just keep yourself in balance, no matter what style you develop, and keep your feet out of your dog's way. One more point, an "about turn" is a "right about turn," always to the right.

In your normal living, when you stop to think about it, you realize that you are not always proceeding at the same speed on foot, any more than you are always going in the same direction. Therefore, you want to be able to teach your dog to stay with you at different speeds, just as you teach him to stay with you when you make different turns. The changes of pace, "slow," "normal" and "fast," also make up some of the requirements of the heeling exercises for Obedience competition at dog shows.

As we have pointed out, you do vary your speeds in normal activities. You might be in town and spot somebody down at the next corner you want to talk to. You could yell, but that would just draw attention to you. Unless that's what you want, the simplest way to get there is to trot or run and close up the distance between you and your friend. Or perhaps somebody is down on the corner and you don't feel like getting into a conversation with her this morning. Again, the easiest way to avoid her is to go very slowly and not draw attention to yourself. In either case, if Buddy is along with you for one of his enjoyable jaunts as your companion, you would like to have him stay with you, with no fuss and bother on your part.

The main thing to remember in practising changes of pace is to try making the changes as smoothly as possible. We like to describe it as "floating" from one pace into another. Start off walking at a normal (for you) pace, change to slow, but do *not* change the size of your step. Arrive at the slow pace by moving your feet a little more slowly. Keep the change smooth—don't hesitate as you start into it and nearly come to a halt. You would be confusing your dog and he would be thinking you're going to stop. Iron out the imperfections *before* you start practising with him. On reversing the pace, from slow to normal, follow the same procedure, remembering to pick up your speed gradually until you are back into your normal walk. Try to do everything as naturally as possible, nothing exaggerated.

The "fast" pace, especially used as a command in Obedience competition, has been interpreted many ways, all the way from a fast walk to a speed race for a 50-foot-dash across the ring. Sometimes we wonder if a stop watch is clocking the time and first prize is going to be awarded to the one who makes the best time in the event! Once again, we feel that the key idea here is *being natural.* If you and your dog can develop your pattern of changing from normal to fast, and back to normal so that you stay together, have a rhythmic step or pace, do it smoothly, and both of you break into a trot or slow run and return to the normal without any problems, you "have it made". Remember the same advice we gave you with the slow pace. Don't change the size of your steps; just increase and decrease the speed of them, and do it gradually. When practising with your dog, later on, vary the sequence of the changes in pace. Keep it interesting for both you and Buddy and keep him guessing as to what comes next.

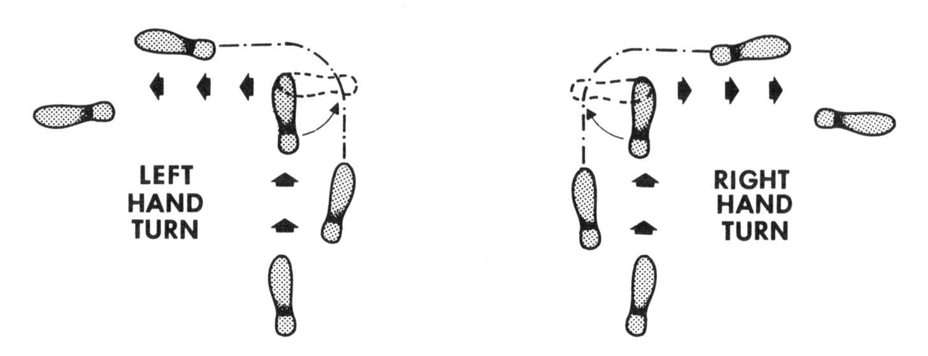

Illustrating footwork for left and right turns

Now, we're going to concentrate on the turns, taking the left one first, again teaching you how to keep your big feet (*or* small feet) out of your dog's way, yet giving him an idea of what you plan to do next. Remember that the left foot and leg are Buddy's guide and that you want him to think of that part of your body as his security and something to love, just as your left hand is your praise hand. You want to avoid any unpleasant association there. Never use that left foot or knee as a correction, or as a physical contact to indicate where you are going or when you are turning. In other words, don't teach him by bumping into him that you are making a turn to the left. We have found that most people accomplish this quite easily by pivoting on the ball of the left foot, bringing the right foot around in a forward step and continuing on in a straight line, using normal size steps. When you start to practise with Buddy, you may find you have to guide him a bit by drawing back slightly on the lead with your left hand to show him the perfect position, but he will learn fast. He will get the message from your right foot swinging across his forward path, *without* banging into your left leg, and both of you will enjoy each other all the time.

Making the right turn is more or less a reverse of the left turn, except that here you are likely to have the same condition as in the about turn, the concern of blocking your dog. To eliminate this, pivot on your right foot and bring your left foot around, away from your dog, and into your first step forward at the turn. Practise this and you will see that there will be no blocking of your dog and he can easily remain in the proper heel position.

Practising and perfecting your footwork in heeling is most important, for it will make everything so very much easier for you and Buddy as you progress in your training. And when you practise and perfect it *before* you subject Buddy to working with you, he will respond faster and happier, for he will realize you know what you are doing and are capable of teaching him!

Before we leave the subject of footwork (temporarily), there is one more important factor to remember. This concerns the way you leave your dog when you have given him a "Stay" or "Wait" command. Ever mindful of the left leg being the dog's guide, it is perfectly obvious that in this case you don't want him to move and follow on this command. So, naturally, you would not move the guide foot first. Instead, step off on the *right* foot as you leave him, giving him an extra cue as to what you plan to do.

Equipment

We're almost ready for you to get Buddy out now and get down to some real work and fun, but first we want to double check on his training equipment to make sure he is going to be comfortable and will have no unpleasant associations on account of it.

For many years the only training collar we ever used was the slip chain "choker," and that is a good name for it. When the nylon training collar made its appearance, we found, through using it on our own dogs first, how really practical, effective, comfortable and sensible it was as a replacement for the chain. Once again, from the dog's point of view, the nylon is: 1—lighter in weight; 2—is not noisy; 3—does not pull hair or cut it; 4—does not stain the coat; 5—is a non-conductor of heat and cold; 6—stays nearer to where you place it on the neck; 7—does not pinch the skin; 8—gives a longer lasting correction when needed (with no resentment); and 9—is actually stronger (by tested "break strength") than any of the chain link collars. There are many styles of the nylon collars available now, manufactured for specific conditions and sizes of dogs. There are the Toy types (small nylon cord and tiny, lightweight rings), and the heavier ones (with *double* cords of nylon and larger, heavier rings), and many variations between the two extremes. There are even the "snap-around" nylon collars that can be put on without having to slide them over the head. Although they are not allowed in A.K.C. shows, this type of collar is particularly beneficial for dogs who have sensitive ears, prick ears, a very heavy coated head and ears, and for those who are hard to fit well because their necks are so much smaller than their heads.

The snap-around collar allows a more accurate fitting of the dog's neck than the regular type. The ideal sizing of the collar is to allow no more than two to three inches beyond the ring when it is pulled up, or tightened, by the "working" ring when used for a correction (even less, of course, on Toys). When the collar is too long and loose and a correction is necessary, the effectiveness of that correction is lost due to loss of timing. You will have to work much harder to put that correction across and your dog will sense it.

The best way for you to learn to put the collar on your dog is to thoroughly study the illustrations, then try it on your dog, always placing him to your left. The ring to which you attach your lead (for corrections) should be on that part of the collar coming straight over the back of your dog's neck, to you. The sliding ring should be on that part of the collar coming from under the neck, toward you. Always put your collar on this way, in case you may have to change the snap of your lead to make a correction, although we hope most of your training will be accomplished on what we call the "dead" ring or "non-working" ring of the collar.

As to the lead, we like to work with one that is from four to six feet in length, is made of a lightweight flexible material, and has a hand loop at one end and a very small, lightweight but strong, snap at the other end. Your choice of snap will probably be determined by which type is more easily manipulated by your own hands. The fabric of the lead should be something that will fold up into your hands so you can get the "extra" out of the way when you don't need it, and also of a material that will not rip your hands (as a chain would), e.g. a strong cotton webbing, a narrow soft leather, etc.

The two extremes in training methods, both using the same type of equipment, are teaching by *showing,* and teaching by *correcting.* We are definitely proponents of the former, *by showing,* as you will see throughout this book. People who preach the latter are those who deliberately set the dogs up into such situations as are *not* wanted; in order to give them an opportunity to correct the dog because he is wrong. This is definitely a negative approach to training.

With the positive approach, the *showing* method, the lead is snapped into the "dead" or non-working ring of the collar. We have found that

Working position of lead on a trained dog

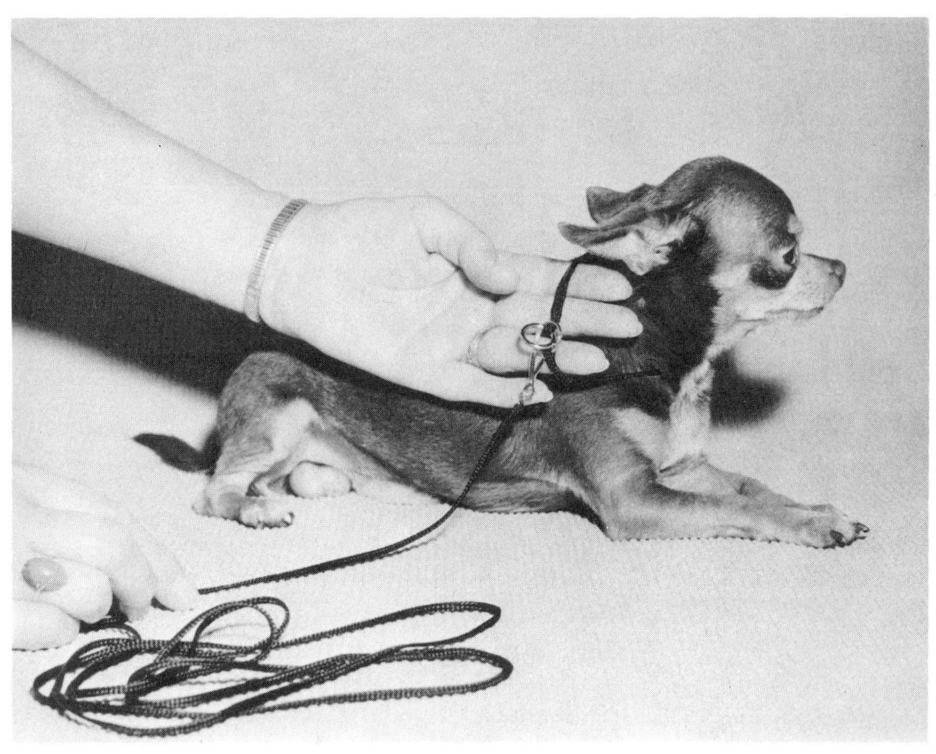

Lightweight equipment for small dog, showing snap on non-working or "dead" ring of collar

this eliminates any unpleasant association when presenting new exercises to the dog, as contrasted to the reactions you get when you tighten that slip collar during the teaching. In other words, your dog is *not* being corrected when he has done no wrong. *After* your dog has learned an exercise and you are sure he knows better, and he is guilty of goofing off or pulling your leg, a properly timed correction on the slip ring and praise can do a world of good. When corrections are needed, most of the time they can be done with the collar still on the dead ring position. This way, there is only a momentary tightening of the lead and collar (even with a rank beginner, no choking effect), and there is no resentment or lack of cooperation on the part of your dog. A bit of praise and kindness and putting his mind right back on his work erases any unpleasantness there might have been.

Lightweight snap and web lead, nylon collar, showing snap on working or "live" ring of collar

Showing action with snap on "live" ring of collar

Throughout the text of this book we will be giving you advice on whether to use the dead ring or the working ring of the collar in your training. However, there will be instances where you, and you alone, must decide on which one to use in your specific case. There are always the exceptions to prove the rule. Whatever happens, don't go overboard with your corrections. If you are not "certain sure," sit down first and think things over; do a little self study to find out just who is at fault, you or your four-footed pal. *You* are the one responsible for making him what he is.

Now that you have proper equipment on Buddy and have practised your own footwork, let's see how you get along when you start to work together. We are assuming that you already have taught your pal what Stand, Sit and Down mean, along with Stay, as described in the K.P.T. chapter. You are now ready to go into motion.

With your dog at your left side, slip the loop of your lead over the thumb of your right hand and fold the lead *into* the palm of the right hand, shortening it until it is slightly snug but not pulling tight on the collar when he is in heeling position. Your left hand is your controlling hand and should be placed over the lead, near the collar, palm down, loosely so the lead can slide through your hand. With your left hand in this position, you are always ready to keep your dog from making a mistake. In case a correction is needed, it can be done with just a flip of the wrist and turn of the hand. In all your training, follow through with the practise of keeping your hands no higher than waist level. If Buddy is a Toy breed or a very small one, turn his collar so that the ring is at the back of his neck, keeping the lead from falling down by his eyes and distracting him.

With the lead fastened in the dead ring, shortened to the proper length in your right hand, your dog at your left side, call his name and tell him to heel, "Buddy! Heel!" As you start to say "Heel," lead out with your left foot in a normal step and encourage him with "Good boy." If he did not move out with you, don't correct, for he has done nothing wrong to deserve a correction. He is only starting to learn from you what *"Heel"* means, so don't add to his confusion. Try again, encourage him as the lead tightens, even laugh and show him what a grand game this is, praising him as soon as he starts to move with you. Avoid any continuous jerking on the lead. This went out of style (at least with our theory of training) along with the bustle, a long time ago. You will see your pup responding to his name and the command much faster than you anticipated. A still further help and guide you may use is dropping your left hand down in front of your dog's nose, as the lead starts to tighten, giving him something he likes to go to in front of him. There will be no need to jerk the lead as you start out—he will go on his own with the command and your left foot.

Now that you have accomplished the starting, and you're "supposed" to be able to handle your feet in the proper way, let's try the about turn next. Give the command "Buddy, Heel!" and start off. After you have taken about a half dozen steps, do an about turn. As you go into the turn, call your dog's name for attention (no command with it) and using your left hand, guide him around, praising him and keep moving. Now, come to a halt, stopping on your right foot, your left (guide foot) being the last in motion. As you are coming to the halt, drop your left hand off the lead and down as though you were going to "tuck him under" for the sit. Raise your right hand upward, directly over his head, with a slight tension on his collar. As this tension is applied and the command "Sit" is given, be ready with your left hand to follow through with the "tuck under," in case there is a hesitation on the sit and it is needed. As he starts to sit, release the tension on the lead and praise your Buddy with your left hand, being very generous with that praise on his shoulder. Don't be afraid of showing him how pleased you are, for he's not a fragile piece of china. Put a little oomph and happiness in it to let him know you mean it.

Perhaps you're thinking you'd rather have started with the "Sit", before the "about turn." We used to teach it first, too, but found that too many people were putting too much emphasis on it and the dogs were becoming like machines with their sitting automatically on every halt, even though other commands may have been given to them. This way you will be achieving that all-important "dog attention" and you will have a dog that is not a machine or a remote-controlled puppet, one that knows his work and is not trying to anticipate what is coming next.

In teaching the "Sit" as you come to a halt, in heeling, the most important factor is proper timing. Your hands and feet must work together, along with your voice command, and the results must become smooth so as to avoid any confusion in Buddy's mind. You must practise this and be able to do it without thinking about it. Some dogs learn more quickly than others, just as some people learn more quickly than others. Your own signpost of progress is to watch for your dog to start to sit as you give him the command, without the use of your left hand. You want to drop the "extra" help of that hand as soon as possible, avoiding his depending upon it as time goes on. The left hand, at the beginning, is only to show your dog what the command "Sit," and the little snugness on the collar, mean. It won't take Buddy long to learn this, provided

Teaching hand position for "tuck under" to owner of adult dog

Teaching SIT to adult dog

Teaching STAND to adult dog

A posed STAND

you have learned *your* lesson and are passing it on to him so he understands what you want.

Now that you know the different turns and how to change from one pace to another, it is up to you to practise all of them and yet remember that variety is so very important. It is one of your keys to "dog attention" and also a good tool to keep handy to prevent boredom. For both you and your pal can get bored very easily if you don't pay attention to what you are doing and also keep *fun* in your training. Mix up your exercises in practise, but insist upon Buddy following through whenever you give him a command. Remember the magic word, "Good!" Practise saying it with a lot of "O's" in it—"Goooood!" Work toward achieving an automatic sit, and a straight one (*now,* as he is learning), on every halt, except when you give the command to Stand as you stop. On the Stand in your heeling, don't be afraid to return to using your left hand on his body as a reminder of what you expect from him, but only when it is necessary, when he has a little lapse of memory.

A good description of a straight sit is one with your dog's shoulder at your left knee (or in line with it), his body close to you but not touching, facing straight ahead, just as you are, parallel to you. Even though you may not be interested in Obedience competition at dog shows, this should be the goal for which you're striving. It is better for you to teach a straight sit now, while Buddy is learning; then you won't have to be concerned about correcting crooked ones later.

When practising heeling, sits, stands, etc., remember to use Buddy's name for attention, especially every time you give him a command to do something, even when you are in motion. Talk to him while you are working. Let him know you are pleased with him and keep his attention on you. Don't let his mind start wandering, or wool gathering. Remember to praise him with your voice, or your hand, or both.

Now to double check with you to make sure everything is clear. Start with Buddy sitting at heel position. Call his name, give the command "Heel," lead out with your left foot, take a few steps and halt (your left foot being the last in motion), bring him into a sit as you come to a stop, and *praise.* Vary the length of time you require him to sit before starting again so he will not anticipate moving as soon as he receives your praise. Start out again from the halt and go into your different changes of pace, calling his name for attention as you go into each one and varying their sequence from one time to another, with no established pattern. Add some of your turns in your heeling practise, along with the changes of pace and sits and stands. As you progress and Buddy progresses, try the sits and stands on both the slow and the fast pace, remembering how you come to a halt and how to work *with* your dog to make it smooth.

Those of you already indoctrinated to training for Obedience Show competition may raise an eyebrow and question why the sequence of exercises is not as prescribed in the American Kennel Club Obedience Trial Regulations. We are primarily interested in helping you to train your dog in a way that will best be accepted by him, making him a happy eager worker. When all the exercises have been learned and you think it might be fun to get into a show to see what you two can do as a team, *then* they can be put together in the order in which they will be judged. We have found that we get much better results in training, in all stages, if we alternate the easier "fun" exercises with the more difficult ones. Now, this may vary with the individual dog and also the individual trainer. If you should find yourself or your dog reacting differently to the exercises, change the sequence so they suit you best, but be sure you cover all of them thoroughly.

In your Heeling practise, if you have an over-exuberant, out-going dog, you may find you have a problem of forging; that is, he may be heeling too far ahead of you. Perhaps it has developed because you have been a bit lax, or your timing on corrections has been "late," or maybe you have a 110 lb. Boxer and you are a little Slim Jane who weighs about 90 lbs. "soaking wet." This must be stopped as soon as possible, before it develops into a condition where it is completely out of control.

We have found that the easiest method of correcting the forging problem begins with the repositioning of the lead. Put your dog in the heel position at your side, and bring the lead around behind you. Fold that lead into your right hand, shortening it up just enough so there is a slight tension (so it is taut) when your hand is resting on your right hip. Your left hand will be free but will be in a position to take hold of the lead near the collar if necessary. Start your heeling, using the necessary commands, and move only four or five steps. Come to a halt, giving the command "Sit," and at the same time letting your dog take up the slack of the lead across the rear of the body. This will keep your pal in position, instead of allowing him to go ahead and get into a spot which would call for a correction. This eliminates the usual jerking and yanking back into position; you haven't had to work hard to accomplish it and Buddy is still your happy pal. Repeat this until there is no need to use your left hand on the lead and it comes across the back of your body with no tightening. Return to this exercise, as a correction, any time your dog may need it, no matter how advanced he might be in his training. Milo has a favorite expression in teaching this: "God gave us a bumper so

Look out below!
How not to descend stairs.

Below: Easy does it—
Proper heeling control

let us make good use of it!" (Of course, we all realize that some are more heavily endowed than others.)

Stand

The next exercise we will tackle is the Stand. You started it in K.P.T., and if you kept up your practise and encountered no particular problems, fine. However, quite often our little pal presents a problem to us and then we have to think up some way of outsmarting him. We try to come up with something that will help him to do the exercise right, avoiding any need for corrections.

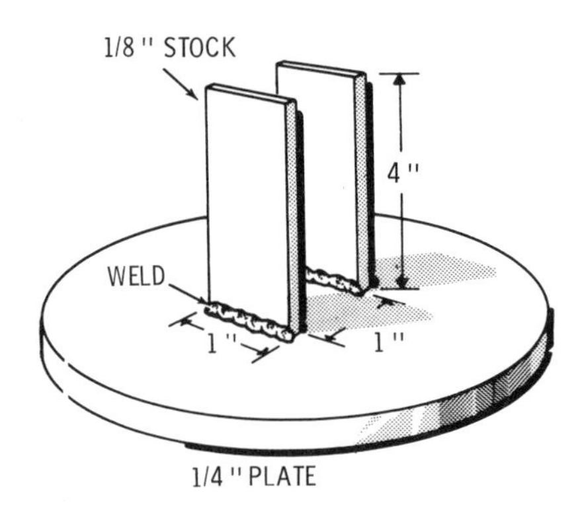

One type of bracket for holding board upright

For this particular exercise we use a plain board from the high jump, placed on the floor or ground along the long edge and supported or propped in an upright position. We use some brackets (see illustration) to keep the board in place. If you already have a regulation high jump, or there is one in a training class which you attend, don't use a board in position between the uprights for this, as we want to avoid any association with a correction in connection with any of the regular Obedience ring equipment. You will want your pup to enjoy his jumping, not get an idea of any kind to the contrary.

Once again, from the dog's point of view, we feel this method is an improvement over the older ones—many of which are still in use—of holding a dog up with a lead under his belly, of blocking his movement with the left hand, blocking with your body, or of posing your dog.

Teaching Stand for Examination over a board

Many times a dog will resent one or more of these methods. If he learns the exercise on his own, it seems to us that he has more self-confidence and is proud of what he can do, as well as being more comfortable as he comes into a natural stand position himself. This also helps him to hold the stand longer without any real difficulty and may pay off later if you enter your dog in the conformation ring. Also, later on, if you progress into the Utility work, where the Group Stand for Examination is for a "minimum of three minutes," you are already well along in the training.

The height of the board you use will depend upon the size of your dog; that is, the clearance between the floor and his tummy, or chest, will determine this. You should have a minimum of two inches clearance and with the large dogs an eight-inch board is quite adequate. No need to go higher (it's easier on you, too!). The object of using a board is *not* to prop your dog up with it, but to give him something to put his attention on, and to keep him from sitting as you give him the Stand command. Try to keep him from jumping the board but don't let it worry you if he does. Don't correct him if he jumps it—just go ahead with your training.

When you have your board, be sure it is sanded and smooth so that there are no splinters. It doesn't necessarily have to be painted; this would depend on how easily *you* are satisfied, not your dog. If your dog is a steady worker and gives you good attention, the location of the board is not too important. However, if he likes to forge, or is overly "full of beans," it is better to locate it about two or three feet from a wall.

With the board in position, bring Buddy up to it, on lead, to introduce him to it. Holding the lead in your right hand, folded up short, kneel down on your left knee in front of the board and tap on it (enough to make some noise) with your left, your "praise" hand, then praise him with the same hand. This lets him know there is no reason for him to fear the board. If it doesn't hurt you, it won't hurt him. Then stand up and back away a few steps, calling his name so he won't be inclined to hop over the board, do an about turn, another about turn and you are ready to approach the board.

With the lead now folded in the left hand, short enough that your dog is in control, come toward the board, talking to him as you are moving. When you get to the board, step over it with your *right* foot and turn so that you are facing Buddy's right side. At the same time, draw back *(no jerk)* on the lead, straight back toward the tail so you don't throw him off on a different angle and not enough to make him sit, giving a signal with your right hand swinging *across* to a position in front of his face, palm toward him but *not* close to his muzzle, as his front feet come over the board. Accompany this movement and position with the command "Stand." The snug lead fastened in the dead ring position will help prevent him from stepping completely over the board, and the right hand will be starting to be used to teach the signal for the exercise. And the board will keep Buddy's mind diverted from any problem he may have in connection with this exercise.

Don't press your luck and keep him standing at this time. Once he stops and stands, tell him how good he is and heap on the praise, and call his name and back away from the board to avoid giving him the idea that this is a jumping exercise. Don't jerk the lead. Get him to come with you by calling him, snug the lead up if necessary. Now, try the whole procedure all over again. Remember all the things *you* have to do

Teaching STAND over a board. (Note handling of lead, position of feet)

STAND over a board, excellent dog attention

and try to improve your timing, getting your feet, your hands and your voice all working together smoothly. Buddy can learn only what *you* teach and you have to be capable of doing your part. There must be communication between the two of you at all times if you are going to be a successful team.

It should be evident by now, why it is important to place the board near a wall in case your dog is really rambunctious and forging. Learn to think and improvise on your own, as you go along in training and come up with different problems, suiting the conditions to your own needs.

After trying the Stand a few times, you will get a response to the command. As soon as you see the start of this, ease off on the lead until there is no guiding with it or tension on it. Using the right hand for the signal leaves the left hand free, so the lead can still be controlled as necessary. When you feel that Buddy really understands what you want of him, eliminate stepping over the board. Try it about two feet away from the board, following through with the command and the signal, being always alert and ready to use the lead if you need to, or even go back over the board if you have to refresh his memory that much. Leaving the board in position serves as a reminder to him of what he should do. Your progress will show as you gradually increase the distance away from the board in your practise of the Stands.

As Buddy becomes more steady in his response, give the command "Stand," then "Stay," and step out in front of him, gradually increasing the distance until he is steady when you are a full lead's length away from him. Be careful you do not pull on the lead at any time. Increase your time out in front of him by seconds only, very gradually. Each time you return to his side, circle around so you come up from behind him and he is in heel position at your left. Gather the lead and hold it up as you return.

Don't be disturbed if Buddy should have a lapse of memory at any time and backslide in his training. We're *all* absent-minded at times. Simply backtrack in his training, even though you may have to revert all the way back to the board. Don't make any corrections; let him correct himself, then gradually progress again, as before. We will not be doing a Stand for Examination in Basic, only the Stand, on signal and command. The "Examination" part will be introduced in Novice training. "Enough is enough." And don't forget, all this is *not* accomplished in one training session. Remember, three to five times on an exercise, then on to something else.

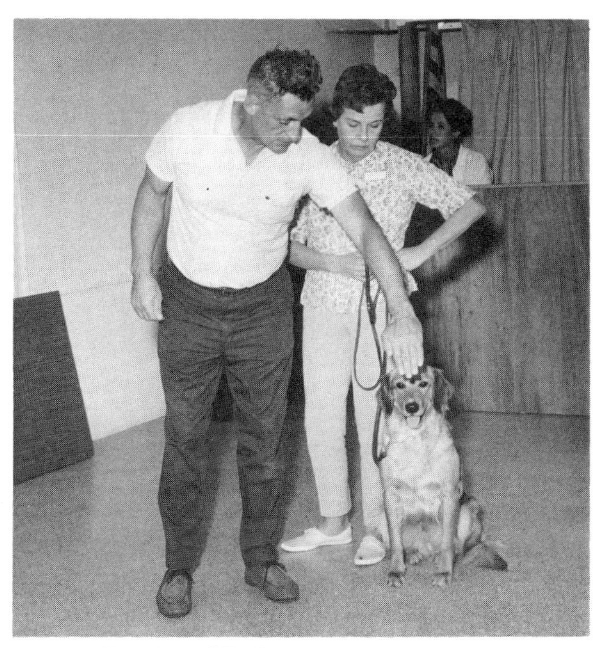

Teaching STAY signal (visible to dog)

Stay

Right now, the "something else" will be the meaning of the Stay command. This is really quite easy to teach and extremely valuable. It is such a practical command to be put to everyday use, in your home, the car, while shopping, etc., as well as being an absolute necessity if you plan to enter into any Obedience classes at dog shows. When you come right down to it, the value of a well-trained dog shows up at home in everyday life, as a well-behaved companion and dog citizen, as well as in the show ring. If he is trained so that he is under control, even under varied and trying conditions, you won't be reaching for an alibi at a show as many do, "If so and so hadn't done that, if such and such hadn't happened, he never would have broken that Stay exercise!" Poppycock!

Another complaint we frequently hear concerns the dog who nearly knocks you down when he greets you in his home, and yet that day or

Group using STAY signal, teaching what STAY means

the day before performed beautifully in the dog show that he got a big trophy (or his master did) for Highest Scoring Dog in Trial!

In teaching the Stay command you will be accomplishing two things, both the Sit and the Stay on SIGNAL. The importance of this may escape you at the moment, but keep it in mind and later on in your training you will remember and realize its necessity.

Sit your dog at heel position. Hold the lead, attached to the dead ring, in your right hand, your left hand being free and in front of your left leg. Be ready for your hand, your right foot and your voice (command) to work together, all at once. Swing your left hand to the left, palm open and toward your dog, in an arc to a point in front of his face where you will stop the motion, at the same time give the command "Stay" and leave on your *right* foot. Go about half the lead's length away and turn and face your dog. Transfer the lead to your left hand and be ready, in case he breaks to come to you, to give an immediate correction. Your timing must be right here, just as he starts to break, not *after* he has broken out of position. When you see him getting ready to move, raise your left hand slightly, bring your right hand in an upswing, palm open, to slap the lead from underneath. As your hand makes contact with the lead, give the command, "Sit, Stay." Don't be surprised if this has to be repeated a few times before Buddy realizes just what it is you're expecting of him. Soon he will be staying and watching you as you turn around and you will be ready to try the next step.

Again in front of your dog, the lead still in your left hand, bring your right hand in a Stay signal toward him, palm toward his face and no higher than your waist at the very most. As you give this signal and tell him to Stay, gently shake the lead from side to side, repeating the signal and command if necessary. If he should start to move, come in immediately with your right hand slapping the lead from underneath as before and with a bit sharper tone of voice in the command this time. As he sits, shake the lead again a little, but don't put any tension on it. After accomplishing a short "Stay," return to Heel position as you did before on the Stand. And then the obvious way of expressing your thanks—Praise!!!!

Later on, teach him to resist breaking position by putting a slight tension on the lead.

Stay signal being put to practical use

Waiting to enter car

Waiting to come out of car

Let us point out here the importance of the direction of the swing motion used for the Stay signal at Heel position. We have found, from the dog's reactions, that a swing of the arm and hand sideways, from the trainer to in front of the dog's head, is much more effective than the old signal of coming from above the dog to right in front of his eyes. The side swing eliminates a fear of getting hit, and there is no blinking of the eyes or turning the head away, and no confusion.

In practising your Stays, be sure you don't confuse him by letting him do something else when you have told him to "Stay." When you give him that command, *that* is what it means and nothing else. He should become as steady as though he were sitting in a pot of glue, and without any forceful methods of training being necessary. Always return to him after you have given him the "Stay" command.

Actually the most important ingredient in the makeup of a good trainer is just good old fashioned "horse sense." This reminds us of an incident we heard of that happened at a training class, where there was a problem dog who was always breaking the Stays. Of all things to try, someone was stationed in a field or bushes behind the group and shot the erring canine with a BB gun when he broke! Just what would be *your* reaction, if you were the dog? We are sure that *we* would have wanted to get all the further away from that spot, and the faster the better.

Recall

The next exercise for us to concentrate on, and a most important one it is, is the Recall—teaching your dog to come to you when you give him the command. We would imagine it might be a toss-up as to which would be used more often, in your routine life with Buddy, the "Down, Stay" or the "Buddy, Come."

Your first step in teaching this begins with the "recall while heeling." Some people refer to this as a "come fore," but we prefer the other term. With your dog at heel position, your lead folded to the proper length into your right hand, say "Buddy, Heel" and start forward about five or six steps. With your right foot on a forward step, call your dog's name and the command, "Come;" at the *same* time drop both hands forward and down in front of your dog's head, at that level, and start to trot backwards. His name and your hands will give you his attention. Drop the folds of the lead so that it does not become tight at any time and keep him trotting until you come to a halt, about five or six steps back. Keep

Dog at Heel position, before Recall

Dog sitting in front, Recall on lead

the lead short enough that it does not touch the floor, to avoid getting Buddy's feet entangled in it, but don't pull on it or jerk it. Bring him to you with your voice, coaxing if necessary, and with his eyes following your hands. As he comes close to your feet in front, command him to "Sit", and at the same time, bring both your hands up by your chest, doing it so that his eyes follow the motion of them as he sits. When you time this right, it activates an almost mechanical leverage. Raising the head up helps to put the tail end down!

You may have to guide him into the Sit with your lead at first, but loosen it completely as soon as possible and never jerk it. You are *not* correcting here for he has not learned anything yet, so he can't make a mistake. You are teaching by showing and guiding. Let that showing and guiding be through voice, the motion of your hands and the collar and lead. Do *not* push down on your dog's back to get him into a Sit, come *up* with the collar and lead if you have to remind him what Sit means. Do not try to straighten him with your feet—they are supposed to be something he wants to be near, rather than something from which to receive corrections. If you get a crooked Sit, or one that is too far away or one too close (any part of your dog touching you or sitting between your feet), then start over and try again instead of correcting. Study yourself and improve your own timing and movements.

When Buddy is sitting in front of you, in the proper position, tell him to "Stay" and holding the lead up out of his way, circle around behind him and come into Heel position. Wait there a few seconds, then go down beside him and really let him know how pleased you are with his performance. Each time you go through the complete exercise, make a concerted effort to improve yourself in your own movements, your commands, your footwork, working all of them together to give the best timing you are capable of.

If you should run into a little trouble and find your Buddy is balking after he has turned toward you and you have called him and the lead has tightened, don't start to jerk the lead and show your temper. Instead, stop moving and squat down to his level, and call him in a pleasant, coaxing tone, keeping the lead snug but not dragging him, using it as a guide. As he reaches you, praise him, turn and repeat the exercise and forget the Sit for the time being. Teach him that it is just as much fun for him to come to you as it is for you to go to him. "Happiness is Togetherness." You can perfect the Sit in Front as you progress in your training, aiming for the Sit to be straight toward you, close to you but outside of an imaginary line drawn across the toes of your shoes, not between your feet.

Down

The next exercise for us to tackle is a *most* important one, for it has been known, many times, as being the means of saving dogs' lives. It is teaching your dog what "Down" means, and eventually having him respond to it on both the verbal command and the signal. Buddy might catch on to this very easily or he might try your patience and make you wonder if he will ever catch on to what you want him to do. Patience, perseverance and praise should be your guide here, as well as in most of your training. You must remember that your dog has to be *shown* what Down means, in a way that he will not resent. You cannot describe things to him in words, as you would in teaching a child. You will be communicating to your dog with your hands, showing what you want, giving the command "Down" at the same time so that he can associate the word with the act of going into the lying down position. Do all of your teaching of this exercise during your Basic and Novice training from a position beside your dog. Some like to teach it from a position in front of and facing their dogs, but this only adds confusion at this point in training.

Inasmuch as a variation of teaching the "Down" is often determined by the size of the dog, we will start with what seems to work best with the larger breeds, such as Great Danes, St. Bernards, Irish Wolfhounds, and Newfoundlands. Put your dog at heel position and have him Sit. Adjust the lead in your right hand so that it will be taut when your hand takes hold of the lower part of the foreleg. Don't forget, the collar is not tightening, the lead is fastened to the nonworking ring. Holding the lead in your right hand, place your left hand over your dog's shoulder, resting the forearm and elbow along his back to reassure him and give him confidence. With your right hand, reach down to the lowest part of his right foreleg and with the back of your hand gently push his foot out and up, just enough to raise it from the floor. Hold it for a moment, then let it back down on the floor and tell Buddy how good he is. Repeat the same thing with the other foot, getting him to relax, using gentleness and good tone of voice, and not letting him get excited. If he should try to stand, come in with a little pressure from your left arm over his back and tell him to "Sit"; then continue as before.

Your next move is going to require smoothness of movement on your part and everything working together, so make sure you know what you're going to do before you try it, even if you have to practise it first without your dog. We would suggest you try it inside your home first, unless you enjoy comments from your neighbors, such as "I wonder what that crazy character thinks he's doing now!" When you start to practise with Buddy, put him in a Sit at Heel position, placing your left arm over his back and shoulder as explained above. Adjust the lead to the proper length in your right hand. Put your right hand and arm behind both front feet and gently push them forward and slightly upward, taking them completely off the floor. At the same time you and your dog are going through this motion, give him the command "Down." A slight pressure with your left hand and arm, especially toward your own body to guide him onto one hip as he goes down, coupled with both front feet taken from under him, leaves him no recourse other than to go into a Down position. Give him much praise when you get him down, but don't expect a lot from him and keep him there for no more than a few seconds. Release him and let him know how pleased you are. You can extend the length of the Down-Stay later, when he gets more steady and is less confused and used to regular practise periods.

If you do encounter some resentment on this exercise (and this frequently happens if your dog is six months of age or older before you start), a very good tip is for you to back him into a corner to teach him. This puts you in control without any necessity of rough handling and your dog will be correcting himself. Your hands will be free to use as directed and you can concentrate on *your* part of the process. If you still don't accomplish what you set out to do, let it go until tomorrow when you are calmer and you have yourself under control. This is one exception to the old adage, where it *is* better to put off until tomorrow what you tried to do today! Don't risk losing your temper so that you force your dog, for right then and there, you could lose all you have previously gained. From then on, you and Buddy might cease to be the companions to each other that you want to be and *should* be.

Now, for those whose Buddy may be in the medium size class, such as a Doberman Pinscher, a German Shepherd Dog, a Boxer, or a Collie, you may find this approach a bit more effective and easier for both of you. Start the same way as with the real big dog, adjust the lead the same way, but with your left arm, reach over his shoulder and pick up his left foot (as you did before with the right hand and his right foot). Next, raise his right foot with your right hand, enough to realize that he is relaxed. Then put these two motions together, lifting his front legs so he is almost in an upright sitting position, sort of "cradled" against you (see Page 37). Let him return to his normal Sit beside you and praise and reassure him so you gain his complete confidence. When you see that you have this, go through the procedure again, making sure your left forearm is resting against Buddy's side as you hold his left front leg. Using some pressure on his side and back, bring him toward you as you stretch both front feet out

Teaching Down at Heel position, lead on "dead" ring

Down at Heel position, lead on "dead" ring

and down, giving the "Down" command at the same time. Try to do all this together in a very smooth, all-in-one motion. Your dog should be lying down on his right hip, toward you, completely relaxed, at the end of this motion. He will be more comfortable in this position and will not be likely to try to get up right away, as may happen if his feet are directly under him. Give him encouragement and show your pleasure, without exciting him and tell him to "Stay." Keep your left hand on his shoulders, exerting a slight pressure downward, if it should be necessary in your particular case. Release him after a few seconds in this position and praise him. Repeat this three or four times, being sure you get the relaxed and comfortable position that Buddy enjoys. Each time will be easier for both of you and the Stay part becomes longer as he realizes what you want.

If you should encounter the problem of your dog trying to back away from you, with the medium or smaller size dog you won't need to hunt for a corner to work him, as with the great big fellow. All you need to do is put him in front of your left knee and proceed from there.

Now, for those of you who have a much smaller size pal, a Toy type, your approach is almost identical to that described for the medium and larger dogs. Again, whether it is easy or difficult depends upon your own ability to put across to your dog, by "showing", what you want him to do. The one big difference in working with the little dog is that the pressure exerted against his back or side to put him down and lying on his right hip, comes from your left wrist or forearm. The size of your Buddy will determine just where this so-called pressure point is. Keep him quite close to your left leg as you work. He will like it better and you will accomplish more. Follow the same procedure as given above, but just tip him over and down instead of sliding him into position. Be sure, when you are teaching this exercise, that you are *not* in a standing position yourself. Get down so that you are on your left knee, or even on both knees (in case of the little Toy dogs). You will not only be more comfortable yourself, you also will gain more from this position because you will be at your dog's level.

When you are down at "dog level", you will be avoiding a further problem that might develop in your dog on account of the feeling he would get when you tower over him. To him, especially if he is a bit insecure, you look like the Empire State Building bending over him. And he certainly can't tell, at this stage, whether or not your foundation is solid or heavy enough to keep you from toppling over onto him. Always

Teaching Down in motion, lead on "dead" ring

remember, too, to praise for a job well done, particularly each small part of a job done correctly.

When you think your canine pal really understands what the command "Down" means, it is time for you to progress a bit further and start teaching the exercise while you and he are in motion; that is, "heeling." Be sure that the lead is still in the non-slip ring of the collar with the rings and the snap underneath the chin. Both hands are on the lead, which has been adjusted to a comfortably short length. Give the Heel command, go three or four steps and come to a halt. *But, as you come into the halt,* give the command "Down" and, at the same time, go down onto your left knee, sliding your left hand along the lead toward the collar, the palm facing the floor, and let your arm stiffen as you take Buddy down. If your arm action is correct, your hand will touch the floor with the lead under it, at the completion of this motion. Try to get all the action coordinated so everything is one smooth movement. Praise your pal and repeat the exercise. You won't need many practise sessions before he is going down on just the command. Drop the hand pressure on the lead as soon as you start to get any response, but don't be afraid to go back to it if he needs a reminder. You are not hurting him or getting any resentment as long as you work on the non-slip ring. Be sure your own happy tone of voice carries on through all your training. As you advance, you soon will be able to give him the command to Stay, after he has gone down, then circle him and return to Heel position.

Finish

The next exercise we will tackle is teaching Buddy to come into the heel position, on command, from a sitting position in front of your feet. We refer to this as the "finish" exercise, for that is the command given by the judge in Obedience classes when your dog has come to you on a

Teaching signal for finish around body

Dog responding to finish around body

Teaching, on lead, the signal for the dog to "finish to heel" to the left

recall or a retrieve, or similar exercises. The American Kennel Club Obedience Regulations, in describing a "finish," state: "The method by which the dog goes to the heel position shall be optional with the handler, provided it is done smartly and the dog sits straight at heel." In other words, he can go to your left and come into a Sit or he can go to your right, circle around behind you and come into a Sit, at heel position. Now, it is quite possible that you may run into some difficulty with this exercise *if* you approach it with a preset idea of which way you are going to have your dog finish. We suggest that you learn what to do so you can try both ways with your pal, and *let him tell you* which way *he* wants to go!

However, before you try it with him to see which way works best, you must first master your footwork, commands, and lead handling, and put them all together smoothly. You might feel very foolish practising thus without him, but just think—you might even be developing a couple of new dance steps! You might even find you are a modern Fred Astaire or Ginger Rogers! Anyway, it is important that you know what you are doing before you try it out on Buddy. Practise both styles before you try him out.

It used to be the thought of many obedience instructors that the size of the dog was the determining factor in the finish, smaller ones to the left and larger ones around in back. Still others had personal preferences as to which they liked best and insisted that each and every one of their pupils do it the same way. In fact, this is still true throughout many areas of the country, with many clubs and numerous classes of instructors who are not affiliated with training organizations. But, again, we prefer to approach it from the "dog's point of view," trying to make it as easy as possible for the dog and the handler as a team.

The idea of testing a dog was initially brought home to us by our first Corgi, "Ronnie." When trying to teach her to finish to the left, as all our other dogs and those of our pupils had done previously, she was balking and putting on her brakes. She apparently objected to moving away far enough to make a circle and come back to Sit in the heel position. But her problem was miraculously dissolved when she was shown that she could circle behind and come in to Sit at heel. This way, she could stay close, all the way around. Even though we attributed this to her natural heeling instinct, Corgis having been bred primarily for herding by nipping at the heels, we later found that it did not necessarily hold true as a breed pattern. Only two, of five we have had, preferred this style of finish!

Guiding dog with lead, finishing to left, showing footwork and lead handling.

Let us tackle the finish to the left first. Imagine your dog is sitting facing you, up close but not touching your toes, your lead folded into your right hand and your left hand on the lead for guiding. To begin with, we want you to concentrate on your footwork. The motion of your *left* foot will be back and slightly *to* the left, so you will stay in balance. Think of your *right* foot as your anchor, for each time you will return to position at that point, not moving the right foot. Got it? Try it again, left foot out and back, then return. Now, let's combine some commands and your lead handling along with the step back.

As you start your step, your command will be "Buddy, Come!" Your left hand will guide him (not drag) in a circle to the left and *away* from you. Command "Heel," and as he completes the circle back to you, your left foot is returning to its original position alongside your right foot. Then, command "Buddy, Sit!" as he comes into heel position. Practise it now, everything all together, until hands, feet and commands are working smoothly and together. Remember, when you start to practise with your dog, you will not be dragging him around but rather, you will be talking him into it and guiding him. Adjust the length of your step

Footwork and lead handling, dog finishing around body

back to allow your dog to make the full circle and come into proper heel position.

In practising the alternate style of finish, the circle around behind you, the right foot goes back and to the right, the opposite from that described above. The lead is also held opposite, as you will be guiding with the *right* hand this time. Be sure your lead is well folded in your hand, as you will pass it from your right hand, and back to your left, as you guide Buddy behind your back and into position at your left side. Remember, as he starts to move past you, return your right foot to its normal position and get it out of his way. The commands are still the same, "Buddy, Come!", to get him moving, then "Heel," then "Sit," as he comes into position. It may take you a bit longer to get your hands, feet and commands coordinated on this one, but "practise makes perfect." (Refer to "left about turn" in the Novice chapter for further help, if any problems develop here.)

Now that you, yourself, can do both methods without too much thinking about it, get Buddy and test him to find out which way is easier for him. Most likely, it will be very evident, as most dogs will go very willing-

Guiding dog with lead, finishing around body

1—"Buddy, Come"

2—"Heel"

3—"Sit"

ly one way with just a bit of talking and guiding, but will resent the opposite way. Don't try to force him one way; see if he goes easier the other way. If, as happens in rare instances, you get a willing response both ways, then and then *only,* make your own choice as to which you prefer, and stick to that one style for his training.

As you progress in the work on this exercise, start eliminating the "extras," the Come command, the foot going back, the guiding and the Sit command. If he should be sitting slowly as he comes into heel position, bounce a command to him every now and then, timing it just as he starts the Sit. It might even be necessary, occasionally (when he starts to test *you* to find out if you mean what you say) to give him a reminder via the training collar, just a quick snap and an immediate release, followed by praise. When you and Buddy have mastered this exercise, all that will be necessary on your part will be to command, "Buddy, Heel!" and he will bounce into position at your left side, according to whichever style of finish you have taught him.

Wait

We now have one more command to teach before closing this chapter on the Basic work. Buddy has already learned the command to Stay. If you will remember, you will realize that he has been given that command *only* when you have left him and returned to him, coming into heel position. Now, in an effort to avoid confusion in his mind and to make his learning easier, we will teach him another command which will keep him steady in position *until* he is given a following command which involves his moving to do something else. This new command, chosen because it is easier for people to remember it, is "Wait." In other words, what we are really implying is: "Stay" until I return to you, "Wait" until I give you a command to do something else. The first "something else" will be the Recall, giving your dog the command to Come.

To teach—Heel your dog a few steps, halt, and give the command "Wait" along with the signal. This signal is similar to that you used for the Stay, coming from the front of your body, palm open and facing your dog, swinging across in front of his head, but *not* stopping directly in front as you did with the Stay. Either hand may be used, depending upon your own comfort and preference. As you give the signal and command, step away on your right foot. When you reach the end of the lead, turn and face your dog, say "Buddy, Come!" and move backward a few steps as you did in teaching the Recall on Lead. Guide him in to you and have him sit in front of your feet, facing you, remembering to use a pleasant tone of voice in your command to encourage him to move. Be careful you don't yank the lead on any of your Recall training, for you want to avoid any "correction" association with this and the Finish. You can vary it so Buddy doesn't fall into a habit pattern. Follow the Recall part of the time with the Finish, as "Buddy, Heel!" Other times, say "Stay" and *you* return to *him,* at heel position, circling around behind him and holding the lead up out of his way. Always follow with PRAISE.

All of the exercises you have learned thus far will now be gone into in greater detail in the next and ensuing chapters. You will see how you can prepare your dog for competition in Obedience classes at Dog Shows. You will see, too, how you can perfect his performance and improve your control of him and enjoy him more as your companion in your everyday life. He will be able to accompany you on walks and on trips in the car without being a bother to anyone. He will become a well-behaved member of your family and the community, one of which you can justly be proud.

Novice

NOW that you and Buddy have learned the exercises that we have presented in the Kindergarten and Basic chapters, you will find how important they are, for, as you will see, they form the very foundation of all the Obedience Training. If your lessons have been learned well, everything will come easy to you as you go along. You will be putting the various exercises together, and your practise sessions will become much more interesting for both you and Buddy. You also will find how really valuable your accomplishments can be, as you progress and apply them to your everyday living.

Up to this point, your education could be compared to the real human kindergarten and the primary grades of the average school system. But we want to keep on with our learning, advancing grade by grade, climbing on up through high school and college. Right now, let's see about getting through the elementary grades.

Dog Attention

As any teacher knows, you cannot make any headway with a pupil who is not giving his attention. It is just as true with your dog. Therefore, it is of prime importance that you learn how to get and keep "dog attention," before you go any further with your training. It is the key to all your training, whether you are aiming for just a well-behaved pal or a dog that will be advanced enough to go into competition in Obedience classes at dog shows.

Dog attention

If you are not familiar with the various class divisions and the titles that can be earned through this competition, refer to the appendix and read the American Kennel Club Obedience Regulations. This is an extremely interesting outgrowth of more or less formal obedience training done in groups or classes. The Regulations have undergone a number of changes, as demands for them became evident over the years since Obedience competition was first initiated in the mid-1930s. Some of the changes have been due to an effort to try to bring together the people whose interests go beyond dog training and Obedience competition, such as Obedience and field work, Obedience and breed showing, and occasionally some who are interested in participating in all three. The chief concern in aiming at such multiple activity is to avoid confusion in your dog's mind. But let us not digress; back to the training—

Buddy knows how to Sit, Heel, Come, Finish, Down, and also the difference between Stay and Wait. He still has to learn that he must give you attention all the time in your practise sessions, whenever you give him any commands, and that he must be alert to anything you might do or ask him to do unexpectedly. Don't *ever* let your practise sessions become cut and dried, with always the same pattern and sequence so he can tell just what you're going to do next. Such performances can only guarantee boredom for both you and Buddy. Put forth a real effort to make the training FUN for both of you. The bond developed between you, as a working team, will become all the more valuable. One more thing—put just as much concentration, or even more, on your efforts in training and teaching Buddy as you expect and demand from him.

Heeling On Lead

We're going to begin with some Heeling On Lead. You will see some repetition of much of the work already, but remember that only through that repetition can you accomplish anything that will be lasting.

Put Buddy in Heel position, give him the command and step off (left foot), take just a few steps and come to a halt (left foot *last* in motion), and have him sit. You are going to start demanding a little more from him now, so don't let him get away with a slow sit. If you see this developing, start to correct it right now. As you come into the halt (*not* after you have stopped) be ready with a quick flip of your left wrist on the lead as he comes to a stop. Always keep your lead folded short enough so that you have immediate control, but not so that you are dragging him. Your lead is still fastened in the non-working ring, so a correction is going to cause no resentment. Be sure to remember the praise and that good tone of voice which brings about Buddy's enjoyment of his work with you. In your practise, vary the heeling as much as you can. He knows how to walk, so don't go all over the place before halting. Put in some left turns, some right turns, some changes of pace and some about turns. Avoid repeating a pattern of exercises, change it around.

Mentioning changes, let us give you another change right now. This will be a slight challenge for you at first, but it will serve a dual purpose. It will help to break the monotony, and it also will be a boon in teaching Buddy that his proper Heel position is definitely *only* at your LEFT side. This is called the "left about turn" and is done while you are in motion. Be sure your lead is folded into your right hand. You will be reversing your direction—turning to your left on this, but Buddy will be guided across in front of you to your right, circling around behind you, coming back into heel position on your left. In order to get him around to your right and behind, as you turn to the left, you move your right hand (lead enclosed in it) behind you, and pass the lead to your left hand as Buddy circles around. Believe it or not, this is really very simple once you get the hang of it. Try it very slowly at first, step by step. If you have difficulty, get somebody to read the directions to you as you go through the steps. When practising, don't hesitate to give an extra command of "Heel!" when you change direction on a turn or an about turn, either left or right. You may accompany it, if necessary, with a slight flip of the wrist on the lead as a reminder to pay attention, but don't get in the habit of correcting all the time. Do it ONLY when necessary.

If you should find Buddy being really distracted by something and not responding to the usual command and lead handling, it is time for a bit more drastic treatment. Make your voice command a bit sharper and your lead correction more severe (be sure it is an immediate release) and time it well. If he shows any hesitation with this, act as though nothing unusual has happened and come out enthusiastically with something like this, "Oh, Boy! That was a good one, wasn't it?" Keep on your merry way, taking his mind completely off the correction. You might find it necessary, if you are sure that Buddy really knows the work and is only goofing off or "testing" you, to make the correction once or twice with the lead on the working ring. Be sure you return to the non-working ring right away and remember, always, to keep it this way when teaching any new exercise.

As you are practising your heeling, we want you to think of another important thing which will help still more to make you and Buddy a team that really belongs together. Perhaps you've been walking too slowly for him, or maybe your stride has been too long, or your steps too short and choppy. In other words, we want you to experiment with this a bit and to work in a style that will get the best response from him, with both of you presenting a "natural" appearance. We want you to work in rhythm. About the best aid we have found toward accomplishing this is to do your heeling to a background of good marching music, loud enough to hear it, but not so loud as to be disturbing. Your own step will be lighter and your spirit lifted, just as it is when you are on the sidewalk watching a passing parade, tapping your toe to the beat of the drum. And this spirit in your own step will transfer right to Buddy, from you!

When testing for the proper length of stride to use with your pal, remember that each and every dog can be as individually different as people are in their characteristics. A good dog, properly put together, built right, is indeed a beautiful sight when moving at his best to show himself off. And we can learn to move with him at his "best" speed, to bring out the best in him, even though he may not be the best specimen of his breed.

Think about your first step in motion, as you start heeling. If Buddy forges ahead, it may be too slow or too small a step. If he lags immediately, probably it is too fast or too long a stride. This should cue you to your first revision of your own habits. For your next self-analysis, you will need the help of a friend, another trainer or, if you are attending a training class, your instructor. It is best for the observer to sit on the floor or a low step or hassock, to get as close to "dog level" as he can, so he gets a good profile view as you and Buddy heel past him. Have him watch the movement of his back line. If he is not moving at the right speed, his back will be "bouncey," the shoulders and hips will be going up and down. Increase the speed gradually until your observer tells you that his back line has smoothed out, almost "floating" in a nearly straight line. You will even be able to feel it yourself, once you've been made aware of it. Buddy, too, you will find will enjoy this pace much more and he will give you better attention in this little trot. When he walks slowly and plodding, he has too much time to think about other things and be distracted by them.

Another "attention getter" to use in your heeling practise is a side step to the right, quickly and without advance warning. If you lose Buddy's attention for a moment, be ready to step quickly to your right and give another "Heel" command. Continue on with your heeling, do not hesitate. Tell him what a good boy he is. At no time, in handling your lead or in making any corrections, should you allow your hands to go above your waist. Use your hands and your wrists, not your arms. If you do not, you not only waste your energy, you lose your timing and you telegraph to your pal that "something" is coming, long before you start. Bring just as much variety into your heeling practise as you possibly can. Surprise Buddy with a left turn when he's not paying attention. Get his mind off it right away with a little sweet talk, but he will have gotten the message that he should pay attention and watch out for what this clumsy ox of a master might do next! Perhaps an unexpected about turn or a left about would be the answer—even a right turn. Always talk him into forgetting any correction or reminder of what he should have done. It is much easier to form correct habits than to reform bad habits, so think and plan ahead for his sake and yours, too.

With some of the dogs, especially the really boisterous spirited types, you are likely to encounter a forging problem. You can cope with this just as successfully as with other problems. About the simplest method is to use the lead behind you, instead of holding it in front, as explained in Basic, especially if you are small and Buddy is big. To adjust the lead properly, put your dog at Heel position, bring the lead across and behind you, then fold it up into your right hand so there is no slack in it when your hand is resting on your right hip. Keep it in that position as you are heeling. If Buddy tries to forge ahead, your body against the lead will prevent him from going out ahead of you, and your arms will not be tired from trying to hold him back. Talk to him and let him know how pleased you are when he is in the proper position.

In practising the slow pace, if you see his head start to tip to smell the floor or the ground, make a sudden change in your pattern along with a Heel command and a wrist flip correction, "Good Boy!," etc. Demand attention all the time and acknowledge when he gives you that attention. Let him know how happy he has made you.

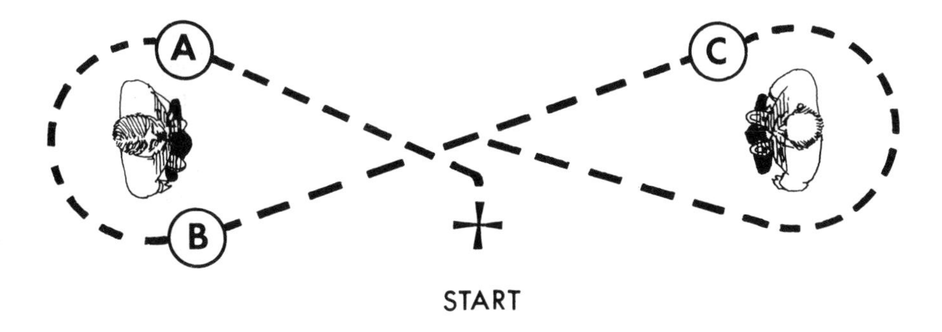

Diagram of path for Figure Eight

Figure Eight

Another variation in your heeling practise will lead into your being able to do what we call the Figure Eight exercise. This is required in show competition and it also has a practical application, no matter where you and your pal go together. It teaches Buddy, still more strongly, to watch in which direction your feet are going. For example, in a straight heeling pattern, you might suddenly decide to make a small circle to your left, then continue on again in the same direction in which you were going. In order for him to keep from getting in the way of your feet, he must hold back a bit, as he is making a smaller circle than you are. In the opposite direction, a circle to the right will demand a quickening of his pace in order to keep up with you and not lag, as this time he is making a larger circle than you are. In one situation, you probably will have to restrain him slightly with your left hand on the lead to show him where you want him. In the other, you may have to coax him up with your voice, even put your left hand in front of his head to give him an incentive and a guide. In both cases, drop all the extra help as soon as possible, but don't hesitate to remind him where he belongs any time you find he is getting careless!

As you get used to working in the single circles to the left and right, your next step forward is to practise the two together—first to the left, then to the right. Next, set up two items (e.g., two chairs), approximately eight feet apart and with ample room for you and Buddy to circle each one. (In a training class and in the dog shows, real people, acting as "stewards," stand for you to heel around them, instead of the chairs).

To begin, place yourself about midway between the two chairs, but about two feet back from the midline between them. This will allow you two or three steps to get yourself and Buddy underway before you go into your first turn. Almost everyone follows the practise of taking the left circle first, avoiding the likelihood of lagging right away. Occasionally, a dog is such an eager beaver to get going that he might benefit from going to the right first, but this is a rarity. If you have faithfully practised your circles, you should not have too much difficulty going around your new "posts." Your chief point for concentration in circling around to the left is to allow the *same* amount of space between you and the "post" for Buddy *all the way around,* until you start the crossover toward the other post, through the center.

As you approach the second post, on a straight line across, be ready to swing into your right circle as you get near it, not after you get alongside it. Here you must concentrate on keeping an even space all the way around between you and the post, walking erect, not dipping your shoulders or brushing against it. Any deviation like this shows up in your own footwork and thus affects Buddy's heeling, so be careful you don't blame him for something for which you might be to blame. Keep your speed and your size of steps the same all the way around both directions of the circles, teaching your dog to make the adjustment of slowing to your left and picking up into a trot on going to your right. Follow the same tips on teaching that we have already pointed out for you in working "circle to the left" and "circle to the right" while heeling. Talking, encouraging and guiding, coupled with your own proper foot pattern will do the trick.

Don't overdo your practise on the Figure Eight as it could become boring, just like anything else. Remember that it is a Heeling exercise and be on the alert to avoid the development of any bad habits. If you should see Buddy sniffing at the chair or the ground, correct immediately, keep him working after the correction and take his mind off it. "Oh, Boy! That was a good one!" and voice praise. Try halting at various places as you go around, even trying an about turn as you get more proficient. Make it fun, but don't lose sight of your goal.

When you and Buddy are working well enough that you can perform satisfactorily, without guiding, without corrections and with the lead over your right shoulder (or tucked into your belt) with a little slack in it, you are ready to try the Figure Eight with people standing as your "posts." This will be a new experience for your pal as he may be very interested in the people and want to claim them for new friends. You must still remain alert and be ready, again, to administer a correction, as above, if he starts to sniff and pay attention to the posts. You must remind him that this is neither the time or place for that type of behavior.

Before leaving the Heeling on Lead and the Figure Eight, we want to bring something else to your attention. We have been dealing primarily with Buddy's behavior and performance and with your commands, your voice, hands and footwork. As both you and he improve, and you gain more confidence in his responses, we would like to see you show it, not only to others who might be observing you but also to him. Don't forget for a minute, either, that he's aware of whether or not you have confidence. Show it by keeping your head up and your eyes forward, instead of looking down at him all the time. You have worked with him long enough now that you can tell whether or not he is in the proper position. You can see a lot with your side vision and can feel a lot with your lead. Give Buddy confidence in you by showing confidence in him.

Off Lead

Now that Buddy is working well on a loose lead, with no extra commands or corrections being necessary, what do you think the next logical step should be with your training? Why, OFF LEAD, of course! And what a big and important step that is, for you *must* be sure he is ready for it. Trying this too soon, or making a mistake in the way you do it, can give Buddy an opportunity to get out of control and you'll have your foundation work to do all over again. If this happens, it may take even longer than before to build up that necessary confidence between the two of you. Be sure that you are ready, and be sure you understand what to do and how to do it before you attempt it. "Look before you leap."

There is one test we would recommend that you give yourself before you attempt to work off lead. Confidence on lead is one thing, but confidence *off* lead is something else again. If you don't have this, your own feelings will travel right down to your dog and he will know whether or not you are sure of yourself and have control of the situation. Test your control by doing some heeling with the lead thrown over your right shoulder, both hands free. If you don't have to put a hand on your lead or make any kind of correction, you can pass the test with flying colors and be on your way, trying the off lead heeling.

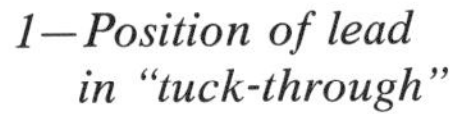

1—Position of lead in "tuck-through"

2—Holding lead, ready to "flip for attention"

To help you and your pal and to make it easier for you, we have a new way to use your lead. It is the means of keeping his attention during the teaching and practise. Take the lead off the collar, put the loop end through the collar, passing it under at the back of the head and toward the tail (pay no attention to the rings). With your left hand, put the little finger into the loop, then take the lead coming through the front side of the collar and hold that, also in your left hand. Fold into your right hand the balance of the lead (see illustration). Adjust the length of the part in

3—Lead released

4—Lead removed

your left hand so that the doubled portion has no slack in it but is not tight, with your dog sitting at heel position. Be sure the lead is put *under* the collar, with the loop *toward* the tail, as this avoids any possibility of the lead falling across your dog's face or in front of his eyes when it is released. If you should find a more comfortable way to hold the lead and accomplish the same results, by all means, feel free to do it your way.

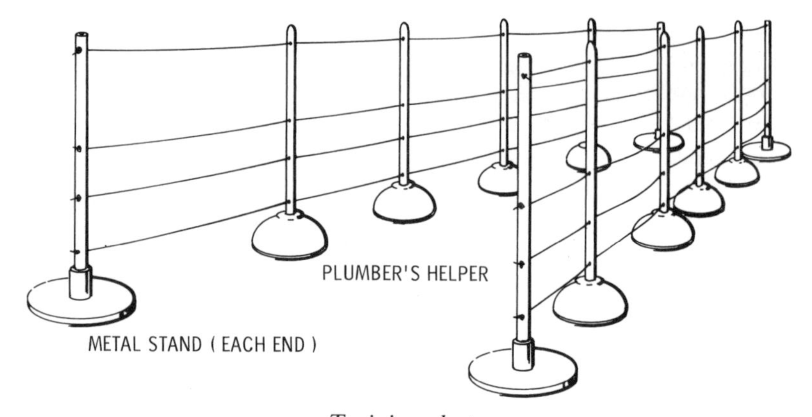

Training chute

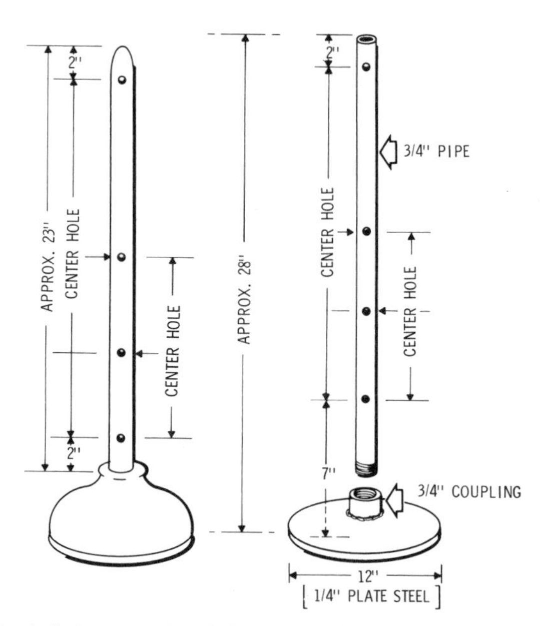

Plumber's helpers and weighted ends (for use in training chute)

In addition to learning the new use of the lead, "tucked through" the collar, we also recommend a training aide that has proved invaluable over a good number of years. You can make up a substitute idea for use in your own training area, if you wish, but a portable type of chute is best, for it can be moved to different positions and various sites and can be used for almost all the exercises to be mastered. As you can see from the illustrations and diagrams, it is composed chiefly of lengths of small cord strung between a series of plumbers' plungers. One word of caution —when you go into a store and ask if they have plumbers plungers with a long handle and the clerk brings one out for your inspection, be prepared for an expression of shock and disbelief on his face when you tell him that's just what you want and you'd like to have eleven more! Then when you tell him you want them for *dog training,* he'll really look at you as though you had bats in the belfry!

Now that you have the training chute set up and you have learned how to tuck the lead through the collar and hold it right, let's put the two together. Heel Buddy a bit first, then heel him through the chute so he knows it will not hurt him. Make it about 4 feet wide so he will not feel crowded as you walk through. Then come into it again, about 2 or 3 feet, and come to a halt. Unsnap the lead, tuck it through and fold up the extra length. Tell Buddy to Heel. After two or three steps, snap the lead UP just enough to get attention, but not enough to raise the feet off the floor, and immediately let it drop off your little finger. Then draw it through and out of the collar, folding it up as you go. After four or five steps, come to a halt still inside the chute, and praise your pal for doing so well. He has been initiated in OFF LEAD heeling, and so have you! Before going further, put the lead through again and get into position again in the chute. At the beginning and until you are sure that you have Buddy's constant attention, also be sure that you start inside the chute and halt when you are still inside it. As you progress, you can do some about turns off lead, but still within the chute. Be sure you master this part *before* you start Off Lead Heeling without the "plumbers helpers" for your guide.

One thing we want to impress upon you, in using the "tucked through" lead, is the importance of drawing it out smoothly, as unobtrusively as possible, then immediately folding it up and out of the way. Don't forget the little "attention-getter" before the release, the little snap upward. Be sure there is no bump thickness on the loop of the lead to catch on the collar as it is pulled through. If you do find this is happening, try turning it so the "bump" is next to Buddy's body instead of against the collar. At this point, we want to absolutely avoid anything that might resemble a correction. We want to establish that complete rapport between you and your pal, your confidence in him and his in you. The elimination of making any fuss and ado about removing his lead will go a long way in helping to establish this.

Don't get any mistaken ideas about the lead not being an important piece of equipment, now that you have Buddy's attention Off Lead. This is one item that you should consider indispensable throughout *all* your training, no matter how basic or how advanced. You may need it for a reminder, a refresher, or for a correction (when *he* tries training *you* instead of you training him!), and you definitely will need it *every* time you teach him something different and new. If it is used for a reminder or guide, use it in the "tuck through" technique, as we have just described.

In practising the Off Lead work, start introducing the turns, the about turns and the changes in pace. Here you will probably see Buddy going a bit wide, lagging or forging. Don't hesitate to tuck the lead through his collar and use the attention getter just as you are starting to make a right or an about turn; guide him on the left turn with it by holding him back a bit; use it as you float into the fast pace, just as you worked in teaching him On Lead Heeling. Remember, too, the importance of your tone of voice—talk to him enthusiastically as you work and let him know how pleased you are. If you need to, and you should be able to judge this by now, go back to working on lead for a while. It won't do any harm and *may* do a lot of good.

Stand For Examination

Our next project will be to teach Buddy the Stand for Examination exercise. This may seem rather pointless to you, unless you are definitely training for Obedience competition in the show ring, as it is one of the required exercises in the Novice classes where you show in order to get your Companion Dog (C.D.) title. But let us take a look at the practical side of the situation. You most certainly want your dog to express no fear or shyness when he meets a person, especially if it should be a relative, a friend, or most importantly, your veterinarian. You should be able to depend upon his acceptance of patting and praise, examination by a breed or an obedience judge, or a more specific and detailed physical examination by a veterinarian, and all of this on a *command* from you.

In the K.P.T. chapter, the foundation was laid for this. In Basic, you advanced still further when you were teaching the Stand-Stay on lead. Your goal now will be to teach your pal to respond to a command and/or a signal to Stand and Stay, off lead, while you walk a short distance away from him, and turn and face him. He should then, in that position, accept a stranger's examination of him. If you prepared him for the type of "going-over" that he is likely to undergo in the breed ring, which may include looking at his teeth, feeling him all over his body, lifting his feet, setting him up, etc., then he surely will be able to accept any type of examination from anybody.

To begin the training, repeat the Stand-Stay, on lead, and then introduce the examination by a stranger, gradually, while you are standing facing Buddy, fairly close to him. You may have to do a little bartering with your next door neighbors or Aunt Nell when she stops in for a visit, as a second person is naturally very necessary. Give specific instructions as to how you wish them to do this, as it must be taken gradually, step by step.

Have the "stranger" approach Buddy from the front and ask that he please not stare at the dog. Let him extend a hand toward Buddy so that he can smell it, the *back* of the hand toward his nose. Here you are simply teaching what is an accepted "safety" gesture which anyone should practise when around strange dogs. If a dog (naturally, not your Buddy!) should make a pass, aggressively, toward the hand, it is easy to close it into a fist and draw it away intact. With the palm extended, under the same circumstances, there might easily be some ripped fingers!

Stand for Examination, off lead

Let the first "examination" be just a touch on top of the head. Then progress gradually until he will accept the hands on all areas of the body, including the mouth, so the teeth can be observed. Encourage his steadiness and willingness to accept such goings-over by repeating the command "Stay!" as needed. Do not expect too much of him, too fast. Increase your own distance from him slowly, until you are at the end of your six foot lead and he is steady. Don't be discouraged if this training should cover a period of a few weeks before you achieve the desired results. Patience will pay off.

Your next step will be to employ the "tuck through" technique of using the lead for getting attention. Walk your pal into a Stand-Stay or pose him, get his attention with the lead, give him the command to Stay, and as you leave him (on your right foot), release the lead and draw it out from his collar, folding it up out of sight or putting it in your pocket. Turn and face him, remembering not to stare at him, then return to him after the lapse of a few seconds. When you have progressed to the point where he is steady on this Stand-Stay off lead for three minutes, then start again with the short Stay, but bring in Aunt Nell or one of your neighbors again and progress as before with the examination.

While you are teaching this exercise, you might just as well start to familiarize Buddy with a signal for the Stand-Stay which will help to make things easier for both of you. This will also be the beginning training of some of your signal work in the advanced Utility exercises.

To start this, put your pal back on lead, making sure the lead is fastened in the non-slip ring of the collar and position it across your hips (as in the method for correction of forging), snugly held in your right hand at your right hip. You might as well also start to teach the Heeling signal and get Buddy familiar with both.

As you lead out with your left foot (and he has become used to following it, as his guide to move), bring your left hand in a swing motion from the outside toward the front of you and ahead of his head and face. (See photo, Page 185). Be sure the palm of your left hand is open and faces toward your dog so he has the full picture of it from his point of view. If you learn to give this signal properly, your dog will see it with no trouble, regardless of how small or how large he is, and you will not have to bend over. If you find it necessary to give the Heel command with the signal as you start to teach this don't hesitate, to make the association so everything is clear to him. You can drop the voice command after combining the two for a few times. This policy can be followed in teaching any of the signals.

For the Stand, as you come to a halt, hold the lead taut but don't pull *up* on it. Give the voice command to Stand, if necessary, as you introduce him to the signal. This starts in front of your body, waist high, with your left arm bent at the elbow, palm open and facing the floor. Keeping your hand in this position, swing your arm outward in this same plane, just far enough that your hand stops in line with, but out in front of, Buddy's head. Try it a few times, being careful to get all your moves working together and timed right, then drop the voice command as soon as possible. (Refer to photos, Pages 226 and 227.)

When he seems to be understanding the two signals and responds without the use of the voice commands, and the lead, start practising the exercise with the lead "tucked through" his collar. Remember to get his "attention" first, then draw the lead out and follow with the signal, then praise him for being so smart! If he didn't make it that time, stop and try to analyze yourself and find out where you erred—then start again, back *on* lead. It might even be wise to go back to the use of the board at this point. You can govern your own rate of progress if you remember to stop and think a little as you are working. Don't be too eager and work too fast to achieve perfection in each exercise you are teaching. Try to keep Buddy from becoming confused and be sure that he continues to enjoy his work, with both of you having fun together.

Recall Off Lead

The next exercise we're going to work on is a Recall Off Lead and is most likely to be the one that you would have preferred to work on *first.* After all, one of the most practical and important things for Buddy to learn is that he must respond immediately to the command "Come!", following his name for attention. It could, conceivably, mean the saving of his life. But the teaching of this exercise definitely should not be attempted before your pal is under control or before he has learned what it is to give you his complete attention. It is very important, too, that there should be no association with any punishment, pain or harsh tone of voice.

We have found that the most satisfactory training aid for the Recall is the chute, or a similar substitute, as this avoids the usual errors encountered and establishes the preferred habit patterns with no necessity for making corrections. Again, it is extremely important to proceed slowly on this, step by step. If you try to go too fast, you will find yourself back at the beginning and with a longer row to hoe next time. You see, if Buddy should get the idea that he has freedom when he is off lead and a distance away from you, you've had it! Go slowly and carefully if you would avoid this disaster.

First take him into the chute on lead and work with him as described in Basic—paying attention to the use of your hands, handling of the lead and your tone of voice, heeling, then backing up as you call him, and getting him to sit as he comes in front of you. When you are sure he knows what is expected of him, you will begin by using the lead in the "tuck through" position again. Working in the chute, command "Heel!"

and move forward at a brisk pace. About halfway along its length, get your "attention" with the little reminder flip of the lead. Withdraw the lead and get it out of sight. Then, using your hands for direction guidance and giving the "Come" in an encouraging tone of voice, back up and bring Buddy in on a trot to you, having him sit in front, facing you, as you come to a stop. Don't work on a "Finish to heel" at this point, as that can come later and we want no extra distractions now. We need to keep his attention and make it as much fun as possible. You can add a finish occasionally to vary the pattern and avoid monotony. Otherwise, just heel him away from his sit or tell him to Stay, circle him into Heel position, and then continue from there. Be sure to use the "tuck through" technique each time you practise the routine.

Your next step will be to get the "attention" from Buddy and withdraw the lead *before* you start in motion, as differentiated from above where you are in motion when you do this. This is also a good time for you to start disciplining yourself to not look at your pal. You are doing a disfavor to both of you by getting into this habit. When you can do this much with no problems, you are ready for a most important step. Remember, as your dog comes to you, use your hands to guide him in and, as he gets near enough to sit, continue the motion of your hands upward toward your chin. His eyes will follow your hands, tipping his head (*if* you have his attention, which you should) and this results in a nice, easy straight sit. Praise him at this point, after he has sat there for a few seconds. You may need to use the Sit command, for a few times, as he comes in. Don't be afraid to revert to it any time you feel it would be beneficial in the training.

Your next step is to take a position with Buddy at heel, inside the chute, and the lead tucked through. Get "attention," withdraw the lead, give him the command "Wait", and leave him, stepping off on your right foot. Traveling half the distance of the chute, stop and turn to face your dog. Call him, saying "Buddy! Come!" Encourage him (if necessary) to come in at a nice trot. Using your hands out in front of you as before, timing their motion with his approach to you, again guide him by raising your hands toward your chin and accompany the motion with the Sit command as he nears your toes. Keep his attention as he comes in and sits, giving him plenty of praise to let him know he has done well.

If Buddy should start slowing down at any time in your practise of the Recall, (he should always come in as though he is really anxious to get there, at a brisk pace), backtrack in your training and see if you can spot your trouble. More than likely, if you are honest with yourself, you will find the problem has developed from an improper tone of voice on your

Recall command. Try varying it and note the difference in his responses. Adopt the one that brings out the best in him, a tone that is pleasant and yet means business to him. Be careful about any show of temper on your part, any grabbing of skin or hair or collar on an attempted correction, as this is unwarranted and absolutely guarantees a setback in the training. Such behavior on your part will certainly not encourage a speedy response and a close sit in front.

As you repeat this exercise in practise, and there is improvement and better control in the performance, you may gradually increase the distance. Back up, though, and shorten the distance immediately if you should start to lose control at all, rather than—just because you want to prove you are BOSS—to try to administer an ill-timed or badly planned correction and have it result in defeating your purpose.

When Buddy does a really good Recall within the chute, about fifty feet of distance, you are ready to try one without the aid of it, free and clear. Start first with a much shorter distance, giving your pal the impression that you are close enough to have complete control. Again, increase your distance gradually. Return to inside the chute for your practise any time that you run into a problem. Don't move any further or faster than Buddy is capable of learning, and don't push any further than what he can take willingly.

If you and your companion have mastered all the exercises we have covered so far, you are now prepared to practise the complete individual routine as defined for the Novice Classes by the American Kennel Club in their Obedience Regulations. You also, by now, will have a dog that is trained and under control to the extent that he should exemplify model canine deportment in your everyday association with him. Make sure in your practise, that you change the sequence of the exercises from one session to another. Don't let it get boring and don't let Buddy train in such a routine that *he* can tell *you* what is supposed to come next.

Also, be sure you remember to *not* follow your dog with your eyes on the Recall. Learn to look over his head or to one side of him. You can still see him.

Long Sit

The Long Sit and Long Down exercise will be the next items to tackle. Your foundation training has already been done in Basic and you will be able to advance much further by yourself, but your soundest training

Practising Long Sit, showing use of board for correction

will take place in an Obedience Training Class or in a group of trainers who enjoy getting together for practise sessions. You need the presence of certain "temptations," if you are going to teach Buddy resistance to them and that he must restrain himself from his desire to romp with canine playmates or argue with them.

To start off, refresh his memory as to what "Stay" means, going back to on lead and with the lead fastened into the non-slip ring. Put him in a Sit, give the command and signal to Stay, leave on your right foot and go to the end of the lead. Turn and face him, being careful to put no tension on the lead. If he should break or lie down, an immediate correction is called for, using the lead and making that correction from *in front.* Increase your time away from Buddy until you have no trouble staying one full minute. (Refer to the method described in teaching the Long Sit and Long Down out of sight in Open on Pages 175 and 177.) As you return to heel position, hold your praise for a few seconds, making the time longer sometimes than at other times. Any time that you are facing your dog, learn to look *over* him, not *at* him.

Practising Long Down, showing use of board for correction

Long Down

Now, do exactly the same procedure with the Down-Stay. We feel it is best to treat this as a second phase of the Stay exercises, rather than as a separate exercise. In other words, don't go overboard with your praise upon returning on the Sit part of the exercise and get Buddy all excited. Give him your praise quietly with your voice and then go into the Down part of the exercise. The sequence may be reversed for variety. You may use both the signal and the command, even if you are in show competition. After you have completed a one minute Sit and a one minute Down and have returned, lay on the praise for a job well done and go to another exercise for some variety. Any one of them will do. Just don't make a habit of always following the Stays with the same one.

Your progress in this exercise, as in all the others, should be gradual. Your distance away from your dog should increase until you are finally about thirty to forty feet away. Likewise, your time away from him should also increase gradually until you reach about three minutes for each. The competition requirements call for a one minute Sit and a three minute Down in the ring, with the handlers standing across the ring, facing their dogs.

Your next step is to get Buddy used to doing this exercise without a lead on. To make the transition easier, put your lead in the "tuck through" position, give the little snap for "attention" after he is sitting, withdraw the lead, give the Stay command and signal, and then leave. Proceed as before, a little at a time, backing up in your training if you encounter any problems. When you put him in the Down position, do *not* use the "tuck through" of the lead as a light tap of the lead might bring him into a sit, breaking his position. He would have made a mistake, but you would have been the cause of it.

When the Stays have become steady, using the lead "tuck through" as a reminder on the Sit, start working off lead entirely. Increase your distance gradually up to about thirty to forty feet and the time up to three minutes. Fold up your lead as you leave and keep it there as a reminder at this stage of training, where Buddy can see it. Later on, you can get it out of sight. Vary this occasionally by putting the folded lead behind Buddy, far enough back so that it will not be a distraction to him. Don't be too ambitious in working for the maximum distance and time. Watch your fellow for signs of nervousness and restlessness and when you sense it is coming, return to him *before* he actually breaks. If he acts like this, he definitely needs reassuring.

After you have reached the distance of thirty to forty feet and a time of a one-minute (or more) Sit and a three-minute (or more) Down, with no problems, you may start to practise a regular show routine, as done in competition. Put your lead on, fastening it into the dead ring of the collar, and heel Buddy into the position chosen for the Stays. Remove the lead, fold it up and place it on the floor or ground in back of him. Give him the command and/or signal to Stay, and without looking down at him, leave him (on your right foot, of course.) Walk away with an air of confidence; don't turn your head for a sneaky peek to find out if he's following you. Don't creep away, either, for both actions are an invitation for him to join you. Make it a normal walking pace. Going too fast will also suggest that he should come along with you. When you turn and face him, be sure you look *over* his head or to one side, rather than staring at him directly. You may, at this time, add more in the line of distraction, by moving around a bit or even talking to somebody. Your purpose is to get across to Buddy that once he is given that command or signal, he is to *stay* there until you return and release him. And don't *ever* forget you have left him. Believe us, when we tell you, we have heard of it actually happening!

ADVANCED EXERCISES

Now that you have made all this progress in your training, you might be faced with a new problem. Your practise sessions, unless you are a real imaginative type of person (Bully for you, if you are!), could become somewhat boring to you and your pal. We are going to present a couple of exercises here that will help in doing away with that possibility and, at the same time, be a basic foundation for some more advanced exercises. They will be fun for both of you and will not interfere with the performance of the Novice exercises. They will also be a further help in keeping "dog attention." This is one thing you never want to lose, no matter what the training or showing stage of your dog.

Jumping

One thing that all dogs love to do, unless they are physically handicapped, is to jump. However it is something that must be approached with gradual steps and with common sense, as we don't want it to become a testing of physical endurance or capability. It is also necessary to keep your dog under control and yet let him enjoy it for both the fun and the exercise. It is not necessary to have a standard type jump as you start to teach this, but if you are interested in building one, suggestions and diagrams, as recommended by the American Kennel Club are in the Appendix of the book. If you feel you are interested in following up your training through the advanced work, we would advise you to get a complete set of the jumps as required for show competition, for the earning of the C.D.X. (Companion Dog Excellent) and the U.D. (Utility Dog) titles. These consist of the solid High Jump, the Broad Jump and the Bar Jump.

We will assume, to begin with, that your Buddy gets at least part of his training in the house. In that case, get a board about 6 or 8 inches wide. If you have a really small dog, make it long enough to fit across a door. Prop it up so that it won't fall over if it should get bumped a bit. You can do your own improvising in your back yard if all your training is done there. If you feed in the kitchen, a good spot for it is across the kitchen door. Thus, there is little likelihood of any unpleasant association with the jump. He can jump for supper.

Our first step is to introduce Buddy to the jump. With the lead fastened into the dead ring of the collar and folded into the right hand, not tight nor loose and floppy, heel him up to the high jump. As you ap-

Guide (left) foot over low jump, lead loose

proach it, kneel down on your left knee, toes of your right foot against it, slap the board with your left (or "praise") hand, and then praise him. Let him know that this new thing is not going to hurt either of you. If he should go over the board on his own, as you approach it, go right along with him and praise him; don't correct him for it. If he should react the opposite way and draw back away from it, shorten the lead gradually and take him up to it, assuring him with your tone of voice, until he is close enough to investigate it on his own. Slap the board, then praise him, until he is relaxed and not afraid that it will jump up and bite him.

Turn around and heel him away from the jump, far enough that you can about turn and go into a trot as you approach, so that your left leg, his guide, is the one that leads over the jump, raising it higher than necessary to clear it and accompanying the action with whatever command you plan to use. Usually the command is "Hup," "Jump" or "Over." Be sure you always use one with the jumping exercise and keep it the same one, once you've chosen it. As you go over with him, be sure you *never* tighten the lead, keeping your hands no more than waist high and the lead slack. If it should tighten, you are very likely to throw him off balance and thus give him an unpleasant association with the jump from the very beginning. As you land on the other side of the jump, call his name and give the Heel command, conveying your pleasure in his performance by the happy tone of your voice. Remember again, even though it's fun, don't repeat it more than five times before going to something different.

Your next step with the jump necessitates a regular jump arrangement, separated from any door or wall support, so you will be able to go around it. This time, unsnap the lead and put it through the collar in the "tuck through" position. Heel Buddy toward the jump, making sure he heads for the center of it. Before getting to the jump, give the little snap for "attention," draw out the lead, give him the Jump command, raising your left arm about shoulder height and as he starts his jump, you step quickly to the right and around the end of the jump. Meet Buddy as he lands, give him the Heel command and lots of praise. Of course, we hope somebody is standing by to give *you* an equal amount of praise for having executed such a graceful (?) step.

The third step in the jump training, preceding the more advanced work when you get into the Open exercises, is to teach the return over the jump. Again we use the lead "tuck through". As you start the approach, get the "attention," then release and fold the lead into your hand before you arrive at the jump. As you give the Jump command, raise your left foot over the jump. As Buddy lands, call his name and give another command to jump, bringing your left foot back and backing up away from the jump, using your hands as you did in teaching the Recall to guide him into a Sit in front of you. You may have him Finish to your left side once in a while, but don't allow it to become a habit. Always keep variety in your training, never letting it become boring to either you or Buddy.

To introduce Buddy to the Broad Jump, adding still more variety to your practise sessions, follow exactly the same procedure as with the single board of the High Jump. However, *two* points of caution here: Do not extend the jumping to use more than one section of the jump. You are still just playing an Open game while training in Novice. Also, *never* allow your pal to return over the high edge of the jump. Remember your own footwork and lift that guide (left) foot high in the air for him to follow. Refer to the Open chapter for advice on using the lifts for the Broad Jump (page 171) to give Buddy a better view of what is in front of him, especially important if he's a bit low to the ground.

Carrying

Our next project is to teach our pal to hold and carry something. Don't jump to conclusions now and assume that we are going to teach Retrieving the Dumbbell while working on the Novice exercises. Far from it! As we pointed out, all exercises must have a beginning, and the beginning of this one is another excellent way to vary the practise sessions, without doing any damage or forcing or accelerating the training. This is another example where step-by-step, a little at a time, pays off in the end with a dog that loves to do things to please you, as well as for the pleasure he gets out of the doing.

If your Buddy went through the Kindergarten experiences with the balls and other articles, you have a head start on those whose dogs haven't. As you will see, we allow *no* unpleasant sensations to be associated with carrying or retrieving, no pain, no forcing or harshness. We want this to be happy, right from the start. If you find you have a problem to begin with, be assured that you are not alone. There are many different types of reaction, just as there are different dog sizes, temperaments and dispositions. A few examples, for instance, are the dogs that refuse to hold anything, those that clamp down on an article and defy you to open their mouths to take it, those that will hold something for a moment and immediately spit it out, and the some that take it, hold it, but will not move with it in their mouths. It is absolutely necessary that you display a lot of patience and common sense here and that you don't expect an overnight miracle.

To begin with, get your dog used to accepting your fingers in his mouth, massaging his gums, etc. You can accomplish this in connection with your regular training exercises. When he is sitting or standing at Heel position, reach over his head with your left hand as though you were going to praise him but bring it, instead, up beside his mouth and gently try to put a finger inside. Talk to him with praise; don't force if he resists and acts touchy. If he accepts it, be happy with a few seconds in his mouth. If not, be prepared to be patient and sit down for two or three more tries. Be sure he is quiet and relaxed, and your attempts will be more productive.

When he will allow your finger in his mouth in this fashion for a few seconds, you may try the next step. Hold onto his collar (*not* in the ring) with your left hand and teach him to accept the tip of your index finger of your right hand, at the front of his mouth. Soon he will be opening it as he feels its pressure against his lips. He will soon become relaxed and willing to accept your finger in his mouth and will have no fear of pain or punishment.

Next, try substituting something for your finger. An easy item to start with is a rolled up piece of plain paper, rolling it over a pencil or something suitable, making it long enough to protrude on each side of his mouth two or three inches. Fasten it so that it does not unroll as you are working. Other excellent substitutes are plastic straws and clear plastic tubing. This latter item is available in a great variety of diameter sizes, one source being tropical fish stores.

As you get ready to introduce this new item to Buddy, be sure you get down to "dog level" with him. You might be on your knees with him by your side, or sitting on the floor by him, perhaps even in a comfortable chair at home (as long as he's not a Great Dane or St. Bernard or a pal of similar size and in your lap!). Don't take the chance of trying it where you are towering over him, thus adding even more obstacles along his path of learning. Make sure Buddy gets a chance to take a good look at whatever you're using. Let him smell it if he wishes to, but don't let him have it to chew on.

With the roll or tube in your right hand, hold the collar in your left hand so you can control his head, and tell him to "Take It!" As he is already used to your finger, let that finger "lead" the roll into his mouth, resting it just behind the long canine teeth at the front. As you encourage him to "Hold It," tip his head up a bit by pressing a finger lightly in the "V"-shaped hollow under his jaw. Almost immediately, command him to "Give" or "Out" and take it, follow with lots of praise. As you repeat the exercise, lengthen the time he holds it. Look for a response from him that will show you he is starting to open his mouth, on his own, to take it.

Now, instead of holding it inside your hand, take hold of the end and bring it up to his mouth, giving the command "Take It!" If he does, fine! Continue progressing gradually. However, if he does not, then go back to the beginning again. You may be impatient now and feel you're getting nowhere, but going back will pay off very satisfactorily in the end.

As he starts to take it on command, gently take your hand away and let him hold it all by himself. Watch him to see if he shows any nervousness or any signs that he will spit it out. Get your hands underneath his jaw, get out the command "Give," *before* he actually spits it out, receive it and give him all kinds of praise again. Both of you have done well, even though the holding may have been only a few seconds. Try to avoid his spitting out or dropping of the article if you possibly can. Sometimes you really have to be fast to catch it as it comes out of his mouth.

Your next progressive step, once you have Buddy holding the roll while you are beside him, is to give it to him, tell him to Stay and leave him, returning right away to have him give it to you again. As he gets the idea, through your praise for a job well done, you can increase the distance and the time away from him. Each time you return, come back and stand in front of him, up close, being careful of the use of your hands as you reach for the roll. With the palms up, reach *under* the roll as you tell him "Give", and gently touch it with a finger on either side of his mouth. This is enough to indicate to him what you want and, at the same time, will help form a habit in yourself that will avoid any unpleasant tugging or pulling against lips or possible sore gums or teeth. This is plenty for you to accomplish with the rolled up paper, plastic straw or clear tubing.

Following the same procedure steps, you may now use a rolled up old glove, tied so that it gives a similar size and shape as the roll. Introduce it, as you did the roll, and progress gradually. If you get resistance from Buddy, go back to the familiar roll again, then try later on with the rolled up glove in another training session. Once you have gone as far with the glove holding as you did with the roll or tubing, you are ready for the next step.

At this point, your goal is to teach Buddy that he can keep hold of something in his mouth, on command, and can move without spitting it out or dropping it. To do this, we will go all the way back to some of the K.P.T. training and will apply it here.

With your pal sitting at Heel position, give him the roll or tubing (vary it occasionally with the glove or even an old corncob), telling him to hold it. With your right hand in the collar, under his chin, the back of your hand directly under his jaw and exerting a slight pressure against it, tell him to Stand, and pull forward a bit to convey what you want him to do. As he stands, repeat "Hold it, Good Boy", then release the collar pressure. Next, tell him to Sit, see that he keeps the article in his mouth, and reward him with praise for doing so well. Repeat this from three to five times.

Now, you are ready to teach him to hold and carry it while he is moving. With the lead fastened to the dead ring and adjusted short by folding it into your left hand, hold the article in your right hand and give it to Buddy. Transfer the lead to your right hand, tell him to Stand (remind him with your left hand under his tummy if necessary), and as he stands give him the Heel command, tell him to hold it and move just a few steps. Encourage him and tell him "Gooood Boy!" Repeat this in several practise sessions until both you and Buddy are sure of yourselves.

When you have mastered this, let's really go for a bit of carrying *in motion.* Remove your lead and tuck it through the collar, folding both ends into your left hand so you have close control. Holding the article in your right hand, heel Buddy a few steps and come to a halt. Get "attention" from him with the lead, then withdraw it and give the article to him. As soon as he is holding it, give the Heel command and move out about four or five steps with him, come to a halt and tell him to "Wait." Step around to a position directly in front of him and receive the article. Then have him go to the heel position. Well done!

Now, provided the lessons are well learned up to this point, it is time to make another substitution, replacing the soft article for a solid, a wooden dowel. The diameter of this dowel can vary greatly, in order to be a comfortable fit for the individual dog. We find that the dogs will accept and carry a dowel that "fits" and will be really proud of themselves, eager to please you. Not all the larger breeds have large dowels, nor do all of the smaller breeds have small ones. Many times we have even found that littermates will vary from 1/16 inch to 1/4 inch from each other. These dowels are usually available at lumber yards, door and sash companies and hardware stores. You can cut them off to the size you want and be sure you smooth off the dowel you use so there is no danger of damage from a splinter. Leave it in the natural wood finish. You may wonder what the point is in getting into such minute details on this subject, but remember, we are trying to approach training from the "dog's point of view" and we have seen it pay off, many times over.

With several different diameter-sized dowels and with Buddy sitting at your left, pick up one of them and put it in his mouth, just behind the lower canine teeth. Hold his mouth closed over it but be careful you don't try to hold it too tight or force it. Tap the ends on the top with one finger of your free hand. If it proves to be loose, or what we refer to as a "sloppy fit," take it out and try a different size; a smaller or a larger one might prove to be the best one. Usually your dog will give you the answer as to which is the right one, for it will feel good in his mouth and he'll be willing to hold it.

Once you have located the right dowel, you have reached an important milestone in laying the foundation for your advanced training as well as introducing some interesting variety to your novice work now.

Fitting dog's mouth for dowel for comfortable carry

You can now practise with the dowel all the exercises you did with the roll, tubing, or corncob and keep up Buddy's enthusiasm in carrying. This will be the key to teaching him to retrieve the traditional dumbbell "on the flat" and over the high jump when you are doing the Open work in the next chapter.

Pivot

Now we have one last exercise to teach your pal to bring still more variety and a bit of fun into your practise sessions in the Novice work. It will also help the two of you when you reach the advanced Utility work, in the Directional Retrieve exercise. It could prove very practical too, if you have Buddy downtown with you on a crowded sidewalk and wish to turn to get at something without using up a lot of room. Of course, if your neighbor should be watching, be prepared for some pointed remarks, like "Since when did you decide to give dancing lessons to your pup?" or "What's the name of that step? I don't remember ever seeing that one before!" Just let your neighbor have his fun. You'll show him later when you start to bring home the ribbons and trophies.

You can work this new exercise, a backup and a pivot, (or turning in place) in with your heeling to break up any sameness in routine. You will also be teaching a new command. We would suggest "Position," "Place" or "By Me," but you may come up with a better one. If so, don't hesitate to use it. The reason for the new command is to teach Buddy that he can adjust and come into Heel position just by shifting his body a little, in case he has been taught to come to Heel around you, behind your body.

The first part to concentrate on in teaching this exercise is the backup. With the lead fastened in the dead ring of the collar and folded up fairly short, take hold of the lead with your left hand quite close to the collar. If your dog is tall (or you are short), it may be easier for you to take hold of the collar itself to guide him. If you have a real small dog, you have to work a bit harder at it to keep him under control and prevent him from turning. Just remember, bending is still a good exercise for the waistline.

With your dog at Heel position, start with a forward motion for three or four steps and then, without halting, start to move backwards. But do it by shuffling your feet, *not* making separate steps. At the same time, give the new command, "Position," and use a slight pressure backwards on the lead or collar. The first few times you will have to be on your toes to control Buddy and not allow him to turn around to come to you or to circle you. Be careful that you, yourself, don't try to move back too far (just a few inches is enough) or too fast. If you encounter problems with his turning, try working him close to one side of the training chute or a fence or wall. Don't try to force. Talk him into what you want and give him lots of praise. Don't demand a sit, either, as you come to a halt. Just go forward and try the backup again. As he starts to realize what you want and begins a little of this shift into reverse, be sure you remember that magic word of praise, "Good!" String it out to "Goooooooood!" When you've tried the exercise about five times, be sure you go to something else and save this for another session.

When Buddy has learned to back up even half his body length, you may start practising the pivot which involves a bit of footwork on your part. You should master the pivot yourself before you combine it with your pal and his backing-up ability.

There seem to be many different interpretations as to how a pivot should be executed. It is actually a *turning in place,* and in fact, is now referred to as such in the Obedience Regulations for the Directed Retrieve exercise: "Handler must *turn* with his dog . . ." (Chapter 2, Section 21). To get a clearer picture of what is expected of you in this situation, imagine a glove on the floor about 25 feet in front of you, a second one located about 15 feet to the right of it, and a third one about 15 feet to the left of it.

The pivot to the right is usually easier for the average person. Stand with your feet close, in a normal position. Turn your right foot to the right, keeping your heel on the ground, lining it up to the right of the glove. Then bring your left foot into a normal position alongside your right foot, turning your body simultaneously to face the right glove.

The pivot to the left, which is the one that requires your dog "backing-up" to adjust into Heel position, is done by turning the left foot to line up to the left of the left glove, keeping the heel down as the turning pivot. Then bring your right foot alongside, to your usual normal position. Dance, anyone? We haven't named it yet but believe it does have possibilities!

Now that you have the idea, practise the pivots until you can do them without having to concentrate on your feet too much, before you get Buddy into the act. You might even check yourself first by performing in front of a mirror. Be sure you focus your attention on your *feet,* not the fit of your slacks or the style of your latest hairdo!

OK, time to get your pal out so he can see how much you've learned. For your first try, do the pivot with him in motion, as you did when you started to teach him. But remember, he should now respond to the command for the exercise. Remind him, if necessary, by a slight guiding with the lead or collar. Be sure you help him along with your voice and praise as you increase the degree of your pivot. You can inject some fun into your new "dance" by following, one after the other, several pivots to the right (also to the left) until you complete a full circle, standing in one spot. Of course, Buddy may get the idea you should have your head examined, but you and he are having fun together, as well as learning together, and that should be your main objective.

Now, it is time to wish you well in your practising and perfecting all your Novice exercises, as well as these last few extras. When you and Buddy have mastered them and can *enjoy* performing all of them, you should be ready (if you so desire) to go into competition at the dog shows and work for your "C.D.," Companion Dog title.

PROBLEMS IN NOVICE TRAINING

On Lead Heeling

Fear of collar, lead, hands (touching, praising).

Be sure you work on the dead ring of the collar so a correction does not become punishment and something fearful. Avoid any correction with the foot or slapping or hitting with the hands or lead. Associate pleasantness and enjoyment with the training.

Fear of handler's feet in motion or standing.

Give your dog confidence in working near your feet. Let him develop a love to be near them. Be overly aware of your footwork in relation to your dog, from *his* viewpoint.

Shies away on being touched.

Avoid correcting your dog's position by grabbing his coat or a handful of hair. Use your lead and collar, always on the dead ring, for any such situation.

No response to his name.

Perhaps you have used it inconsistently, e.g. only in training sessions, or maybe you should try a shorter name, one that allows you to get better tone inflection.

Never any "dog attention".

You must *give* of yourself in order to *receive* from your dog. There must be love expressed, fun in training and variety to make it interesting.

Easily distracted by anything that moves.

It is natural for a dog to see motion. As above, to keep his attention, the work must be fun, full of variety and you, yourself, must express enthusiasm. It *is* contagious.

Sniffs floor or ground constantly while working.

Perhaps you have no rhythm as you move, or you may be moving too slowly to keep his attention on you. If his mind is not focused on you, it gives him a chance to sniff and enjoy the smells to his heart's content.

Loss of control when lead is tightened.

This has likely developed from corrections and working on the live ring of the collar. Use the dead ring or even go to a plain buckled collar to erase the resentment.

Tries to bite your heels while in motion.

This occurs most frequently in small dogs as your heels may be coming up right in front of his face as you are walking, and even to a greater extent when you are trotting. Learn to keep your heels down as flat as possible as you move.

Crowds while heeling.

Check yourself to see how you are holding the lead. You may be pulling it across your body and guiding him in too close. You can practise heeling every once in awhile by putting him on one side of one line of the plumber's helpers, with you walking on the other side of it. Guide him away from your body a bit with your left hand on the lead until he knows what you want.

Small dog lags at the start and continues to lag.

Check the position of your left foot as you take the first step. You may be throwing it a bit to the left, thus making it seem like a block to the forward motion of the small dog. Concentrate on that first step and try to make it slightly to the right.

Straight heeling is fine but fears turns.

Check your footwork to see that you are working *with* your dog, not against him. Keep your feet out of *his* way and never use your knee for a correction.

Lags after a left turn.

Check your footwork, practise more "circles to the left" in your regular heeling.

Forges after any turn.

This may have developed from too much correction on the turns. Be more patient and *show* and *guide* into the correct position.

Confused when making a change of pace.

Smooth out your changes of pace, try to "float" from one into another and don't be too abrupt on your halts.

Forges on a halt.

You are probably stopping too fast, expecting too much from your dog. Check your halt to see if you are stopping on your right foot, bringing the left one (your dog's "guide" foot) up to it as the last one in motion.

Wants to race and play on fast pace.

You may have overdone the speed of your fast pace, did not make it smooth. Show what you want, keep your dog under control, enjoy it, and don't overdo it.

Starts to sit or lie down on slow pace.

Perhaps your normal heeling practise is confusing to your dog, for you may be slowing down, coming to a halt, in the same way as in changing to a slow pace. Make a distinction between the two—"float" into the slow pace. Be definite on your halts.

Fine with homework but shows fear in class.

Double check your tone of voice to see that it is the same in both places. Make sure that *you* are not the one who is afraid, thus transmitting your fear to your dog. If noises behind him are disturbing him, take him for walks around shopping centers to help him get used to such things.

Confusion on the about turn.

Instead of using the lead and correcting, as you start to make an about turn in practise, call his name without a command, bringing his attention to you.

Confusion on left about turn (for practise).

If you are a bit unsure about this yourself, check the detailed instructions again as given on Page 62. Make the change of the lead and your turn smoothly, call his name as you turn and be sure you don't stop half way around. If your own turn is smooth, your dog will come through fine for you.

Starts to sit doing the about and left about turns.

As above, your own unsureness and hesitation when you are part way through the turns is reflecting in your dog's performance. Smooth out your handling and he will do as you wish.

Figure Eight

Fear of strange stewards as "posts".

Perhaps there has been an unpleasant experience with a stranger. Introduce him to the strangers before you start to work, using only one stranger at first along with someone he knows, and holding a conversation with both of them. Be sure the tone of voice is pleasant and reassuring.

Sniffs the stewards.

Do not be too quick to blame your dog and make a correction. There might be a very valid reason for this. There could be an interesting kennel odor on their clothing, or perhaps they have a bitch in season at home. They may not feel well, or may have some type of medication on, or even an unusual cologne or perfume. It also might be caused by your crowding your dog and forcing him in too close to the stewards. If all possible causes are ruled out, and you are sure he's just goofing off, a sharp quick snap of the lead (dead ring) and immediate release, accompanied by his name, should do the trick.

Swings wide on outside turns.

There probably has been a good bit of correcting here, rather than guiding and showing. Watch your own footwork and pattern—be careful that you are not making your "circle" via pivot points and don't swing your hips and dip your shoulders. Make your circle as smoothly as possible, walking erect and natural. It is much easier for your dog to follow you if you don't try to be a contortionist.

Crowds handler on inside turns, or forges.

This has probably developed because you have slipped somewhere along the line and have not guided your dog with your left hand on the lead, near the collar. It also could have come from your crowding him, and not leaving enough room for your dog between yourself and the steward. Check for either of these possibilities and backtrack in your training to remedy it.

Lags on first inside turn.

As above, check the space you are leaving for your dog, guide him and show him where you want him. You may be forcing him to lag.

Is good at home, confused in class.

You are probably using chairs, or trees, or posts for your stewards when you practise at home. Try to vary the sessions at home by sometimes having real live people as stewards.

Tries to go in front of steward, not around.

Still the same situation as above. Be sure you are giving ample space for your dog to move around the steward. Talk to him as you are working, until the proper habit pattern is established, then gradually eliminate the extra chatter.

Works fine for instructor, not for owner.

Owner should pay really close attention to instructor's handling of the lead, his footwork, and especially to his voice. Try to find the difference, then change accordingly.

Slows down, lags, after one or two circles.

Vary your regular figure eight exercise in this manner: Make the first circle around one steward, then run away from the stewards, run back toward the stewards (making sure your dog stays up beside you), *walk* around the other steward, run away again (opposite direction), turn and run back, *walk* around the first steward again. Repeat this as necessary to remind your dog he is to keep up with you at all speeds, in all places, when he is heeling with you.

Recall

Will not turn when name is called.

Check again to see how you have used your hands, his name, and the command. Be sure your on lead work is satisfactory before you try off lead.

Doesn't come in close before sitting.

Again, check the use of your hands. Use them to guide him in by direction. Use no force or corrections.

Jumps on handler before sitting.

Use your lead properly and on the dead ring, have authority in your tone of voice and command him to sit.

Comes in and goes right to heel position.

You probably have been too quick to give the command to finish. Don't be afraid to use the command Stay or Wait occasionally at this point. Hesitate before having him finish, don't always do a finish. Keep him guessing as to what is next.

Is afraid of movement of hands.

Be more careful of what you do with your hands. Resist impulses to reach out and pull your dog in by grabbing his coat or hair. Don't overcorrect with a choke collar.

Does not obey command to Stay.

If you have taught "Stay" for the Stay exercises and also for the Recall, your dog may be confused. Change and make the distinction of teaching "Stay!" (until I return to you) and "Wait!" (until I give you a command for something else, as "Come").

Moves forward as handler turns around.

Go back to teaching on lead, within controlling distance and work on having him wait for the command to Come.

Comes half way, then stands and looks.

Staring or glaring at your dog may have caused this. Try looking above his head as he's coming to you. Put an encouraging tone in your voice and give him the "green light" all the way in.

Comes half way, then lies down.

You may have gone overboard in teaching the Down. Never teach it to your dog while doing Novice work, while you are facing him. Go back to on lead teaching of the Recall, right from the beginning, to get the idea out of his head.

After being left, moves on instructor's or judge's commands.

Return to within controlling distance of your dog. Teach him that he is to move only on the command, following his name for attention. Carry on a conversation, talk about anything (even if you have to risk being accused of talking to yourself), then give the command that is his cue to move. Increase the distance gradually, after he has learned his lesson well.

Starts on command, then sits and stays again.

This, too, indicates confusion on meaning of Stay. Change to "Stay" for staying in place, "Wait" for staying until told to move.

Turns head as if afraid of Stay or Wait signal.

Change the style of your signal, so that it doesn't come down toward his face and eyes as though you were going to hit him.

Will stay until called then runs away.

Go back to training on lead, on the dead ring, and show him what is expected of him on the Recall command. Don't pull or yank him. You can even make good use of the chute here, an obvious guide.

Will not Finish on command, OK on sit.

It could be that the answer lies in your tone of voice, or you might possibly be glaring down at your dog. Perhaps you were not thorough enough in your teaching.

On going to Heel, the Finish, keeps circling.

Perhaps too much emphasis was put on this when teaching it, without variation of other exercises. Good lead handling and control is needed to correct this, as well as good timing on the Sit command. Maybe working in front of a mirror will help your timing.

"Walks" all the way in on the Recall.

Your voice control and elimination of staring, some enthusiasm, hand clapping, etc., will do most to help on this. You may have to go back to working on the lead, using *no* corrections.

Comes in too fast, bumps into handler.

Use one of the boards from the high jump, held erect in bracket supports. Stand close to it, on the opposite side from your dog. Your timing must be *right* on this. Give a sharp Sit command just before he arrives at the board. Do not allow him to jump the board to come to you. *You* go to him at Heel position, praise.

The Finish

Balks on doing a Finish to Heel.

Have you tested him to see which way *he* prefers to finish, to the left or to the right (around behind you)? If you have been insisting on his going as *you* prefer, you may find it easier for him to perform this exercise going in the other direction. Check it.

Going to right, dog sits behind handler.

Smooth out your lead handling, guide him all around to the proper position, and *praise* him when he gets there. Practise of the left-about turn is a big help.

Going to the left, dog sits facing left side of handler.

In teaching the finish to the left, there *must* be ample room allowed for the dog to make a complete circle away from you and coming up to your side from slightly to the rear. Teach this pattern properly and there should be no problem of his ending up in the wrong position.

Leans on handler when coming into Sit.

You may have been tightening your lead, and pulling it across the front of your body as you were teaching the Finish. This would encourage the leaning and could also be responsible for a crooked Sit.

Going to right, dog circles and comes all the way around, sitting in front.

You must have slipped up on your lead handling and the timing of your Sit command as you were teaching. Do not wait to find out if he is going to do it right—don't allow him to make a mistake. Guide him with the lead, command him with your voice, at the *right* time.

Stand

Does not respond to Stand and Stay command.

Backtrack on your teaching the Stand, using the beginning K.P.T. method, which should eliminate any confusion as to just what you want of your dog.

Stands but won't accept touching by a stranger.

Reintroduce him to the stranger, using the board in the brackets, and putting him over it. Don't allow even a beginning of examination or touching until your dog is relaxed in the presence of the stranger. Include conversation between the two of you, being careful to see that there is no staring at your dog. Take it in small easy steps, don't rush.

Tries to bite if head is touched.

Start back from the beginning, K.P.T. work, then work over the board, combining talking and laughing with the examiner before any touching is attempted. When the examiner comes close, be sure he moves his hand from the *front* of your dog's head. Don't let it come from the side, from behind, or from over the top. Always let your dog *see* the approach.

Will not allow touching of the mouth.

This should be worked on at first at home, in familiar surroundings. Taking a tidbit from your hand is a start. Then get him used to accepting the feel of your fingers, rub his lips a bit, touch his teeth, all the while talking to him and praising him. Do not try to open his mouth until he is not bothered by this much.

Shies, pulls away on touching hindquarters.

Progress gradually, getting your dog used to feeling your hands go over him on the Stand—first down his back from the neck to the tail, then down over the tail, then over the hind legs, and then on down to the hocks. Take it easy, as it will take a bit of time, and you don't want to force the issue and risk losing all the ground you have gained.

Sits when slight pressure is felt on hindquarters.

This may have developed from your method of teaching the sit. Did you use pressure on the hips to make him sit? You should have relied on the collar and lead, with your voice command. Now you will have to backtrack in your training and reestablish the idea that a touching on the hips is *not* a signal to sit.

Moves forward on Stand as examiner approaches.

Use the board in the brackets to develop steadiness on the Stand, to teach him he is to "stay put" when he has received the command to Stand Stay.

Backs away as examiner approaches.

Use the board in the brackets for this, too, and squat down beside your dog to reassure him as he is approached. Don't tower over him. Increase your distance away from him gradually.

Wets on the floor when touched by examiner.

This is an evidence of nervousness, so don't try to pose your dog in a Stand until he gets used to your hands touching him while both of you are moving. Let him think you are just reaching down to praise him. Repeat until you can stop, turn and face him, and touch him. Going into motion this way will take his mind off his old problem and it will be forgotten shortly.

Moves toward handler after examination.

When examination is completed, do not talk to your dog before you have returned to heel position. Never call your dog to you from the Stand to praise him. It will not hurt, in training, for you to give some extra Stay commands as needed, in order to steady your dog.

When handler returns to Heel, dog also turns.

As above, don't talk as you are moving back to your dog; don't stare at him. You may have to return to practise On Lead, where you have control of him and can keep him steady with a taut lead.

Sits as handler returns to Heel.

Vary your routine upon returning to your dog, so that he never knows what command you are going to give him. Part of the time, tell him to Heel, and walk away a few paces before halting and having him Sit. Other times, finish with a Sit. And still other times, praise where he is as you come into Heel position, and follow with a few minutes of complete freedom and play. Keep his attention on you, waiting for his next cue.

Off Lead Heeling

Is unsure when lead is removed.

Use the tuck-thru position of the lead, and stay in motion after alerting him with it for "dog attention". Do not expect too much from him too fast.

"Dog attention" lost upon removal of lead.

Go only five or six steps, after removing the lead, then give a command for a Sit, or a Stand, while you still have his attention and he is under control. Increase your distance occasionally, very gradually, but never do a lot of Heeling without putting other variations in it. Nothing could be more boring to dog and handler alike and we certainly don't need to teach our dogs to walk. Mother nature takes care of that very nicely.

Runs away when off lead.

This happens most often when a dog is confined to a small space at home or chained up, or when he has been severely over-corrected. A dog needs freedom to move (but *not* to roam the neighborhood), ideally provided by a fenced yard or run. Sometimes the running away starts when he is allowed to "try" heeling off lead when he is not ready for it. In any case, it means a complete working-up again from the beginning, *on* lead.

Sits when handler changes to slow pace.

Again check your footwork. Don't get into the habit of slowing up on coming to a halt, nor of "jumping into" a halt abruptly. Walk as normally as possible, as though you were taking a walk by yourself. Make it smooth, changing from one pace into another.

Wants to race and play on the fast pace.

Return to On Lead (the dead ring) and work all changes of pace, no more than a few steps in each one. Change them all around, first one, then another. Be sure you use the lead to guide, no corrections, yet keep him under control.

No dog attention Off Lead, sniffing floor, ground.

Perhaps he has had too much Heeling practise, not enough emphasis on "dog attention" and variety of exercises, resulting in boredom. "Smells" are much more enticing and interesting. This means back to On Lead work again, and a concentrated effort on your part to make it interesting and fun for your dog.

Goes out of control, "explodes" with praise.

There are varying degrees of praise that can be given, and it is up to you to know what is best for your own dog. Sometimes a quiet word of praise is as effective to one dog as a loud and physical hand praising is to another. Sometimes just a sweet smile is enough. Give as much as your dog reacts to best, without losing control of him.

Seems afraid when chain collar is used.

Very likely you started training with a chain collar and also using it on the live, or slip, ring. He still associates it with unpleasant noise and pulling of his hair, so the obvious solution is to change his collar to a nylon or a plain buckled collar. Think of your dog first and *his* comfort.

Long Sit

Will not stay in the Sit position.

Go back to teaching the Sit-Stay on lead, increasing the distance away and the time you are away from your dog, gradually.

Breaks Sit and goes to sniff other dogs.

Use a correction board on either side of your dog and gradually increase the time you are away by the count method.

Breaks on a slight noise or distraction.

Perhaps there has been no gradual introduction to noise in his training. This should be done with much thought and careful planning. The volume and suddeness of noise should be minimal at first, and should come first from in front of the dog, then from one side, then from the other, and lastly from the rear. Stay within a controlling distance of your dog whenever this is going on until he is quite content and relaxed.

Using board to correct breaking on SIT

Dog moves as handler moves away.

Double check your command, your signal, which foot you're leaving on and the timing of it all.

Dog cries when handler is away.

The simplest way to correct this is to teach your dog to hold something (such as a glove) in his mouth, and use the count method for gradually increasing the time you are away. As soon as he cries, tell him to hold the article. Praise him as he becomes quiet and you take it from him. After he catches on to the idea, leave it in front of him to remind him that he'll have to hold it again if he cries. Soon you'll be able to remove it altogether.

Runs away as soon as handler leaves.

Go back to training On Lead again, using the tuck-thru of the lead, no rough corrections, until you can go completely Off Lead again and you can depend on his doing the Sit-Stay reliably.

Breaks Sit and visits the instructor, or if in a show, the judge or a steward.

Even though this may be good for a laugh by the onlookers, it's not funny to the owner. You might consider it embarrassing and well it might be for your dog may be looking for some love, affection and companionship that he hasn't found with you. Take an unbiased, fair look at yourself from your dog's viewpoint and be honest. Just *who* is to blame?

Long Down

(Note: Many problems on the Long Sit are repeated on the Long Down; same suggestions are advised for eliminating them).

Does not stay Down.

Your dog needs more work on the Stay command and you should back check to see if he seems to be in a comfortable position.

Breaks position as his handler returns.

Do not glare at your dog on your way back to him. Don't hesitate to reassure him with a Stay command as you come back, to let him know that he is to remain in position until you release him with another command. When you are in training, you are not being judged and marked off for extra commands. Give your pal all the help you possibly can and he will make you proud of him.

Teaching holding of the dumbbell for satisfactory throwing *(See p. 164)*

Open

BEFORE tackling the more advanced exercises which will be given in detail in this chapter, let us do a little organized checkup on our accomplishments and those of Buddy, up to this point.

Go through all the Novice exercises—do it impartially and objectively. If you can perform all of them with no "major" errors, only a few "minor" errors (or possibly none?), you should be ready to forge ahead. However, be honest with yourself and your pal, for you'll be doing neither of you a favor if you try to do things for which you have not prepared yourself.

If he needs continual guiding with the lead, second commands, lags or forges and pulls the lead, has to be corrected, doesn't Stay or Wait, doesn't move on the first Recall command, and doesn't work happily, then it is quite obvious that neither of you are ready for any advanced work. Your first goal should be to perfect the Basic and Novice work so that both of you can do all of it and do it well, enjoying it as you do it. Your foundation must be solid, if you're going to build anything worthwhile on it, as the success of each step depends upon how well the preceding ones have been learned.

Although the exercises we present in this chapter are those prescribed by the American Kennel Club for Open class competition at Obedience Trials, working for the C.D.X. (Companion Dog Excellent) title, they are also practical for everyday living.

Heeling Off Lead and Figure-Eight

As Heeling Off Lead is only a continuation of the Novice exercise, let us do a little review first, just to refresh your memory. A few minutes of practise On Lead should tell you whether or not you have your pal's attention and if both of you have remembered everything. Before going Off Lead, use your lead in the "tuck-through" position, go through all your exercise with all turns and changes of pace and include halts during each change of pace, Normal, Slow and Fast. We hope you were able to do this with no problems at all, no major mistakes or corrections, and as a happy team should perform. Each time you practise Off Lead Heeling, lead into it with a short session On Lead (using the dead ring), then with the lead "tucked-through" the collar.

Follow this same procedure, also, in practising the Figure-Eight exercise—(1) On Lead, (2) Lead tucked through, (3) Off Lead. Again, refresh your memory as to the important things to watch out for. Keep your own posture upright (no dipping the shoulders as you turn and no staring at Buddy to check on his position), keep your steps even and in rhythm, no pivoting to get past the "posts," and make your halts as smooth and normal as possible.

When you think you're ready to try it Off Lead, work for the same perfection in performance as you did for On Lead. It will be up to you to decide when you want to release the lead from the "tuck-through" position. It may be while Buddy is still sitting at Heel, before you start in motion, or perhaps you will find it will work better for you and Buddy after you are already in motion. Be ever watchful for new problems that might appear that have never before raised their ugly heads, and be quick to squelch them right then and there.

Distractions are always much more of a threat Off Lead than On Lead. If you notice any start of lagging, forging, crowding or wideness, don't hesitate to go back on lead for correction if it is warranted.

After you and your pal are performing quite to your satisfaction, start to bring a little variety into your practise sessions by varying the distances between your posts or stewards that you circle, far apart and close together. The Regulations recommend that, in the ring at a dog show, the stewards stand approximately eight feet apart. From what we have observed occasionally, we wonder what kind of an elastic tape had been used, if any, to check the distance. Anyway, it makes for more fun when we change it around for practise! And your pal won't be able —just from force of habit—to tell when you're going to start your circles, so he will give you much better attention. You might even change it so you "figure-eight" (or serpentine) around three or four posts in a line and return the same way. Be ready for anything, as you could readily encounter a similar situation when you and Buddy go for a stroll or on an errand, and there is a considerable amount of pedestrian traffic. Still another idea to introduce into your Figure-Eight practise, to get attention and help to keep it, is to add an occasional about turn and left about turn.

Drop On Recall

In the Novice work, you have taught Buddy to Drop or Down, but up to this point, if you have followed your instructions carefully he has been going Down only when he has been at your side, at Heel position. Our project now is to transfer the "Down" command so it will apply when Buddy is in any position, and also when he is in motion, and in such a way that you will get an immediate and willing response from him.

Remember that, from the very first, your fellow has learned that your left leg and foot are his guide, as well as your left hand on the lead. Both will be used in the first step of teaching this exercise.

Put him at Heel position, fasten the lead in the dead ring and have the rings at the bottom, nearest the floor. Adjust the lead length in your right hand so there is no slack and place your left hand on it near the collar, the palm facing down. Your timing is very important on this, so think it through first and be sure you understand it before you try it out. As you speak his name and give the command "Down!", your left hand should slide down the lead to the collar (straight arm); at the same time you will have dropped to your *left* knee, alongside him. As your knee touches the floor, so should your left hand and Buddy should be lying right there beside you and getting a lot of praise. If your Novice work was learned well, you should encounter no difficulty, as he should respond well to the command.

Your own speed and timing are prime factors here in getting prompt reactions. Don't try to keep him down any length of time. Praise and release, go a few steps and try it again from a Sit. Remember to repeat no more than five times. If you have done this right, there should be absolutely no resentment.

When you see that Buddy is responding to the command promptly, continue as before, down on your left knee, but without touching the lead as your hand goes to the floor. Your hand following through in this motion is an important thing to keep in mind, as Buddy will eventually be reacting to a hand signal as readily as the verbal command. When practising, proceed from one halt and Down to the next, with just a few steps in motion in between.

Your next step will be to proceed just as you did at the beginning, with one big difference. This time you and Buddy will be *in motion* as you go through the routine. Again, take a few steps between each Down, be sure you are enthusiastic with your praise. As he progresses, try him as you did before, following through with the complete motion, but leaving your left hand off the lead.

When you are quite confident that Buddy's responses are all that you dreamed of, it is time to test him with some added distractions. Take him for a walk, keeping him at Heel position, but not turning your head to watch him. He, most likely, will be watching you very intently at first, but soon his mind will wander, especially if he spots anything different or sees something move. At this point, when he least expects it, give him the Down command and *take* him Down if he hesitates or makes believe he never heard the word before. This should be a surprise to him and should teach him that he must always be attentive and ready for anything you might do and any command you might give.

These three exercises, all intergral steps in teaching the Drop on Recall, have been done *on lead* and with the lead attached to the dead ring. Our next step is to repeat these three, in the same order, but with the lead off and "tucked through" the collar, as in the Novice training. Let us go through a bit of "refresher," in case you may have forgotten. Tuck the lead through, give a slight snap on it to get Buddy's attention, release it and draw it out from the collar, then follow with the command for the work to be done. If you do not get the response from him that you should, there should be no doubt in your mind that, somewhere along the line, *you* missed the boat, and you must backtrack to find out where. Start over again, from the beginning, and you will be able to spot where you fell down on the job. Work harder and praise more on that part, and then you will progress faster and will be on your way again, both of you accomplishing more and also enjoying it together.

For the first time now, you are ready to try the Down command with your dog facing you. For the first step, sit your dog, tell him to Stay, leave him and turn and face him (only about a half-lead's length away), holding the lead in your left hand. He should be giving you good attention by now, so just be sure of what *you* are doing and concentrate on that.

Teaching Drop on Recall from in front, lead on dead ring. Note position of hands.

Drop on Recall signal

Drop on Recall signal, showing direction of motion.

You are now going to introduce Buddy to a *signal* for the Down, along with the voice command. This motion will be the raising of your right arm upward, but completely away from your body (to keep it free from blending in with your clothing as a background), the elbow reaching no higher than even with the shoulder, the forearm and hand extended straight up with the palm of your hand facing your dog. Having his attention, it is good to start making a distinction that he will understand as to whether or not you use his name. Associate his name with a "moving" command, as "Buddy, Heel," or "Buddy, Come." *Without* the name, give a command to *stop* motion or to do something *without* moving out of position, as "Down," "Stay," etc.

Now that you are within easy controlling distance, only two or three feet away, with the lead comfortably shortened in your left hand, give the command "Down!" and immediately drop to your left knee, left hand hitting the floor, simultaneously bringing the right arm up with the motion for the Down signal. Repeat this from three to five times, and then increase the distance to a full lead's length away, provided you have had success with the shorter distance. When Buddy is responding satisfactorily at this point, with no added help, you are ready to try the Drop off lead.

With your pal sitting at Heel, tuck the lead through his collar, get his attention and then release and remove it. Give him the Stay command (and/or signal), walk away about five or six steps, and turn and face him. Do not stare at him—just look in his direction but over his head. Call his name and command him to Come. As he is moving, about half-way to you, simultaneously give the command "Down," the signal to drop, and go down on your left knee with your left hand touching the floor, exactly as you have been doing before on lead. Go directly to him and praise him at that point for having gone Down in that spot! Do not speak to him before you get there, for this could encourage him to break that position and might be the beginning of a bad habit.

After the praise, tell him to Heel as you make an about turn and walk back to where you started from. Repeat this up to five times and after each good drop, increase the distance a little. Never get so far away that you have lost control, for you must then backtrack in the training. This means a loss of time, and it might be damaging to your own patience.

When you have progressed to the point that you can go about thirty feet away and Buddy will go down on your command and signal and your dropping to your left knee, it is time to start eliminating, one by one, the extra signals and help you have been using. If your teaching has been done right, this should not take long. The first thing to do is to get the lead out of sight, so there is no visible reminder. Next, leave out the left hand going to the floor and dropping down on your left knee. Then try the exercise with just a command to Come and a command to Down, remaining in an erect position as you give them, completing with another command to Come (*after* he has been in the Down position three or four seconds), and finally ending with a finish to Heel.

When you have accomplished this much, your next step to try is the same routine, but using the signal only, no voice command. If you should see a hesitation at any time, or a slow response, remember that your left hand and left knee are still available to use as a reminder. Don't let your practising become a dull routine at any time, with the same pattern being repeated over and over. Vary the location of the Drop; alternate by using the command only, then the signal only, using the two together as needed; intersperse the Drop on Recall with occasional Straight Recalls; and remember to change to another exercise when you have gone through this no more than five times. This procedure will help you to keep "dog attention" and make it interesting training for both of you. Buddy will be constantly alert, for you will always keep him guessing as to what is coming next.

High Jump, Maximum Height

In approaching the teaching of the High Jump and the achievement of maximum required jumping height, as set forth in the American Kennel Club Obedience Rules and Regulations, let us re-emphasize the importance of progressing one small step at a time. We prefer the presentation of the jump by itself, rather than combining the retrieving of the dumbbell over it, as we feel that it is easier for the dogs to learn when they are concentrating on only one thing at a time. Of course, we must always remember that we may be faced with an exception to the rule.

Before you are ready to start teaching your pal any of the jumping exercises, you will need to provide yourself with the proper equipment. You will find diagrams and plan drawings of suggested construction design, as contained in the A.K.C. Obedience Regulations, in the appendix in this book (Pages 362–3). You will see that for the High Jump, to provide for the various requirements of all the breeds, they advise four 8-inch, one 6-inch, one 4-inch and one 2-inch width boards. This allows height adjustments every two inches, all the way from the mimimum of 8 inches to the maximum of 36 inches.

Although the explanation will be for teaching the maximum height of 36 inches, remember that the approach and method will be the same for all sizes of dogs, from the smallest on up to the largest. The increase in height should proceed slowly, only 2 to 4 inches at a time. The introduction to the 8-inch high jump has already been done in the Novice training, and if Buddy is required to jump only 8 inches, relax! You have it made, and you can gloat over your accomplishment as you watch the larger dogs practise and improve on the exercise.

Let us begin with the jump set at 12 inches. Approach the jump at a little trot, Buddy at Heel position, and don't bother to *sit* him first. He learned that in Kindergarten or Basic, and we want him to think about the *jumping,* not the sitting. Also, we want him to enjoy this and have fun, though we don't want him to get out of control. As you come up to the jump, give the jump command (whatever one you have chosen). Keep the lead loose and don't raise your hands above your waist. Lead over the jump with your left foot and jump with him. Be sure you *jump,* yourself, rather than *step* over, as your actions are an incentive for your dog to emulate. Don't let him get into a lazy habit just because you feel that way!

Gradually increase the height, 2 or 4 inches at a time, no more. When you can no longer easily (and safely) jump with Buddy, continue the same procedure of approaching at a trot. At this point, change your lead and put it into the tuck-through position, ready for the release just before he starts to jump. Make sure he comes up to the center and as you, yourself, get to it, do a sidestep that will take you around the upright (watch that lead, don't tighten it!), and you and he will meet and continue at Heel position on the other side. Be sure he gets his word of praise or pat on the head. Then turn around and do the same thing on the way back.

Your next step in teaching the high jump, *before* you ask your pal to jump the maximum required height, is to leave him on a Sit and Wait, a distance from the jump and facing it. Go to the other side, place your hands on the top board, call his name and tell him to jump, *at the same time* raising your hands high in the air and trotting backwards far enough to receive him in front of you. Raising your hands high helps him to keep his head up, giving him more lift, and also makes him concentrate on you, rather than worrying about the jump.

Learning where to place your dog, in reference to the jump, may take a little study and effort on your part, but it will be well worth it. You should learn your dog's individual jumping ability and help to make it easy for him. He must be in balance from the start of the jump to the landing. He should be far enough away to allow him to take a few steps and adjust his approach so he takes off on *both* front feet, giving him the push *up* that is needed, combined with the thrust forward from the hind legs. If the distance is not right, you will most likely hear the ticking of the nails of his front or hind feet or even, in some cases, you may find he is using the top of the jump to assist him in getting over. He may be too close or he may be too far away. Often, a matter of 6 to 12 inches can be the answer. Be sure to keep checking this as you increase the jump height further, as it can change with a change in the height.

When a 16-inch height has been reached (or less, if you have a Toy size), you must start to teach your pal that when he jumps, he must also return to you over that jump. To prevent the occurrence of any mistakes and the necessity of confusing corrections, we will put the plumber's helpers in place. This will guide him back properly and develop the correct habit pattern from the beginning.

Start toward the jump with Buddy at a little trot, give him the jump command and watch his landing on the other side. As his hind feet touch, call his name and give the jump command again (these two commands are to be eliminated later), back up and let him return over the jump to you. Be careful that you don't get overanxious yourself and call him back too soon, before he gets in balance to make the return jump. He might try to "pivot in air" to get back to you and he could hurt himself.

As long as you advance slowly and continuously, and provided your dog is sound and healthy and his legs and joints are normal, you should encounter no difficulty in teaching the High Jump and in reaching maximum required height. But *please,* heed a word of wisdom right here. *Don't* make the mistake of trying to find out how high he can jump! Also, teach him to jump *only* when he has been commanded to jump. An excellent way to do this is to heel him up toward the jump and just before you get there, give him a "Heel" command and do a right turn, going right past the jump.

Retrieve On The Flat

Very often, the Retrieve exercise is found to be the most difficult to teach, unless you are fortunate enough to be owned by a dog who loves to retrieve anything and everything. This need not happen, however, if you look at each small step from your dog's point of view. And that first step has already been mastered in the Novice training, teaching the Take, Hold and Carry, using several different types of articles (a dowel, rolled-up paper, glove, corncob, etc.). There are six steps to teach *before* actual dumbbell retrieving starts.

Step Number 1: Review what you have taught Buddy in the Novice chapter, making sure he will accept and carry each article with no help, before you prepare to advance in teaching the Retrieve.

You will find it much easier to keep your dog's attention while you're working with him if you set up the chute of the plumbers helpers, or a similar guide, especially when he is off lead. You don't have to work so hard to maintain control of him.

Step Number 2: The aim of this step is to teach your dog to take one of the articles *in motion.* Some dogs will actually prefer to take something while in motion, rather than while sitting. This can be done either *on lead,* or *off lead.* It will be much easier on your back if Buddy is a fairly large breed, but maybe you need some of that bending exercise anyway. Don't be disheartened, though, if you have a wee one, for you can accomplish the beginning of this "in motion" from a kneeling or sitting position (we mean *your* position here, not your dog's).

Take one of the articles in your right hand and hold it about six inches ahead of your dog's nose. As you get him to move, tell him to "take it" and try to get him to move toward it and take it in his mouth. You might find he will try to turn his head away from it. If so, use your left hand at the back of his head, middle finger in the collar, with a little pressure and with the little finger on the left side and the thumb on the right side of his head so you can guide it and keep it from turning. Then you can effectively direct him to "take" the article from your right hand. As you see Buddy begin to respond by opening his mouth and "taking," with no controlling of the head, try to accomplish the same thing with an increase of the distance from his nose to the article, encouraging him to move out and reach for it.

Step Number 3: Now you should be ready for teaching Buddy to take the article in association with a box, a table, a bench, some books, or such—in other words, surfaces at different heights from the floor. Start by selecting an item which is about the same height from the floor as his

Teaching Take and Hold

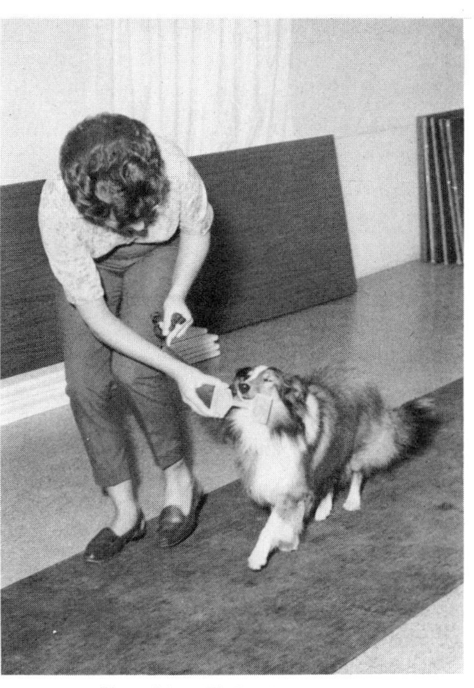

Teaching Take in motion

Carrying while Heeling

chest is. Introduce him to it by heeling him up to it and, as he smells it and looks it over, praise him to let him know all is well. Approach it again, carrying the article in your right hand. When within about twelve inches, hold it out in front of him and toward the box (or whatever you are using) and give him the command to "Take it." When he does this, with no hesitation, you are ready for the fourth step.

Step Number 4: Here, you will repeat the same approach as before, but, as he takes the article, run backward and call his name, telling him to bring it to you. Encourage him, clap your hands and, as he nears you, reach under his chin with both hands and give your command for him to release the object to you. Never come down to your dog's head from the top or the sides to take anything from him, and don't pull it out of his mouth. Also, be consistent in whatever commands you use to have him take an article and release it. Be sure your tone of voice in your commands conveys your pleasure and your praise. Speaking of commands, Milo and I were very favorably impressed one time a number of years ago when an exhibitor's command to release a dumbbell or a scent discrimination article was "Thank you!"

Step Number 5: Your next step in this progression is to have Buddy take the article, hold it, give him a signal and/or command to Wait, leave him, and go about ten feet away from him. Do an about turn so you are facing him, call him and receive the article when he gets in front of you. This step can be repeated and the distance *gradually* increased until he is carrying an item about forty feet to you. Just a reminder: we are *not* including the "Finish to Heel" in any of this teaching and practise, as we want to keep his mind on the *new* work and also keep him happy. He learned the return to Heel a long time ago and *if* trouble should turn up in that area, it should be worked on when you can concentrate on that, and that alone.

Now we're ready for the Big Step, Number Six! But before this, we must get the proper dumbbell to fit him. This will teach you how to fit Buddy for a comfortable dumbbell so he will be most happy with it, and you and he can continue on with your training and follow through with the completed exercises of "Retrieve on the Flat."

There are many types of dumbbells available, and many people who have the talent and equipment prefer to make their own. As long as there are no definite specifications as to the style, we find that we owe it to our pals to give them a type that will make the carrying easy, thus increasing their enjoyment of the exercise. The American Kennel Club

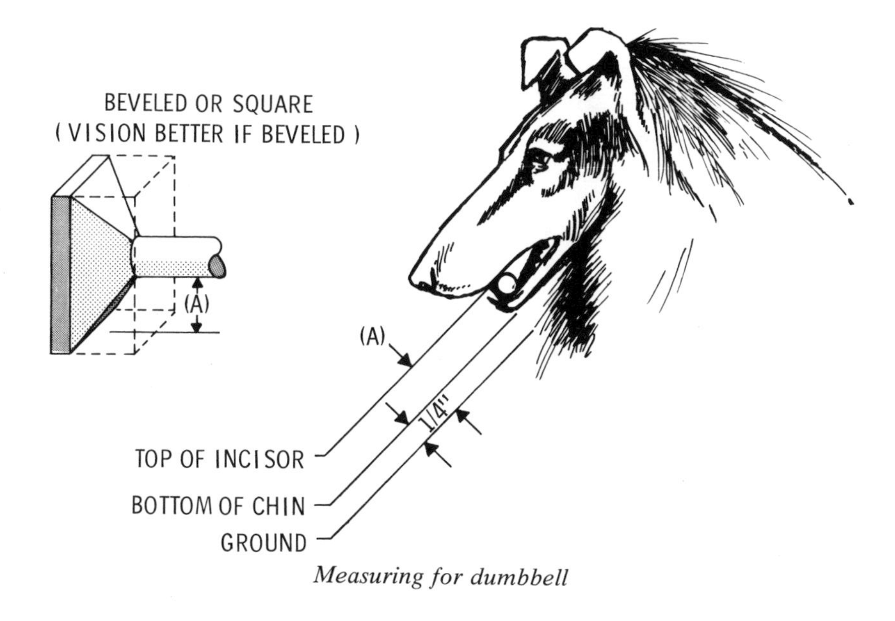

Measuring for dumbbell

does specify that the dumbbell shall be in proportion to the dog and that it shall be made of one of the heavy hardwoods.

We already have found (in Novice) the dowel diameter which fits best. Now we must put the ends on it which will raise it from the floor to allow a comfortable pickup with no painful scraping of the bottom of his jaw or the end of his nose against the floor, rough grass stubbles, loose sand, hot asphalt, cinders, etc. This means that the *clearance* from the dowel to the surface it is on should be great enough to allow his jaw, plus the lower canine teeth, to pass under it without having to squeeze under or maneuver it to try to avoid the scraping. Let us now make an actual measurement so we can plan the size of the dumbbell. Please refer to the diagram to clarify it in your own mind. Take the distance from the top of the *lower* canine tooth to the bottom of Buddy's jaw, then add about one-fourth inch. As an example, let us say that you are using a one-half-inch dowel and this measurement you have just made is one and one-quarter inches. Multiply the latter by two and add the one-half for the dowel and you come up with the total of three inches, which gives you the ideal size of the end pieces.

The shape of the end pieces can also be very important in the design of the dumbbell, both on account of excessive weight and blocking vision. The purpose of this exercise should not be to test how heavy a weight your dog can carry. Nor should we handicap him by putting

Fitting for dowel size

Checking for comfortable fit

Checking for vision between ends

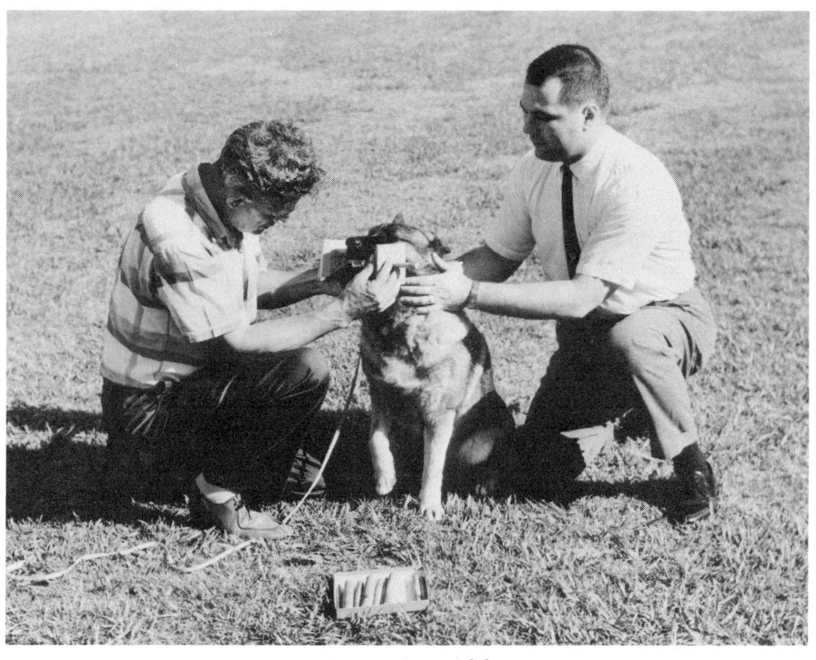

Fitting for width

A beautifully fitted dumbbell

"blinders" up in front of his eyes and make it difficult for him to assess the task in front of him. We personally prefer the tapered end design for the majority of the breeds, as it is the answer in both situations.

The length of the mouthpiece is the next item to consider, as the bells should not press against the lips, nor should it be so long that it can pull down on one end if it isn't picked up dead center. Usually, about one-fourth-inch clearance of the lips on each side is ample. However, it is best to give more than this amount to the breeds that have whiskers—Miniature Schnauzers, wirehaired Terriers, certain specific trims on Poodles, etc. Try to avoid any pressure against the lips when teaching the retrieve. If you have no means of making your own dumbbell, now that you have all the dimensions needed, find a dealer or a friend, or even a friend of a friend, and get one made especially for Buddy. If your pal is a really big fellow and you come out with a measurement of more than 4 inches across the ends, make an exception here. We have found that the ends are too heavy for the size of the dowel when they go beyond the 4 inches and are much more likely to break when thrown. An excellent wood for the ends is poplar, and another (even better) is basswood. The time may come when you have to toss it on concrete, and a split dumbbell is not the easiest thing for your pal to carry. Besides that, such a situation usually brings *you* a few more gray hairs!

Now that you have your properly fitted dumbbell, *don't* go out in the backyard and see how far you can throw it, then try to send Buddy to get it. The gradual, step-by-step progression of training is so important here. Go back to your numbered steps of retrieving the other articles and don't be in a hurry to go from one to the next. Be sure one step is accomplished and executed with ease, happiness and no confusion before you attempt the next. Continue to use the other articles, too, as well as the new dumbbell.

If you should see that Buddy starts hanging his head as though the dumbbell is too heavy, as you move backwards and call him in to you, no doubt you have been moving too fast and he has become confused and doesn't understand what you expect from him. Your objective here is to get his head up and his mind off those things on either end of the dowel mouthpiece. Try this: As he starts toward you with his head down, call his name and sweep your arms up in front of him to just above your shoulders, drawing his attention *up* with the motion of your hands and arms. As soon as he raises his head up, stop and receive the dumbbell and be sure to let him know how pleased you are. Make the carry just a very short distance at first, a few steps, until he gets the idea. Remember how you used this motion to teach the Sit, coming to you on the Recall? Rest assured, it will come in handy, many times over, on other exercises and certain steps of the exercises.

Step Number 6: We will assume, at this point, that you are now ready to make use of the table, stairs, bench, cardboard cartons of various heights, or a stack of books, in teaching the "Retrieve of the Dumbbell." Begin with something at your dog's chest level from the floor, and be sure you will be able to lower the height gradually so that eventually it can be practically as low as the floor. This may sound silly but Buddy will react to it exceedingly well. We've seen it work fabulously hundreds of times. A friend of ours even designed and built a layered box that could be changed by adding on or taking off 2-inch or 4-inch boxes, each one being fastened to the one below it (see P. 160). For convenience, we will refer to the item you're using as a table.

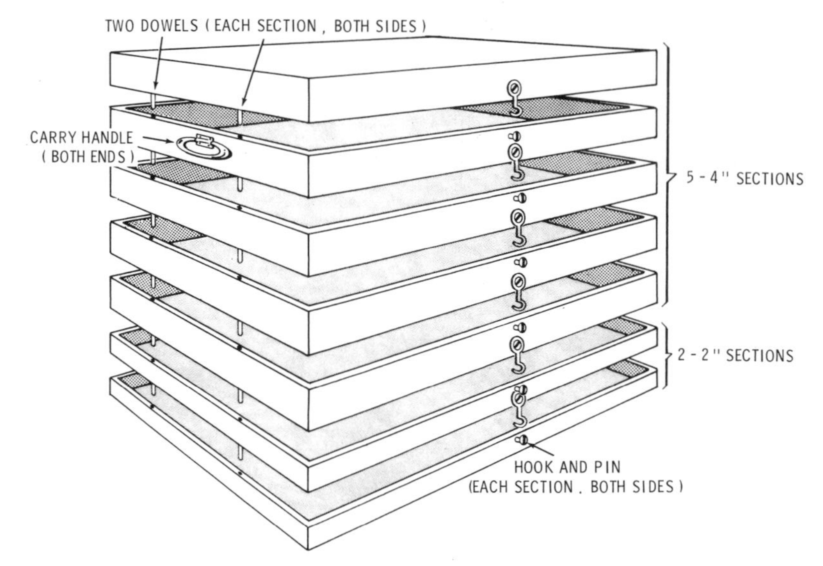

Diagram of layered box for use in teaching Retrieve of the Dumbbell.

First, moving forward toward the table about 6 feet away, have Buddy take the dumbbell in motion about 2 feet in front of the table. As he takes it, move backward and urge him to carry it to you, making use again of the motion of your hands upward to about chest level, as he approaches. Keep your hands together so he focuses on the one spot moving up. He will sit in front of you, his eyes on your hands, if you have done this correctly. Receive the dumbbell and lavish the praise on him! Repeat this hand motion each time on any of the retrieves until we advise you to start eliminating it.

Your next step is the same, but you will go closer to the table, only about a foot away from it. Then have him take it as you hold it over the front edge of the table, still in a motion approach. Next, have him take it while it is resting on the front edge, but with the fingers of your right hand still touching the end of the dumbbell.

When he will do this, have him take it with your hand near, but not touching it. Your next step is to command him "Stay" or "Wait," move about 6 feet to the table and place the dumbbell near the front edge. Return to him, give him a pat and some praise and then command to "Fetch it," moving with him about halfway to let him know what you

1—Taking at chest height

2—Level lowered by books.

3—Level down to one book.

4—Success at ground level

want. Coax and encourage him if it is necessary, but if he goes forward on his own just stand still. If he is still unsure, go with him and show him what you want. The faster he learns he can leave you on command, the faster you and he will progress through the other steps.

This was Step Number 6, substituting the dumbbell for another article to carry back to you. Now we'll go on to the balance of the steps, continuing to use the dumbbell. Be very careful you do not jump over any of them, or try the next one before you and Buddy are ready for it.

Step Number 7: Repeat as in Number 6, but this time, you do not move forward. As Buddy picks up the dumbbell, immediately let him know how happy you are. Put your feelings into your voice with that magic word "G-o-o-d!", clap your hands and raise them as he comes to you, to help guide him into the straight sit that you want to become a habit.

Step Number 8: At this point you should be ready to lower the table slightly, to the "first notch." Be careful that you don't expect too much and make the difference too great for him to accept it easily. If you watch carefully, he will indicate whether or not the change from one height to another has been too much.

Step Number 9: When you have reached floor level with the pickup and retrieve and Buddy is enjoying the leaving you and bringing back the dumbbell from about 6 feet away, you are ready to reach for distance. Continue with the "Stay" or "Wait," placing the dumbbell, returning and sending to retrieve, as you have done previously, gradually increasing the distance up to about 25 feet.

Step Number 10: This will be his introduction to the dumbbell in motion. Holding it in your right hand, both of you move forward a short distance, and, as you are moving, slide it out in front of you about 6 or 8 feet; at the same time, give him the command to get it (*same* command you have been using). Encourage him, have fun, and let him know how pleased you are when he picks it up and brings it to you.

Step Number 11: When he can do that one well, you and Buddy will now be in motion when you toss or slide the dumbbell out about 8 to 10 feet in front of you. However, send him out to get it just as soon as it lands. Increase the distance gradually on this step until Buddy is going out about 25 feet and proudly bringing back his dumbbell.

Step Number 12: When you and your pal have accomplished all this, through 11 steps as described, you should be ready for practise as prescribed in show routine. Tell Buddy to "Wait," throw the dumbbell about 25 feet in front of you, wait a few seconds and then send him to get

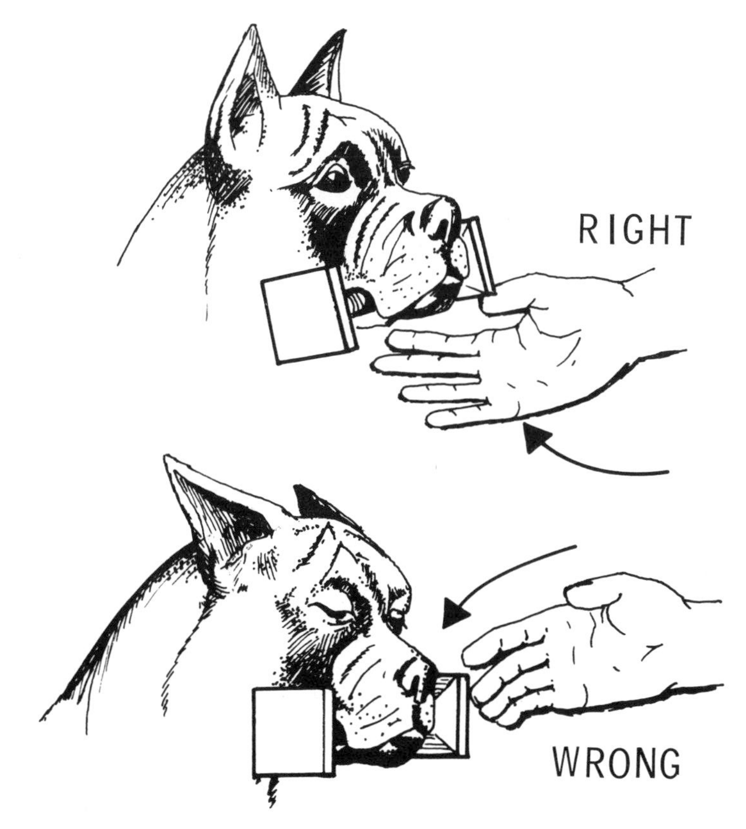

Showing right and wrong way to receive dumbbell

it, receive it, wait a few seconds and then give the command to finish to Heel. Don't always have him do this finish, however, or you will find he is anticipating or becoming like a robot.

At this point we have a few "Don'ts" to bring to your attention again:

Don't reach for distance too quickly.
Don't yank the dumbbell out of your dog's mouth.
Don't glare at him when he is returning to you.
Don't use a corrective tone of voice.
Don't be afraid to backtrack to wherever necessary.
Don't be afraid to return to use of the lead for attention.

Retrieve Over The High Jump

When teaching our dog to retrieve the dumbbell over the maximum required height of the high jump, we must again realize that the proper introduction is necessary and the exercise must be broken down into small, separate steps.

The retrieve on the flat, by now, has become as easy as the proverbial duck soup, as he can easily see where the dumbbell lands and whether or not it bounces or rolls and in what direction. It is a different situation, working over the jump, for Buddy can't see the dumbbell even though *you* might be able to. It is extremely important that you hold a few practise sessions yourself, just throwing it over the jump so that it will land in the best spot for your pal to see it in front of him as he makes the jump. It doesn't make much sense to create a double problem to begin with, making it necessary for him to *hunt* for it before he can pick it up and bring it back to you. "Don't put the cart before the horse."

Perhaps we can help you with a few of our ideas, gained from many years of experience and of trying just about every way possible for throwing the dumbbell. The object, of course, is to try to keep it from bouncing or rolling. Sometimes this is really difficult, with certain types of floors and surfaces. It also depends on the shape and weight of dumbbell.

Study the diagram on the facing page closely and notice the placing of the fingers and thumb over the bell on the end. It is important *not* to curve the fingers around it; don't grab it as though your life depended on your hanging onto it. If you have done any bowling, your swing and follow-through can make it easier. Just be sure, though, that you stand up and don't move your feet, as you're not approaching a foul line. Even though Buddy may require only a low jump, try practise throwing over about a 30-inch jump, as this teaches you to get a slight arch as the dumbbell goes over it.

Now, to go through it slowly. Put a marker down for the ideal landing distance, about 10 feet beyond the jump and to one side, so you can see it from where you will be standing, about 10 feet away from the jump, facing the center of it. Standing with feet together, and the dumbbell

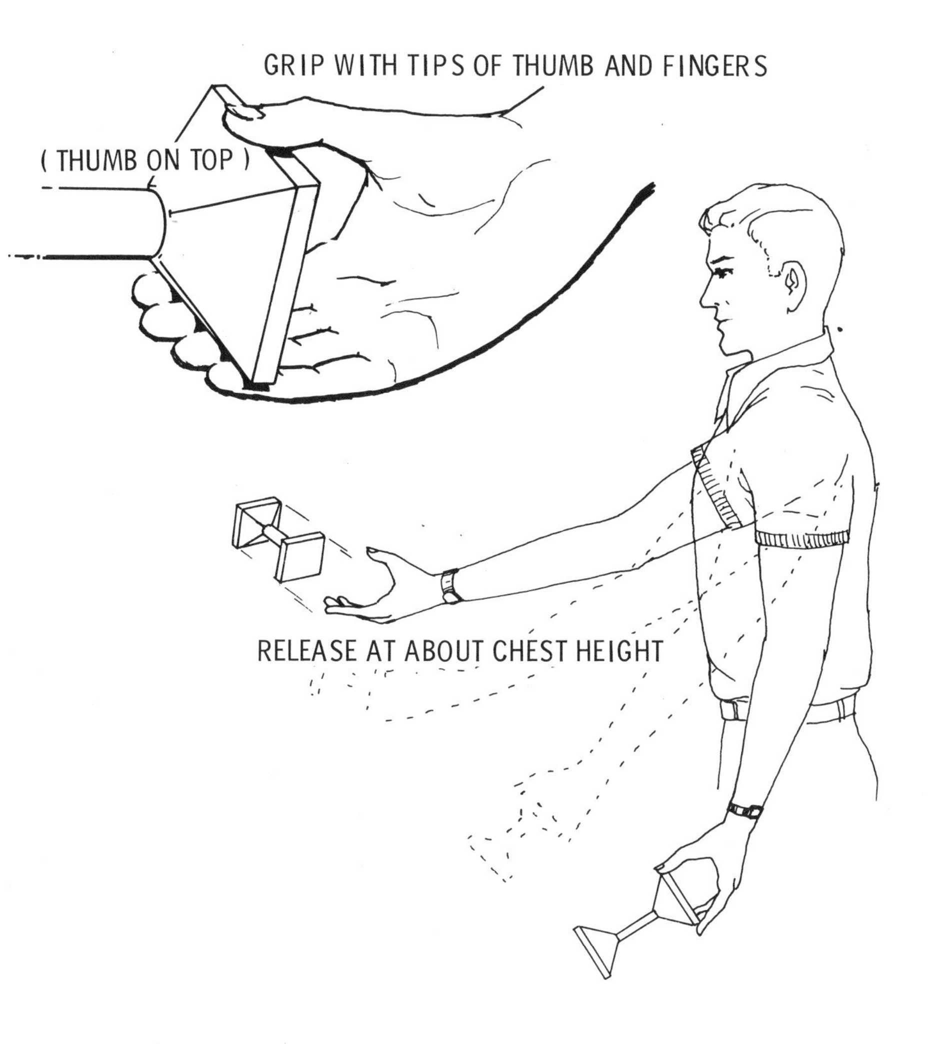

Showing recommended technique for throwing dumbbell

Holding dumbbell

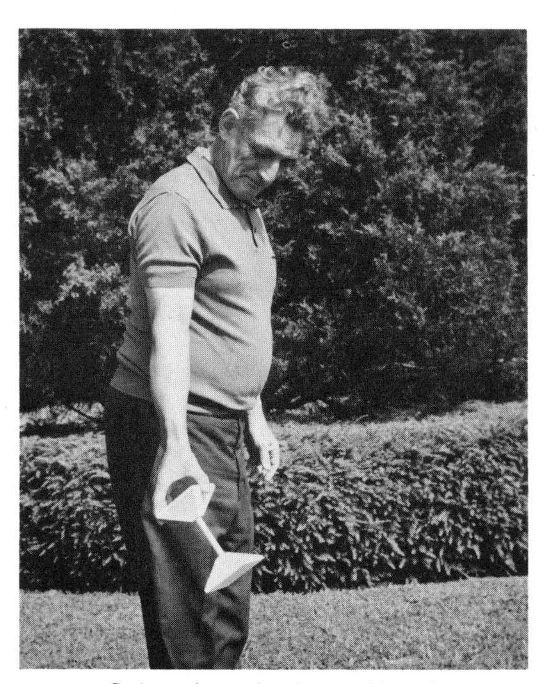

Swing of arm begins at this point

Release of dumbbell, shoulder height

in your right hand, heft it a bit first and swing your arm two or three times to get the "feel" of it. Be sure you have no bend of your arm at the elbow and don't turn or flip your wrist as you release it, for this will give it a spin and the landing will likely be on the end, causing a bad bounce. As your arm comes up about chest height, simply open your hand and let it sail out and over, continuing your arm swing up, to make it smooth. If you happen to be left-handed, make an extra effort to practise this with your right hand. Remember that guy on your left side and don't take a chance on swinging it past his head. He just *might* turn his head or jump up into the dumbbell as you're swinging it. You wouldn't want to go get something and bring it back to your mother if she had hit you in the head with it, would you? Remember your dog's point of view!

When you can throw the dumbbell consistently and place it where you want it, just ahead of where you think Buddy will land, you are ready to practise with him. It shouldn't take you long to master this if you concentrate and if you learn to relax as you make the swing.

Teaching the Retrieve over the High Jump may seem like some unnecessary backtracking, but it will pay off and avoid confusion. You will be starting again, as in teaching the High Jump, over an 8-inch board so that he won't have to worry about how high it is. You, again, will introduce Buddy to it, but this time he will be carrying his fitted dumbbell in his mouth. Approach the jump at a trot and guide him over with your left foot as you give him the command, stepping back and calling his name, stopping and receiving him in front of you, accepting the dumbbell as he releases it for you, and then adding all that praise for a job well done!

For your next step, with the dumbbell in your right hand and Buddy heeling, trot toward the jump. When about 6 feet from it, toss the dumbbell over and give him the command to get it, continuing your own forward motion, if necessary, to get the idea across to him as to what you want him to do, even if you have to put your left foot over again. As his nose nears the dumbbell, give him plenty of praise ("G-o-o-o-d!") and clap your hands to let him know that's what you want and follow through as before. Keep the jump at this low height until Buddy will retrieve the dumbbell for you without any of the extra help. Then you can start raising the jump *slowly.* Don't get carried away and speed up the raising of the jump height, even though your dog may prove to be a "jumping fool."

Remember, as the height increases, vision decreases (as far as his being able to see the landing of the dumbbell is concerned) and you don't want to chance any loss of your pal's confidence in you. This could enter the picture, if you might be advancing too rapidly. As the height increases, if you are careful to retain Buddy's confidence, you will find that he will continue to perform this exercise for you, even though he has no idea where the dumbbell is until he has jumped. As you progress, remember to keep both your dog and the dumbbell within controlling distance. Eliminate your extra commands as soon as they "become extra," but keep the praise coming.

Another reminder here, as you have been increasing the height of the jump, you should have been keeping the same pattern of practice, that of approaching the jump *in motion.* Don't take any chance, at this point, of turning the practise into the formal style required in show competition. Always endeavor to keep it *fun,* no matter what! Keep your Buddy relaxed, as well as yourself. Not until you have reached maximum height, approaching in motion and with no extra help, and you and your pal are completing the exercise with no problems, are you ready for show routine.

Retrieving over solid jump

At this point, refer back to the detailed instructions that pertained to determining the distance for you to stand away from the jump in order for Buddy to be able to take off "in balance," on both front feet. If you have not found you needed the aid of the "plumber's helpers" before, this will be an excellent spot to start using them, as a preventive measure. Now that *you* are not moving, you are not within controlling distance of him when he is on the other side of the jump. Fan out the two lines from either side of the jump, and this will be a natural guide to channel him back over the jump with no opportunity to start a bad habit of returning around the jump. It is so much easier to establish correct habits from the beginning, rather than to have to correct bad ones and retrain all over. As he gets into this approved return habit, you may decrease the effect of the aid by fanning them out wider and wider. You may also start to train him for the possibility of a bad throw of the dumbbell on your part, by deliberately tossing it a bit to one side or the other, increasing the distance off course as he grasps the idea you're trying to convey. The "plumber's helpers" will be there to remind him of the correct path for the return.

When you feel that Buddy has the proper idea and the correct habit more or less established, you may start elimination of the aid. You may find it advisable to first lay them flat on the floor or ground, still there as a reminder, or you may try removing them completely. Remember that you can always resort to them again if you see your pal has become confused and unsure of himself at any time.

If you notice a loss of interest in the exercise at any time, take stock of yourself and ask, "Why?" Perhaps you've been repeating it too many times before changing to something else, maybe it's been your voice, maybe you've become too serious. At any rate, start backtracking a bit by getting your lead and using it in the "tuck-through" position again, guarding against anything that will contribute to any further boredom or lack of attention. Ease off on your own eagerness. You are trying to accomplish too much too fast. Be sure you call a halt to any training session before it becomes work or boring and both of you take a rest.

Following are a few "Don'ts" for guide lines in a nutshell, so to speak, on this exercise:

Don't throw the dumbbell too close.
Don't throw the dumbbell out of sight.
Don't crowd the jump.
Don't correct with your tone of voice.
Don't glare at your dog as he returns.
Don't correct on retrieve (*stop* and show what you want).
Don't correct your dog for ticking (or hitting) the jump—Check *why*.
Don't correct when your voice and hands can show what you want.

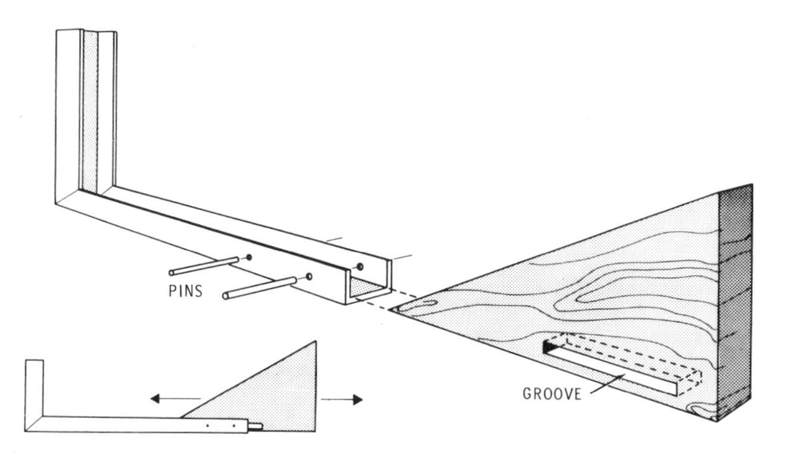

Broad Jump lift. This particular lift, to be used on the first board, is designed to allow a gradual lowering of the jump to normal position as the dog becomes more accomplished in his performance.

Jumping the Broad Jump

Practically all dogs love to jump but we still must approach the training of each type of jump in a gradual, logical series of steps to accomplish the most satisfactory results. Even though the construction of the broad jump makes it low, due to the fact of the extended distance to be spanned, it is most important that your pal learns to exert himself enough on the takeoff to give some *height* to his jump, thus affording ample clearance of all the boards he is required to go over (see A.K.C. Obedience Regulations in the Appendix). One might easily compare his style to that of the Olympic human broad jumpers.

For construction plans of the broad jump, refer to Page 351. Also, please pay special attention to the design of the "lifts," which we find are a very important addition to our training equipment. If you would imagine what the jump actually looks like, from the level of Buddy's eyes, actually get down on your hands and knees, or on your tummy if he's real small, if you need to prove it to yourself and see what the surface really looks like. Would *you* be able to estimate how far you'd have to jump to clear it, if that were all you could see? Now, put a lift under each section, as illustrated, and observe how much more is seen from the level of *his* eyes.

As you see, there are four sections to a set that comprises the full broad jump. One lift will elevate each section, so if your dog is required to jump all four, you will need four lifts. Our directions will be for the larger breeds, but you will be able to eliminate the third and/or fourth board as you reach the maximum required for your dog, if only two or three boards are needed. (Refer to the A.K.C. Regulations.)

For the beginning, we're going to retrace our steps back to the introduction to the single sections of the broad jump that we did in the Novice training. Set the sections up as single jumps, using a lift on each one and allowing ample room for you and Buddy to move between each one, probably about 12 to 15 feet. As in teaching the High Jump, it is still important to remember that your left foot is his guide and should be the one for you to use to lead with, going over the jump. Raising that left foot is another thing for you to exaggerate, as it gives him the idea of jumping high enough that the carry-forward in distance makes it much less effort.

Come up to the jump as you did with the High Jump the first time and introduce him to it, then turn away before actually trying it. Approach it again, giving yourself enough distance that the two of you can go into a little trot, then up with your left foot, giving the command, making sure the lead *never* tightens to throw him off balance. Keep your hands no higher than waist level and the lead loose. Make sure that Buddy has the benefit of seeing the entire width of the jump in front of him, not just one end of it, so think of *his* position as you make your approach. When you give the command "Hup," "Over," "Jump" or whatever you decide upon, make it a happy tone and put a "lift" into it. Do not, unthinkingly, use his name as he is about to jump, for this brings his attention back to you, rather than on the job at hand. Come in with your magic praise word "G-o-o-d," as soon as the jump is made and repeat the procedure over each of the single jumps. Progress in this manner until Buddy is jumping each one alone and off lead, with yourself dodging around the end of the jump, but keeping him under control with your Heel command as you approach in a trot, and bringing him back to Heel position as soon as he has jumped.

Your next step is to place two of the sections close together, parallel to each other, and with a small space between, creating a wider jump and making a longer distance necessary for clearing it. Continue approaching the jump at a trot or in a smooth fast pace. When on lead, remember to check to make sure it is loose so that your pal is not

Teaching broad jump in motion, showing:
Loose Lead
Left hand guiding
Lifts in position to elevate jumps

thrown off balance. As the jumping improves, gradually increase the space between the two sections until it is about equal to the width across one of the top boards. Be sure you do not add a board or increase the distance until your pal can do what is in front of him with no help from you.

When the jumping on command is under control over two boards with no corrections or extra help necessary, you may proceed gradually with adding the other sections and increasing the distance, working off lead. Get Buddy's attention, if it becomes necessary, by slipping the lead under the collar in the "tuck-through" position, or simply putting your fingers under the collar in the same manner and reminding him to pay attention to you.

When you have successfully completed the maximum distance in this manner, you are ready to start removing the lifts, one at a time, first taking away the one on the highest board, furthest away. As Buddy gets to the point that he can clear all the jump without any of the lifts, you and he are ready to try working toward show routine.

For this, you will go back to the use of one jump only. Place your dog facing the jump, slightly to the left of center and within ten feet of it (adjust this distance to less than this if it is best for him), and tell him to Wait. Leave him, go to the right side of the jump, and turn to face it. Call his name and give the jump command, at the same time taking a step forward (toward the jump) and raising your left arm and hand shoulder high in a sweeping motion to give him something to follow, encouraging him to jump forward, rather than toward you. Your own stepping forward at this point is another linking step between your running alongside him and his jumping from a fixed Sit. It can be shortened gradually, as you see fit, just as the signal with your arm can be decreased until no signal is needed.

To teach a good habit pattern on the return to you, as required in show routine, your own timing is of prime importance. First, you must remember to make a right turn (90 degrees) yourself *as* your dog is going through the air, to be in the proper spot for his return. Then, be ready to speak his name just at the moment his *front* feet touch as he is landing. No other command is used with this, just his name for attention. As he comes to you, use your hands as you learned to do in getting a straight sit in front of you on the Recall. Complete the exercise with the Finish to Heel. Don't ever completely drop the name for attention, but don't make a habit of using it. Many times a little reminder or refresher is worth its weight in gold.

Follow through with the same sequence of steps as before in gradually increasing the distance of the jump until you and Buddy have accomplished the maximum he is required to jump and are doing it in the show routine pattern. However, don't be afraid to introduce a bit of variety into it to keep it interesting and avoid his becoming a robot. In other words, don't always have him jump from the Sit; approach it occasionally with him in a trot. Don't always have him Finish at the end —just turn and Heel him away. Remember to keep your commands happy and enjoy it all with him. Be sure you stay aware of the best distance from the jump to leave your dog and don't be afraid to back up if you run into any problems in the jumping. When you find where it started, work it out at that point, and *then* move forward again.

Basset Hound clearing broad jump with ease

Just one more reminder: As in all the other exercises, don't repeat more than three to five times before you change to something else or call it off completely.

Long Sit

The regulations for the Long Sit in the Open class call for three minutes from the time the judge says "Leave your dogs" and the handlers go out of sight to a designated area, until he says "Return to your dogs." Naturally, the time out of sight will be more than three minutes and will vary according to how far from the ring the handlers have been sent. With this in mind, we want to gradually work up to the point where it is not unusual for Buddy to have to wait for four or even five minutes before you get back to him. In order for him to feel secure while you are out of sight, it will be necessary for you to build up his confidence gradually.

Your best way to approach this is to first refresh his memory, as per the Novice training, on the meaning of the Stay command. His confidence in your return to him should have been built up in training for the Novice stays, even though you remained in sight. In beginning practise, first do the regular Novice Sit, but increase it gradually from one minute to three minutes, with you in sight.

To start the "out of sight", first choose a place to practise that will lend itself to easy exit and return. Avoid going through a door, as you may worry your pal too much with this situation, at least at the beginning. You can go around the corner of the house, garage, shed, etc., if working outdoors, or into another room if you are inside the house, but be sure the door doesn't get closed. Now, ready to start?

Put Buddy into a sit position, tell him "Stay!" and leave (on the right foot, of course), walking straight away from him, not looking back, even though you'd love to take a peek. Go completely out of sight, then turn right around and go back to your dog. This is your first step in planting complete faith in his mind that you *are* going to return to him. Repeat this about three more times to make sure he understands. In practise and teaching this, we recommend this should be one place you should withhold your praise until you have finished and are ready to release him from his Stay position. This is to avoid any excitement and exuberance *before* you have let him know it is OK for him to move.

When you start to increase the time you remain out of your dog's sight, be sure you understand him and his individual personality and work accordingly. Use the common sense you were endowed with and don't push ahead too fast. If you encourage any breaking of position at this point, you can make up your mind right now that you can turn right around and go back and start all over again!

About the simplest method that we have come up with, for gradually increasing the time out of sight, is by counting. After the immediate return, next time out of sight increase the time by counting to five, then return. The next time, increase the count to ten, if Buddy seems relaxed and steady, gradually increasing the time by an additional count of five more, or, in some cases, by ten. Remember to break the practise after three to five times and go to something else, gradually increasing the time in future practise lessons. The Long Down (which comes next in the text) would *not* be a break in the routine. Go to something else for variety. When your dog is steady on the exercise, he should have no difficulty holding this position for anywhere from three to five minutes.

Long Down

If Buddy has learned to stay on the Long Sit, with you out of sight for at least three minutes, you should encounter no trouble teaching him to remain in the Down position while you are out of sight, provided you don't do anything carelessly to alarm him. When Buddy is in a sitting position his head is higher (naturally) than when he is down and, as a result, he has a better view of your exit. He can see more and follow you further when in this position. To compensate for this, don't drop out of sight suddenly over a hill or try to get out of sight too quickly. If he should get upset, his only recourse is to raise his head up so he can see you. Unless he's unusually large, he probably would break his position and sit up to get a better view. Be sure you help to keep him relaxed in the Down position by leaving as smoothly and naturally as possible, and by increasing your time away from him gradually, as in the Long Sit. Pay strict attention to the counting system and don't assume that you should go forward faster in the progress of this exercise, just because Buddy has already learned to stay on the Long Sit for at least three minutes.

On returning to your pal from out of sight on the Long Down, even at the very beginning, be ready to give a Stay command, as you don't want him to develop a habit of breaking his position to show you how overjoyed he is over your return. He gets just a little bit more excited when he is down, for some reason or other. It seems to become a really *big* event to him. If you should see his feelings are starting to cause him to sit as you return, don't correct at this point, but come right in with the command, "Down, Stay!" As he gets used to the exercise, he will settle down and become more relaxed and the "Stay," as you come back to him will penetrate and keep him in position. As in the Long Sit practise, don't give any praise until that session of that exercise is terminated, then really "lay it on"! When practising the Down following the Sit for formal competiton, reserve your praise for the completion of the Down, not between the two.

ADVANCED EXERCISES

As at the end of the Novice training, we now have some other exercises for you to work on which will help lead you into the next phase of training, the Utility work. This not only will help prepare you for your next step, but also will bring some variety into your training to relieve any possible boredom without interfering with your Open work.

Take, Hold and Carry: Even though Buddy has learned to Take, Hold, Carry and retrieve the dumbbell, it is good to teach him to Take, Hold and Carry other items made of other materials, as he will be required to do just this in the Utility exercises. In addition to this, he also will be able to help you when you're enjoying each other's company in your everyday living together. It will be more fun for both of you. Some of these additional items can be a leather glove, a white work canvas glove, some kind of a metal article and some kind of a leather article. The main thing is that you will be trying to put across to him at this point that he should Take, Hold and Carry *any* item you ask him to, on your command.

If you need to refresh your own memory on introducing any of these items to your pal, refer back to the technique we used with the dowel, then with the dumbbell. There may be one exception, however, especially if he did not go through Kindergarten Puppy Training and get used to the feeling of a metal article in his mouth. When he experiences this sensation the first time, he may react to it very unpleasantly when his teeth first contact the metal. Many dogs find the taste or feel of metal in their mouths extremely distasteful and become very disturbed by it. DON'T force the issue!

One way we have found to successfully combat this is to apply one or two coats of clear plastic spray to the mouthpiece of the article, making sure each coat is thoroughly dried before applying the next. (We have found Krylon plastic spray satisfactory.) This takes away the cold metal feeling and makes the article very acceptable to your pal. Use this one for your practise sessions, and as the plastic wears off, he will gradually become accustomed to the feeling of the bare metal.

When you and Buddy have mastered the Take, Hold and Carry with all the articles, put some additional fun into your work with an occasional retrieve of them. Make sure this bears no resemblance to show routine. Do your throwing while both of you are in motion, and send him out at the same time as the "throw." Keep him eager and keep it fun! *And,* don't wear him out just because he loves it so much.

Getting used to bar, above solid jump, low position

High and Bar Jump: Using the striped Bar in combination with the High Jump is a most important step, leading to the advanced work where the Bar Jump is a hurdle all by itself. Buddy must be made to realize that he is not performing in a clown suit when he is given the signal to jump over the Bar, although it does look funny when he runs under it. Let's have that for the trick dogs in the circus—it's their job to make the people laugh!

On Page 180 are diagrams of brackets we use on the boards of the High Jump that will hold the Bar in place above the solid boards, as well as pictures of the Bar in position. Always start a new jump (and with the Bar, it *is* a new jump) at a minimum height. You can gradually increase the height as you go along in practise, but don't rush to see how fast you can reach the maximum required height. When you first start with the Bar, do it with the same steps you did on the other jumps, beginning with introducing Buddy to the Bar. (And we don't mean the kind where they serve liquid refreshments!)

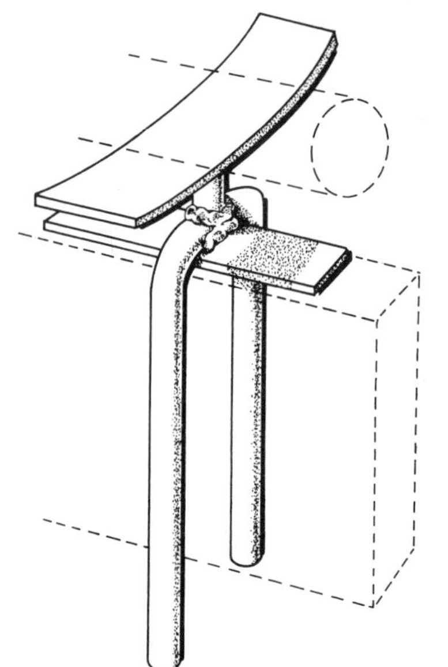

Design of bracket to be used for holding striped bar on solid jump, for introduction of dog to the bar of the Utility jump. Purpose of the design is to allow the bar to be knocked off in either direction, avoiding possible injury to the dog.

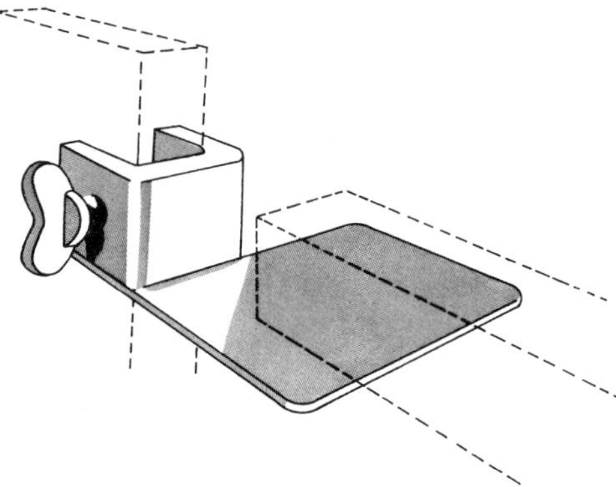

An alternate design for the bracket holding the Utility bar above the solid jump, which allows the solid boards to be removed one at a time without moving or changing the height of the bar, gradually working to a completely open space underneath.

Short bar on brackets used with solid jump to familiarize dog with the bar of the utility jump

Same jump lowered, beginning of teaching bar jump for a large dog

If you find him knocking the bar off, it could be caused by one or more of several things. Maybe you raised it too fast; perhaps you had him too close to the jump for a proper takeoff; or maybe it was just the opposite situation, too far away. Whatever the reason, lower it again and start going over it with him again, raising your own leading left leg high as you hop over, to help give him the idea. Always double check yourself and what you are doing, before you start to put the blame on him. If he should be frightened by the noise made by the falling Bar, take him with you as you replace it and let him know there is nothing to harm him.

When he understands that he should jump over the Bar, in spite of all that space *under* it, you can increase the distance away from it, and then teach an angle approach to it with a signal from you to indicate the direction, coupled with the jump command. An excellent aid here is the chute or "plumber's helpers," as illustrated on Page 104. If you can go this far, getting your dog to respond to your signal and command at a distance to do the Bar Jump, while you are still working with the Open exercises, you will have accomplished a great deal and will have progressed a long way into your Basic Utility work. This will be the foundation for the Directed Jump exercise.

Solid jump with utility bar in place illustrating position at maximum height for large dogs, before starting to remove boards gradually

Signals—Heeling (On Lead): Again, to put a little more variety in your training sessions with Buddy, and looking ahead toward your next degree (that of Utility Dog), let us try to teach your pal just three of the signals used in the Heeling. You will also find some very practical uses for these signals in your everyday life.

The dictionary uses the words "signal" and "sign" interchangeably in several definitions, including the one pertaining to its application here, as a "natural or conventional gesture or motion used instead of words to express some thought, command, or wish."

We have several things to consider here, but first and foremost, it is Buddy! Realizing that motion is of prime importance in getting attention, that motion (given by your arm and hand) *must* be a gesture that can be easily seen by him, from *his* level or position. It must be deliberate and smooth, so there will be no confusion in its meaning, and definitely should not be a quick flip that he could easily miss. To start properly and be able to guide and teach what you want, you naturally must work *on lead.* Also, combine your signals with your voice commands until the association is well established and he knows that he is to respond properly to *either* the signal *or* the command.

Let us start with the signal to Heel, trying out in front of a mirror first so you can see what Buddy will be looking at, checking on the appearance from *his* eye level. Remember that your signals should be distinct from their background (e.g., keep your arm *away* from your own body at all possible times). Start your signal with your left hand and arm from the far side of your dog and forward of his head, sweeping smoothly toward your left side, dropping it to a normal position to finish. A too frequent error is often committed here, in that a signal starts behind the dog's head and he is lucky if he catches the end of it. If done as described, he can see it from start to finish. Practise it several times so you're sure you have it smooth and ready, to harmonize it with your dog, your lead and your footwork so that the action is timed well.

Refer to the Novice training, if you need to, for a review of the details for the Stay and Wait signals.

Signal for Heeling

Signal to Stay

Signal to Wait

Come: Now get your imaginary dog in a Sit position, facing toward you and waiting to be called. Which arm and hand you use is optional, so it might be a good idea to try both to see which one seems best for you. Raise your arm out and upward in the same plane as your body, palm open and facing your dog, to nearly shoulder height, then bend your elbow and bring the palm to the front and center of your chest, returning to your normal position, all in one smooth motion. (Illustration Page 189.) Practise this with both left and right, and then adopt the one that is smoother and easier for you.

Finish: Now you have your imaginary dog sitting in front of you, up close, waiting to go to Heel. The way your dog finishes will determine which hand and arm you use to give this signal. With your dog finishing to your left, you will use your left arm and hand. Start this signal, palm facing the floor in front of your body and to the *right* of center, giving him the opportunity to see the motion sweep across the front of your body (in case he's looking away from you). Make the motion an outward circle or oval to your left, returning to normal position. If your dog finishes to the right and circles behind you to come into Heel position, simply reverse the signal and use the right arm and hand. (Illustration Page 190.)

Now, let's get Buddy, put him on lead, and, being sure it is on the dead ring, we'll try putting all of these together.

Remember that you are teaching now and your hand and arm waving, as you start out, means absolutely nothing to him. For all he knows, there suddenly appeared a batch of flies or mosquitoes for you to start swatting and brushing away! Don't push too fast, too far, or expect too much from him. Don't give him so many different signals that he becomes confused. Try to master one or two before you go on to more.

Timing of your signal and its smoothness, along with a normal tone of voice in your commands, will go a long way toward clarifying in his mind what you expect him to do. As you see him beginning to respond to the signals, start dropping the voice commands, but be ever ready to return to them as needed. It is much wiser than to use corrections, as it helps him to understand where he went wrong.

With Buddy at Heel position, the lead in your right hand, give the Heel signal at the same time as your left foot starts to move forward in your first step. Combine the voice command at first, also give assistance (lightly) with the lead at the beginning. As you practise, eliminate the

Recall Signal

Signal to Finish around body

"extra" helps as soon as you can, one by one, as soon as you see him starting to respond to the slightest movement of your arm and hand.

In teaching the Wait signal, the command and signal should be given simultaneously, but there should be no other motion started on your part *until* your signal hand has returned to its normal position. When you have reached the end of your lead, turn and face your dog, but wait a few seconds before giving him the Recall signal. If he should be overly anxious to move, you still have your lead in your hands and can get your message to him through it. He must realize that he is not to move until the signal is given. If you should need to get his attention, speak his name, then give the signal and command simultaneously, making sure you don't stare at him any time he is facing you and coming in to you.

After he is sitting in front of you, prepare for the signal for Buddy to go to Heel, making sure your signal hand is free of the lead (but *you* shouldn't have to be reminded of this!). One special note of caution here in the handling of the lead in teaching the signal to Finish to Heel position. It is most important that there be no tension on the lead at any time, lest it be misinterpreted as a correction and become associated with that signal. Be overly careful that you do not let the lead become tight at any point here. Don't be afraid to use his name for attention, if necessary, and the command with the signal, as needed, but be careful that you don't get into a habit of turning your body as you give the signal. The fewer your own body movements are, at this time, the less bad habits you will have to break yourself of later, and you also will be giving Buddy fewer "extra" movements for his cues to performance. The signal is to be the movement of an arm and hand only.

Good luck, keep it fun!

PROBLEMS IN OPEN TRAINING

Heeling

Refer to Novice Problems for Off Lead Heeling problems.

Dog seems bored and weary, has no interest in the training.

It is very likely that the dog has had "too big a dose" of one exercise (or perhaps more than *one* exercise). He will tell you what his feelings are, if you but learn to understand him. Remember to work your dog on one exercise only from three to five times when you are practising, then go on to something else.

Dog loses interest in Heeling, although he starts out fine.

There cannot be too much emphasis put on the importance of variety in your practise sessions. Make it interesting enough to keep *both* you and your dog from becoming bored. Your dog doesn't need practise in just walking—he already knows how to do that!

Dog works fine when there are no other dogs around to distract him. If off lead, he loses interest in his owner and goes off to investigate the dogs.

It is quite obvious that "dog attention" was overlooked in Basic and Novice training or was forgotten when Open training started. The one and only solution here is to back up in the training, go back to working *on lead* and teach "dog attention". This is something you want to hang onto, through all your training.

Dog usually works fine except when in the show ring, where he hangs back as though he were looking for another command or something.

Probably when working at home and in class, it was easier to slap the leg to get the dog's attention and bring him up into correct position, instead of putting him on lead and showing him where he should be heeling. Many people have the habit of slapping their leg, using it to get their dog's attention. However, it is actually teaching your dog an extra signal, one which cannot be used in the ring in competition. If you teach without it, you won't have to worry about making a mistake and your dog won't be confused when you siddenly have to stop it. Don't blame your dog for your poor teaching.

Dog's heeling is fine but when he sits on a halt, he rolls over onto one hip, making a crooked sit.

Return to your *on lead* heeling practise, being sure that the lead is attached to the dead ring. Take only five or six steps and, as you are coming into the halt, snap the lead and release it immediately (making sure the direction of the snap is straight back, toward the tail). Don't give him a chance to sit long enough to roll over onto his hip. Start right out again and repeat about five times before going into something different, making sure you give plenty of praise for each "G-o-o-o-d!" sit.

Figure 8 Off Lead

Review Novice Figure 8 problems.

Dog lags on outside turn.

Probably your own path around the steward is not smooth and you are pivoting rather than going into a smooth circle, thus forcing your dog back into a lagging position. Learn to come across between the two stewards in a straight line and start your turn when you get in front of the steward's right foot, keeping your body erect, shoulders straight, avoiding any dipping of the body.

Dog shies away from steward's feet on the inside turn.

This could well be due to some thoughtless (and inexcusable) use of the feet for correction, making your dog suspicious of all feet he comes near. There's only one piece of advice here—STOP DOING IT.

Dog crowds handler on inside turn.

This is usually what happens when the handler does not allow ample space for the dog between himself and the steward as he goes around. The dog had probably been corrected on lead for lagging in this situation previously, so now is trying to avoid the need for a correction by crowding the handler. Check to see what you, as the handler, are doing to cause this, then change your own practise to overcome it.

Dog refuses to move after the first halt.

Return to working *on lead,* preferably in front of a mirror. Vary the position of the halts. Check to see if the dog's forward motion is blocked or hindered in any way by the position of your feet or your body, then adjust yourself accordingly.

Dog swings out and sits in front on the halts.

Check your footwork as you come into a halt, also the position of your body. Don't turn or twist your body to look at your dog, as this might be causing the crooked sit. Remember, on halting, your left foot is the *last* one in motion.

Dog swings very wide on the outside turn.

If your dog is one of the small varieties and you are doing everything else correctly, check to see how high you are raising your heels in walking around the steward. Also, your foot may be swinging out toward your dog, forcing him away from you.

If your dog is medium to large in size, be especially careful as to how you start the outside turn. Be sure you are not pivoting or dipping your shoulders.

Drop on Recall

Dog moves forward three or four lengths of his body on the command or signal to down.

Your dog has not learned thoroughly the basic training leading up to the proper response to your command or signal as he is trotting toward you. Go back to your preliminary work *on lead,* on the dead ring, dropping to your left knee as you are heeling him, being sure you give the command and/or signal at the same time. Progress gradually to dropping him from in front of you, within controlling distance, to increasing the distance slowly as you and he become sure of the response.

Dog usually drops before the command or signal is given.

A dog does what he has been taught to do. Very likely, there has been too much emphasis on show routine in the practise sessions here, too much dropping of the dog in the same place. As in all the training, variety, mixing things up, not only keeps your dog and you from being bored but also prevents forming a habit pattern. Teach your dog so that he understands that regardless of where he is or in what position, when he gets a command or signal from you to Down, it means just that, and *now.*

Dog drops but gets right up and comes in.

Again, in practise, a habit pattern has been established by calling the dog as soon as he went down and he is anticipating it. He knows that's the next thing to do, so why not do it and get it over with? Vary your practise to get him over this habit. Play a "waiting game" after a drop, return to him and heel him away instead of finishing the recall. And don't drop him on every recall. In other words, keep his attention by keeping him guessing and responding *only* to your commands when they are given.

Dog goes down from a Sit or Stand in any position, but seems confused when receiving the command or signal when in motion on the recall.

Go back to working *on lead,* on the dead ring, and practise the Down as you are heeling, in the different paces of slow, fast and normal, dropping to your left knee with him, and giving him plenty of praise with each drop. Then tie this in with the next step of dropping him as he starts toward you from a very short distance away.

Dog makes a big arc coming in on a regular straight Recall or Drop on Recall, instead of coming in on a direct line.

Set up a chute (directions and illustration, P. 104) in your training area and do your Recall practising in this. Make it 30 or 40 feet long and go a short way into it, then leave your dog and come to a halt yourself while you are still within it, so the entire exercise is practised within the confine of the chute. Avoid *any rushing* toward the dog to make a correction, for this is probably what has caused the condition.

Dog drops OK, but doesn't respond to the next command or signal to come.

This is usually caused by one of two things, sometimes a combination of both. Check the tone of voice used. Is it an "invitation" to come to you, or does it hold a threat of punishment in it? Many times this also happens when the handler stares at his dog. Look *above* his head as you call him and you can still see him.

Retrieving on the Flat

Dog tries to grab the dumbbell as it is thrown.

As much as we try to emphasize fun in the training, there is a place where a line should be drawn, as too much play can defeat your purpose. Apparently, the playing became more important than the retrieving in this case. To correct this, hold the collar (*not* the ring) with your left hand as you toss the dumbbell with your right hand. Lengthen the time gradually before giving the retrieve command, then mix up the waiting time.

Dog leaves the handler as the dumbbell is thrown.

Proceed the same way as in the above problem.

Dog runs out to the dumbbell, then plays with it.

With this problem, start to correct by tossing the dumbbell no more than six feet in front of you, within controlling distance. As he picks it up, get immediate attention on you. Don't give him time to think about playing. Increase the distance slowly, never chancing a possible loss of your control of him.

Dog picks up the dumbbell but keeps mouthing it and dropping it on the return.

It is most likely that the dumbbell is so ill-fitted to the dog's mouth that it is extremely uncomfortable for him to carry. When he tries to readjust it or change its position, he naturally drops it. Pay more attention to the individual needs of your dog and get him one that fits and is not objectionable to him.

Dog retrieves but picks up the dumbbell and carries it by the ends.

Probably the dowel mouthpiece is too close to the floor or ground, not allowing enough room for the dog's lower jaw and teeth to get under it to pick it up, without scraping and hurting. Check the instructions in the text for measuring to estimate this clearance. In starting with a corrected dumbbell, first get him to take it out of your hand while both of you are in motion, presenting the mouthpiece to him. Next, put it on the ground in front of him and give him the command. You are in control here and can make a correction if he should still go for the ends.

Dog retrieves but will not come in close, nor will he release the dumbbell.

Perhaps, not realizing what it is like from your dog's point of view, you have been taking hold of the dumbbell from the sides and pulling or yanking it out of his mouth. Naturally this HURTS, and he is going to try to avoid a repetition of the experience if he possibly can. If he's doing it as a game, no doubt it is the result of playing "tug-of-war" with you, probably from the time he was a puppy. Sometimes play practises can cause trouble later on. In either case, be sure you form the habit of bringing your hand *under* the dumbbell to receive it and let your dog *give* it to you, dropping it into your hands. He will, as soon as he realizes that you're not going to hurt him.

Dog goes out part way to the dumbbell, then turns around and returns.

Very likely there has been too big a jump in the training, trying to get a long retrieve before a short retrieve had been learned satisfactorily. He may feel insecure when he goes away from you, not being sure just what is expected of him. Go back to Heeling, and while both of you are in motion, throw the dumbbell and send him at the same time. Make the toss a fairly short one at first. The motion combined with a good tone of voice, will help to put the idea

Taking dumbbell, proper approach

Accepting dumbbell

across to him. Do not try to reach for distance or formality until you are sure your dog knows what you want.

Dog loves the retrieving but is easily affected by any distractions like hand clapping, loud speakers, flash cameras, etc., and will return without the dumbbell.

These distractions should have been set up in your training classes and will still have to be set up so they are present during your practise sessions. Work your dog *on lead,* doing some heeling, while this is going on, making sure he pays little attention to it, giving his attention to *you.* Then try some short retrieves in motion, during the same distractions, using the magic praise word "G-o-o-o-o-d!" as he brings the dumbbell to you.

Dog will not look for the dumbbell if it is not immediately visible, returns without it.

This may have started from your habit of always throwing the dumbbell in the same place as you practised. For correction, locate an outdoor area to work in that has short cut grass but is bordered by taller grass. Start with short retrieves on the low cut grass, gradually increasing your throw until the dumbbell lands in the taller grass. Should you see him showing signs of "forgetting" where it is, take him immediately to it and show it to him. Give lots of praise. No correction to the dog. Aim for the same spot on the next throw, changing the location when he has found it by himself. Encourage him with your voice, reward him with praise and soon you will see he is enjoying your new "search" game.

Dog refuses to open his mouth to allow anything to be put in it; will clamp it shut so tightly it cannot even be pried open.

Understand, first of all, that the dog is reacting from fear and suspicion, trying to avoid any physical pain being inflicted upon him. Instead of trying to force the mouth open, take a plastic straw or small plastic tubing about the same length, and proceed—as we say—to "thread the needle." This means to find the small space between the teeth, along the side, and start to work the tubing through the mouth at that point by gently rotating it slowly, until it emerges on the opposite side. Three or four attempts should accomplish this easily. When the dog will hold the tubing, continue the training as outlined on page 119.

Dog retrieves but omits the sit in front, going right to heel position.

Work inside the chute, crowding the side your dog uses to finish, as he goes for the dumbbell. As he brings it back and gets near you, give a sharp command

"Sit!" Receive the dumbbell and heap on the praise, forgetting the finish. Maybe you have been emphasizing the finish every time, to the point that your dog thinks this is the BIG thing for him to do, thus creating the problem. Never dwell on anything your dog already knows, concentrate on the *new* things you are teaching.

Retrieve over High Jump

Dog does not jump for a retrieve, but has no problem with the retrieve on the flat.

Probably the emphasis has been put on the maximum jumping here, instead of leading up to it gradually. Lower the jump to no more than the dog's chest level for height and work within controlling distance of him. Don't be too anxious to increase the height of the jump—take it slow and easy.

Dog jumps in both directions but drops the dumbbell before making the return jump.

Check your dumbbell first to see if your dog has clear vision between the ends of it. If he cannot see clearly, he cannot focus on the jump to judge accurately what he is going to have to do. If there is any question in your mind on this, get him a new dumbbell that will remove any doubt.

Dog jumps on the way out but brings the dumbbell back, coming around the jump.

Check for vision while carrying the dumbbell, as above. Practise over a lowered jump with the chute placed so that he will be guided back over the jump.

Dog touches the jump on the way out but clears it well on the return.

Ask somebody to watch your dog's front feet as he takes off to make the jump, to see if he gets his lift from one front foot or from both of them together. If it is only one foot, he is not in balance to make the most out of his jump. Adjust your own position in relation to the jump, as you are probably standing either too close to it or too far away. Your dog's performance will tell you when you hit the right spot. Remember, when he leaves you, he is jumping from a *sit.* When he returns, he is already in motion.

Dog jumps and retrieves perfectly, except when the jump is set near or at maximum height.

Start working from the lowest board, observing the use of the front feet and adjusting the distance from the jump accordingly, until the jump is at chest level of your dog. Increase beyond this only two inches at a time and check to see when the ticking or a refusal to jump occurs. If this continues when the jump is above chest level, or above his eye level, take him to a veterinarian to have his eyes examined. He may be having difficulty focusing on the jump to judge the distance properly. Also, have his hips checked, if you are not sure of their condition.

Dog jumps, retrieves the dumbbell, but starts to play with it instead of returning with it.

As in the same problem in the Retrieve on the Flat, work it out with your dog within controlling distance. Lower the jump and toss the dumbbell only a few feet, keeping it so you can step over and insist on the retrieve. Add the chute, angling it out a bit from the jump, so your dog will be guided back immediately on your command. Increase the jump slowly, but only after there is no need for your stepping over, and no need for any extra commands from you.

Dog acts afraid of the jump, both directions.

There must have been some unpleasant experiences in training for the jump, to create this condition, such as a tight lead on going over or being dragged over it. You must start over again, back at the beginning, to build up confidence in your dog and remove the fear. Work with the jump, one board only, inside the chute. Introduce him to it so he will understand that it is not going to hurt him. Jump with him, over and back, always keeping the lead loose and on the non-working ring of the collar. Keep your tone of voice light and happy as you give your commands. Don't raise the jump until your dog will do the same when off lead. Eliminate your own jumping as early as possible. Build the confidence gradually and don't bother with formal sits and finishes. Keep it fun.

Dog jumps and retrieves but seems unable to adjust on the return so he can sit in front. He usually goes past, then stands there confused.

Each dog has his own individual personality and ability and it is the responsibility of the owner or trainer to know their own dog and his limitations. Take note of the distance needed by your dog on the return jump and adjust your starting position so it is just a bit behind that. Work *with* your dog, not against him.

Broad Jump

Dog jumps only when handler jumps with him, not on command to do it by himself.

Back up in your training to using only one board. Take the dumbbell with you, position yourself and your dog properly in front of the jump. Give him the command "Wait!", toss the dumbbell out beyond the jump and give him the command to jump as it leaves your hand. Take your finishing position at the side of the jump immediately and receive your dog and the dumbbell as he returns to you. Repeat as many times as you feel it is necessary before you add more boards to increase the distance. When he will do the maximum distance required, using the dumbbell, try eliminating it but use the arm motion if needed, doing without it later. Return to the combination of the dumbbell throwing once in a while to keep it fun and to provide variety.

Dog steps on first board or "tiptoes" between the boards, won't jump the required distance.

Once again, think what the boards look like to the dog from his eye level, especially if he's rather "low to the ground". There is just a white mass in front of him and he may not be able to estimate *how* far it extends. In other words, he cannot accurately adjust his thrust on takeoff to assure a safe landing beyond the jump. Refer to page 171 in the text for instructions on the construction and use of the lifts to increase the angle of the broad jumps and bring it up where your dog can see it better. A higher jump will result in a greater distance span, too.

Dog "cheats", covering only a small part of the jump, cuts across the corner to return to the handler.

This has very likely happened as a result of improper use of the lead in training, putting tension on it toward the handler. Naturally, if you constantly pulled him in that direction, your dog has gotten the idea you wanted him to come to you the shortest and fastest way possible.

Start over again in your training, off lead, and jump with your dog until he stops crowding you. Then, as you both approach the jump, raise your left arm shoulder high as you give the command, and go around and to the side of the jump. When he will do this, leave him in position and go to the side of the jump, continuing with the arm motion as you give the command to jump. If he starts to jump at an angle, step forward in between the last two jumps, decreasing the size of the step as your dog becomes sure of what you want, and then try your show routine.

Dog "ticks" or touches the last board.

Recheck the distance from which your dog is starting. Is he taking off on both front feet or only on one? Try changing the distance, within the ten feet allowed. Sometimes one foot more or less is the answer.

Dog makes a big swing as he returns, resulting in a crooked sit and sloppy return.

The correction for this is quite easy but it does depend entirely on *good timing.* Give your dog the command or signal to jump and watch his front feet. *As they hit the floor,* come out with his name at that instant with a firm, sharp voice. Use *only* the name, no command with it. This brings his attention directly to you and with no time for his usual nonsense and mind-wandering. Throw it at him every now and then to keep him sharp. He won't know when you're going to surprise him with it. Keep him guessing!

Dog jumps but often romps and plays instead of returning properly.

Your best bet here is to decrease the size of your training area, using a fence or hedge if outdoors, a wall or corner of a room if inside, and setting up sections of the chute to limit the other boundaries. Keep your dog within controlling distance in teaching and correcting. Use his name (as above) go get his attention back to you when he lands. Do *not* correct with your hands or with the lead. *Show* him what you want him to do and give him PRAISE to let him know he is pleasing you.

Dog jumps and returns but goes directly to heel position.

Before your dog gets a chance to start around you (or swing to your left), give a sharp "Sit!" command. Block him with a section of the chute if necessary. Give him praise and do *not* complete the finish, simply turn and heel him away to another exercise. He probably has had too much routine practise of finishing every time he comes to the front of you, so he's just anticipating and is doing "what comes naturally."

Dog tries to run away and acts afraid of the jump when he's given the command to jump.

This has evidently been caused by unnecessary roughness and mishandling of the lead in teaching the exercise, trying to pull or force him over the jump. Go back in your training, being careful to use a *loose* lead, fastened to the non-working ring of the collar and jump with him. Don't bother with sits or finishes, keep in motion and keep it fun. Make sure your tone of voice is gay and happy, smile as you give your commands. As he starts to gain confidence, take the lead off and progress to the "tuck-through" of the lead on the approach, continuing to jump with him until he is really enjoying the exercise. Go into the formal *very* gradually, after you have accomplished this much.

Long Sit and Down

Dog breaks as handler goes out of sight.

Start back at the beginning, using a count system, out of sight for only a count of five. Increase the time out of sight very gradually, adding only five counts at a time, as your dog is ready for it. Make sure, as a tie-in to your Novice training, that you can first be able to leave your dog at least fifty feet away, *in* sight, before you even try to go out of sight.

Dog stays OK but cries and whines the whole time the handler is out of sight.

To prepare for this correction, first teach your dog to take and hold a leather glove (he should know this already). Teach him to do this in all three positions of sitting, standing and down for periods of up to three minutes. Again using the count system, put the glove down in front of your dog and leave him, counting no more than 15 (maybe less) out of sight and return to him. Be sure you return immediately if he should start to make any noise. Pick up the glove and tell him to take and hold it, leave him and return at the count of 5. Receive the glove and heap on the praise, avoiding correction of any kind. Repeat this until he will stay for a full three minutes with the glove in his mouth; then start over with the short count, increasing the time gradually, with the glove laying in front of him where he can see it. Even when he apparently has learned what not to do, refresh his memory once in a while by having him hold the glove in his mouth, always remembering the praise.

Dog changes his position when handler has gone out of sight.

The most effective way to treat this is to refer back to the Novice chapter and make a distinction between the commands "Stay" and "Wait". If taught properly, you should be able to get a steady and firm Sit and Down when you give the command "Stay!", for you will have conveyed the true meaning of the word.

Dog starts to roll one way and the other, after handler is out of sight.

This should have been corrected as it was starting, but it is not at all hopeless. You can set up the correction according to the size of your dog, using two boards from the high jump (2″ for Toys, up to 8″ for large breeds) and supporting them upright by means of brackets or other supports (*not* the uprights of the jump). Place them parallel to each other, wide enough apart so that your dog can sit or lie down lengthwise between them. Increase the time you are away gradually, checking by counting. As your dog becomes steady and relaxes, remove the boards. But take away one at a time, laying them flat before removing entirely. Repeat the use of the boards occasionally, as necessary.

Dog is steady on the stay, but breaks position and acts cowed when handler reenters the ring to return to Heel position.

This could have resulted from confusion in learning what "Stay" really means. In this case, it means going back to the beginning and teaching it all over again, with more understanding and patience.

The other possible cause, and one that can be remedied easily (with a little concentration and habit breaking on your part), is the dog's reaction to your eyes, your staring at him as you return. Try returning to him and fix your gaze upon something above and beyond him. You can still see what he is doing, but you are not meeting him "eye to eye". No dog enjoys this and it makes them very uncertain as to what is expected of them. It also transmits any of your own apprehension and nervousness to your dog.

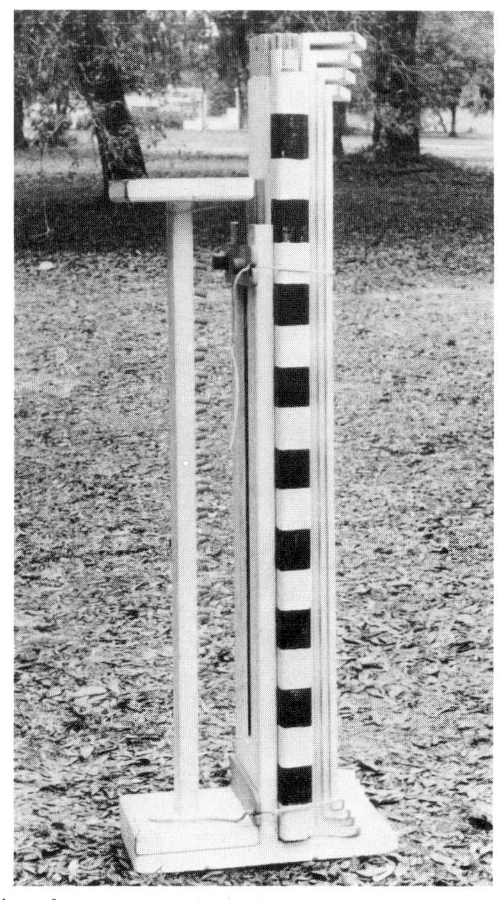

A well-designed, compact unit, including all three jumps and brackets

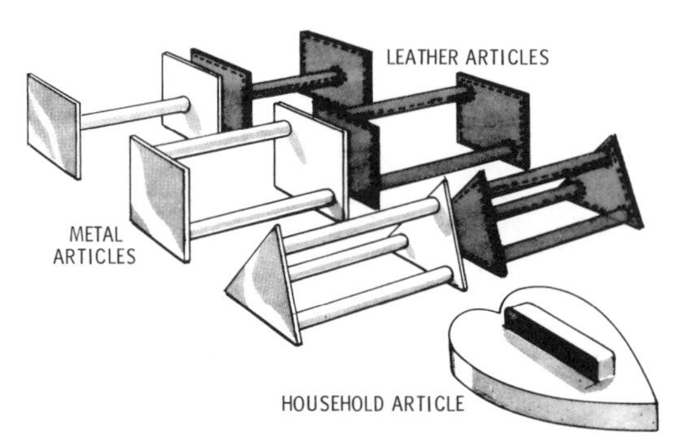

Various designs used for scent articles

Type of scent discrimination articles, diamond shaped ends

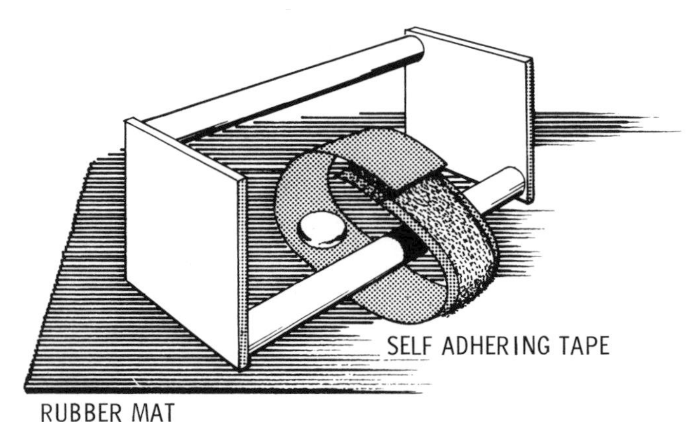

Section of scent discrimination mat, showing one article anchored with "Velcro"

Utility

TO BEGIN this chapter on the advanced training, let us first consider scent, and how dogs react to it, so that you can better understand your dog and how he works. We will delve more deeply in it, however, in the tracking chapter.

Scent Discrimination

Even though scent itself is a very elusive thing to "corral" for observation, the study of different types of scent has revealed certain facts that help us when we try to figure out *why* our dogs react a particular way under certain conditions. There are facts that seem to be very obvious, when we given serious thought to the subject, even though we have no "black and white" proof, as such.

We do know that certain scents can be very attractive to dogs and make for an eager worker. We also know, from watching and working with many dogs, that a scent can be extremely uncomfortable to a dog's nose. It is the *why?* that we cannot answer. We do surmise, however, that in many cases it is because it is too strong or too fresh. The dogs themselves indicate this to us when they go out to a group of articles, looking for one with their owner's scent, locate it fairly easily, then proceed to kill time before they are willing to pick it up and carry it in their mouths. When it has cooled off or sort of faded in intensity, it is no problem. We have tested this by having a handler scent an article *very* lightly and for just a few moments for a particular dog having this type of trouble. Voila—the solution!

A dog's ability to smell things is so many times more keen than a human being's that it is difficult for us to even try to comprehend it. With such a complex and extremely sensitive organ, is it any wonder that some scents would be very distasteful and uncomfortable to him? Many scents that we humans come in contact with are so strong that we turn away from them, and try to remove ourselves from the area where they are, if possible. So, what about our dogs whose noses are so superior to ours in performance? Isn't it conceivable that they are trying to do the same thing?

At this point in training, we are primarily interested in offering you a method of teaching Buddy what you expect of him when you ask him to go to a certain group of articles and find and retrieve one certain article which has your scent on it. We also will give you our technique of applying your scent to that article.

At present, in show competition, this exercise calls for five leather articles (all alike) and five metal articles (also all alike). However, for teaching, we also include five wooden articles, as formerly required. We start out with the wooden article, for it is so much more like the dumbbell that Buddy is already very familiar with from the Open training. Even if it is a different shape and size, he needs little introduction to it, for it is still the same material.

To begin, choose three articles from your set, one of each material, and mark them so that you can identify them easily. These will be your only articles for practise sessions, until you are directed differently, and the wood article will be the first one you'll be using. Keep the balance of the set put away until you are ready to work with them.

Motion is one of our greatest aids in teaching a dog, so we will take full advantage of it in our step-by-step approach in learning the Scent Discrimination exercise.

With the wooden article in your right hand, holding it by the bar (rather than on the ends), and with Buddy at your left side, move forward a few steps, and while *both* of you are in motion, toss it out in front of you about ten feet. As it is about to land, send him out to get it, using whatever command you have chosen for this exercise. As he tips his head to smell or to pick up the article, remember to encourage him with the magic word "G-o-o-o-d"! Clap your hands as he's bringing it back to you, receive it and praise him. Don't include a "sit" or a "finish". We want to keep his mind on finding and retrieving the article as he is learning.

When you have repeated this from three to five times, pick up the leather article. Hold it in front of Buddy and tell him to take it and hold

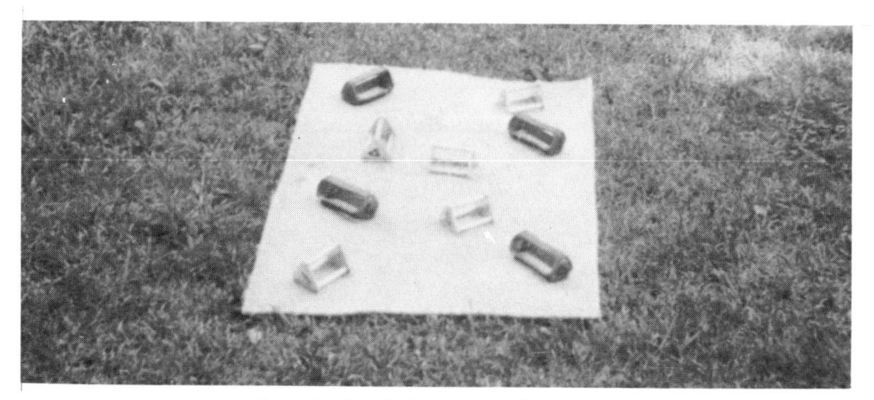

A typical article mat for home use

it. He was familiar with wood, but both the leather and metal may require a little introduction, being such new and different materials to him (unless your advanced Open training has already accomplished this, along with good foundation training in the Kindergarten stage).

Work with the leather article, then with the metal, just as you did with the wood, until Buddy happily retrieves each of the three materials. Now, to begin the work of Scent Discrimination—

At this point you should have the scent discrimination article mat or board made up. It is the greatest aid for teaching your pal what it is that you expect him to do, and teaching it in a very short time. If, to show him the proper way to do the exercise, you were to go out to the articles, get down on all fours and smell the articles, and then get one and bring it back, you'd look pretty silly, wouldn't you? With the scent discrimination board, it is simply a matter of association and well-timed praise, to let him know he is doing the right thing. Refer to the illustration and instructions for ideas for the construction of one. Space the articles from 6 inches to 10 inches from each other, depending upon the size of your dog. Also, put two or three of them on a cord, about 6 inches or so, to allow them to be moved by a nudge of a nose. Avoid using a very light material for the mat, or a sheet of metal. The former can, conceivably, be picked up and carried by your dog; the latter can make your dog afraid as it might be cold and is definitely noisy. Now, armed with the mat, the chute and your three practise articles, we will go to work.

Set up the chute so that it is no wider than the width of your mat and put the mat inside it, about midway the length of it. Avoid any contamination of the articles with your own scent. Enlist the help of an interested neighbor or friend in setting up the mat and carry it out, if you do it yourself, by the edge, keeping away from direct contact of any of the articles. Have your four metal and four leather articles attached, as well as a couple of the wood articles at the beginning. These will be removed completely as soon as Buddy learns what it is all about.

Of first consideration now is the proper way for you to put your scent on an article, regardless of its shape, size and material. Remembering what we observed about scent being too strong or too weak for the comfort of the individual dog's nose, we have found it advisable for *anyone,* in teaching this exercise, to do their own testing to find out how much scenting of an article is best for his own dog. We now advise experimenting by counting to find out what is best for your own dog, also checking to find out whether your left hand or your right hand may give better results. Doctors will tell you that one side of your body will vary from the other, as far as perspiration is concerned, among other things.

Take the wooden article and hold it by the mouthpiece (not the ends) in your right hand. Do not rub it, just hold it firmly and count to five. Place it on the floor, about ten feet away and then send your dog for it. Carefully observe his reactions, watching to see how long it takes him, and if he does much smelling, if he licks his nose or does any snorting or sneezing. Then repeat, changing the count to more, and then to less. Then try it using the left hand. Experiment over several practise sessions, until you come up with what you feel is your most satisfactory combination.

Now enter the chute with Buddy at heel position, proceeding at a normal pace to the other end, over the articles and mat to let him know there is nothing to be suspicious of. Make sure he walks through them, too, and does not jump over them. Control him with his collar or lead, if necessary and let him tip his head to investigate if he should be so inclined. Repeat this two or three times. Then, upon entering the chute, when you are about 10 feet from the articles, toss the article you're holding about half way to the mat and send him for it as you toss it. As he nears it, come in with your "G-o-o-o-o-d!", to let him know he is right and is doing what you want. On his return, receive it and give him his praise.

Dog working on article mat within training chute

Next, tell him "Wait" or "Stay", walk out to the mat and turn to face him. Place the article just in front of the mat, making sure he sees what you are doing. Return to him and send him for it. If he should smell the other articles or even try to pick one up, DON'T correct him! But be on your toes and ready to say "G-o-o-o-d!" when he gets near the one you placed out there. This is the beginning of teaching him to use his nose the proper way, without errors and eliminating the need for corrections.

Proceed in this same pattern in your practise, placing the article on the mat in various different locations. When he can do this without any help, you may then go through the same procedure with the leather and metal articles, one at a time. After he is finding both of these, you may start to loosen one article at a time, making sure that *your* scent is on *only* the article he is supposed to find. When all the articles are loose and Buddy is having no difficulty finding the right one, you may remove the mat, but don't hesitate to return to using it if necessary.

Here are a few "Don'ts" to keep in mind while you are training this exercise:

Don't glare at your pal.
Don't overscent the article.
Don't yank the article out of his mouth.
Don't include the Sit and Finish (Focus his attention on the article instead.)
Don't put your hand over his nose to "give him the scent". (This only loads his nose up with it and makes all the articles smell alike.)

For the last step, you will require help from a second person, in order to get your dog to go out to look for the right article which has been placed while you and Buddy are turned to face away from the articles. It may be advisable to return to the mat for a few times here, as the introduction of a second scent could be a confusing factor. When all is

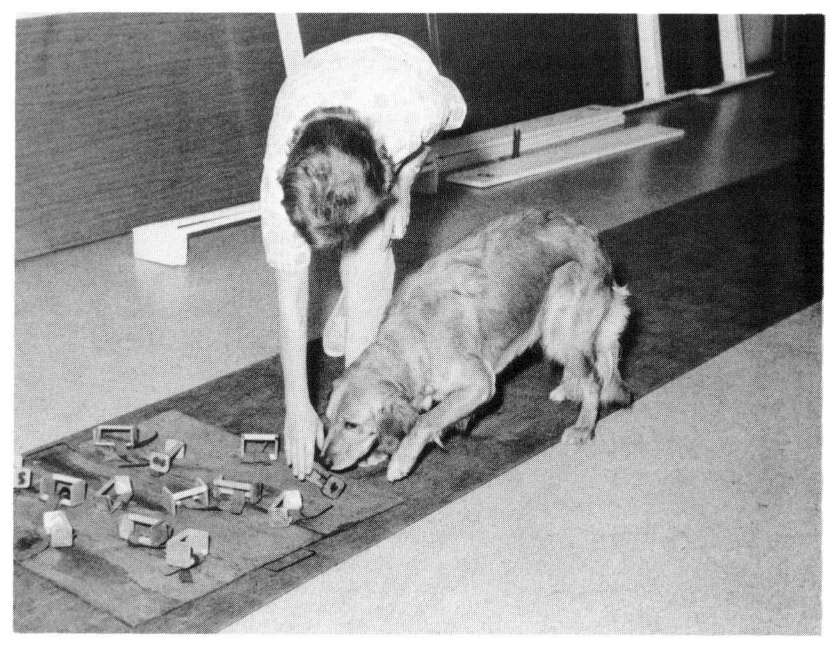

Showing right article to dog

Working on articles on mat

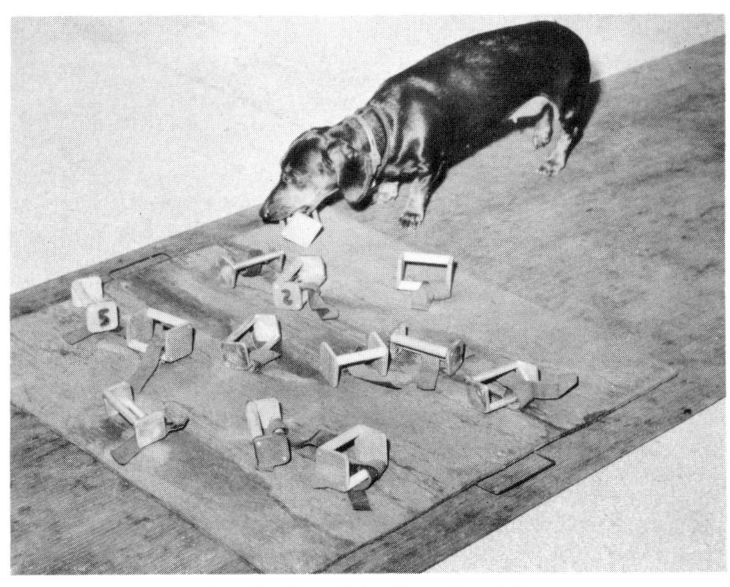

Dog finding right (loose) article

well and going smoothly, it is time for you to start practising your "turn and send", leading into the way you will have to execute it for ring competition at a show. With your back to the articles and Buddy at heel position, do an about turn smoothly, making sure he turns with you. As you face the articles, continue with a forward motion, making believe you are going to take a step. At the same time, give him the command you've been using for him to go out and find the article. Remember the magic word and when to use it. After working several times in this manner, drop the make believe step and simply turn and send. You may next remove the mat, then one side of the chute, then the other. However, if any confusion whatever is observed, always be ready to revert to any or all of the training aids.

Before leaving this exercise entirely, I would like to add this note on scent, in relation to the articles and your working with them. To begin with, a dog's ability to distinguish different scents is so keen that we humans cannot even comprehend what he can do in this field. But we should be very aware of it and observant of our pal's reactions when he is trying to tell us something.

Many people, even now, try to "give their dog their scent" by holding their hands over their dog's nose or in front of it. In reality, they are doing him an injustice and making the task much more difficult for him.

To begin with, your dog already knows what you smell like and, if the proper association has been made in teaching the Scent Discrimination exercise, he knows what you want him to do. More than likely you and he have lived together since he was a young puppy. He started recognizing your scent when you first began to care for him, feeding, watering, grooming, exercising and playing with him. Your scent was on everything you used in his training, the collar, lead, dumbbell, etc. So why, in Heaven's name, when you've progressed to Utility training, should it be necessary to remind him of what you smell like?

If you insist on "giving him your scent" by holding your hands over his nose or in front of it, you are only loading his nasal membranes with it. You are sending him a short distance within a very short span of time, so that *everything* he smells still smells like the scent he's already carrying in his nose! And *you* put it there! If he is going to do the job correctly and with ease, he's going to have to do it with a clear nose, just as you and I prefer to tackle a problem with a clear head. After all, this is a "discrimination" exercise, so there must be something there to "discriminate." Sometimes dogs will take matters in their own hands, so to speak, and will snort or sneeze or paw their noses on the way out to the articles, in an effort to clear out the nasal passages. I'm sure you've seen this happen, but maybe you were not aware of why they were doing it. They can tell us a lot, in their own way, if we but watch them, think and ask ourselves "Why?"

In case you may be wondering about de-scenting your articles effectively, we have some simple tips that should come in handy, especially if you have back-to-back shows on a weekend or are on a circuit with several shows in a week or so and don't have extra articles to replace the used ones. One easy way is to spread your articles on a newspaper overnight, where the night dew can get to them. We don't pretend to know what chemical process takes place but we have reason to believe that some element in the printer's ink could very well be a contributing factor. Be sure you do not handle the articles when you pick them up in the morning. An inexpensive pair of kitchen tongs will serve the purpose well.

Another, even more sure method is to spray the articles with a pressurized can of ether or Quik-Start (for cold motors, available at service stations) and let them air thoroughly before putting them into the carrier. Washing, baking, boiling, etc., only serve to impregnate the article still more, many times adding a most unpleasant smell, as far as your dog is concerned.

The case in which you carry your articles should also be given careful consideration. It should receive the same care in de-scenting as the articles, and it should be of a solid material—wood, plastic, or something similar. Never use a mesh or wire or anything with open weave, as this only allows your scent to re-enter the case and spread over the articles as you are traveling in your car. Also, avoid putting the tongs and the canvas gloves in with the articles as they do not get de-scented. If you smoke, the fumes from the tobacco can also spread over the articles if they are not properly protected.

One other piece of advice to think about when you are traveling to shows away from home. Even though you think it's nice to impress somebody with your new cologne, or your special after-shave lotion, think about Buddy first! *He* may not exactly appreciate the change, and you may throw him off his usual reliable performance completely. (*Don't* blame him until you've definitely cleared yourself of any possibility of contributing to his failure!) Keep yourself as natural as you have been in your practise sessions at home, even if it means that you take the trouble to bring along some of your regular soap from home. If Buddy approves of the way you smell, that's all that matters!

Directed Retrieve

The Directed Retrieve exercise was added to the Utility work by the American Kennel Club in an effort to correlate retriever field trial work with Obedience trial training and furnish a basic exercise which might lead into an interest in both phases by the average exhibitor. It is not intended as a qualification or requirement for entry into field trials, as much, much more goes into this type of training. If you need any proof of this, just make a point of attending a retriever field trial sometime. It is one of the most thrilling demonstrations ever staged of the ability of a dog and the "know-how" of a trainer and handler; and the rapport between the two can only evoke applause and amazement from any onlooker.

To get back to our new exercise, one of the important things you must first master is your own footwork on the "pivot" or turn. According to the best recommended interpretations, a pivot is a turning in place or position, *without* taking a step. In other words, if you turn on one foot, heel or toe raised, then slide or shuffle the other foot to line it up into position, and do it smoothly, you "have it made." A step could be construed by a judge as "changing your position", and thus could be a valid reason for a minor deduction on your score. Practise first before you try it with your dog.

Your next step is to teach Buddy, unless he has already learned it in your previous training, to shift his position according to your pivoting, be it left or right. If he has been taught to go to Heel by circling to your right and behind you, your training will be a bit more involved as this type of movement is not allowed in this exercise, in connection with the pivot. You also will have to choose a new command to teach for this to avoid confusion. Some words we might suggest are Place, Position, By Me, etc.—just do not use a word that has already been used in training. If Buddy is accustomed to going to the left, your teaching will be easier and should take less time.

To start this procedure, it is necessary to put your dog back on lead so that you have control of him as you show him what you want him to do. Hold your lead so there is nothing hanging down to distract him and keep your left hand on it as near the collar as you can. Using the command you've chosen, working in first a forward motion, then back two or three steps, see if you can get him to back up just a few inches. This is the beginning of the adjusting to the pivot to the left. Don't take steps back yourself, just go into a sort of little shuffle. You might find it helpful to reach down with your right hand and exert a slight pressure against his chest, but body contact is not usually necessary. You can make a game out of your practise and pretend you're working on a new dance step! Both of you will enjoy this.

Teaching Buddy to adjust his position to you as you pivot to the right is quite easy, as it is much more normal for him to move forward a bit to get to the right spot. As you start this, move forward a few steps and pivot to the right as both of you are in motion, giving the command and halting as you complete your pivot. Keep Buddy close to you, Heel position, as you go through these practise sessions, and reward him with plenty of praise as he begins to get the idea. Vary your pivots, left and right. Soon you will find he will respond so well that you can do a full 360° circle, first in one direction, then the other. Of course, he may look up at you as though he's wondering if you've gone "off your rocker", but it's more fun that way, anyhow! "G-o-o-o-o-d!"

Now, we will go to the actual retrieve. You will start working with only one of the required three gloves which shall be "short, predominantly white, work gloves." The cotton canvas garden gloves do fine, even if they have blue cuffs. And don't worry about your dog being able to manage them, even if you have a Toy breed, as we have seen little Yorkshire Terrier puppies in K.P.T. carry these gloves across the room, heads held high, as proud as Punch!

Remembering that our dogs are sensitive to motion, let us again capitalize on this and start out by tossing the glove out for a regular retrieve. As you toss it, using your left hand and starting the motion with that left hand alongside the right side of his face, give him the command you are going to use for this exercise, just as the glove drops. Make it a fun affair, lots of praise and spirit on your part as he returns to you with it. When he will do this with no extra urging or commands from you, start working by having him "Wait", and go out on a 45° angle to your right, drop the glove about 25 feet out and return.

Now, you are going to pivot to the right. Give your command to have Buddy bring himself into the Heel position, and then give him a "line" or direction to follow with your left hand and the command to retrieve. To give him a "line", put your left hand along the right side of his face, with the thumb down (this, to avoid any accidental jabbing into his eye if he should swing his head unexpectedly), holding his collar with your right hand under the left if needed. Face his head toward the glove and give the command for him to retrieve it. You may give your hand a little flip upwards as you send him, but don't extend it out in front of him. Leave your hand in position until Buddy has left your side. Your hand

Giving a "line" signal to a dog on the Directional Retrieve

position is only serving to line his head up with the glove. You may also bend your knees a bit to get into a better position as you give him the direction, but this does not mean you may squat down beside him.

When you have mastered the glove retrieve to the right, proceed the same way in practising the retrieve to the left, the pivot to the left giving the direction as before, still using only the one glove. Only when you have perfected both left and right separately, will you go to left and right together. Should you run into any difficulty on either of these single retrieves, such as not going out in a direct line or dillydallying along the way, set up the "plumber's helpers" to guide him and encourage him with hand clapping and praise all the way on his return to you.

Next, set up the combination of left and right gloves, using the distances and arrangement as described in the Obedience Regulations, and positioning yourself on a line midway between the two jumps. When starting to work with the two gloves, draw Buddy's attention to each of the gloves as they are dropped and send him for the *last* one dropped. If he should bring the wrong one or try to bring both, you have gone too fast and confused him. He apparently has not learned to follow your "line" in giving him the direction. Back up in your training, as far as is necessary and bring your chute back into action again to guide him. Never ask Buddy to get the second glove after he has retrieved the first, simply because it will save *you* a few steps. Each time you send him, be sure both gloves are dropped and vary your pattern of sending him.

When you add the third glove, the one in the center, it would be a good idea to set up the chute for this so that it goes directly to this center glove. When you send to the left or right, simply step back from the end of the chute so that it does not interfere with your giving the direction and step just into the end of it when sending for the center glove. Again, be sure you ask for only *one* retrieve of the three gloves before replacing all of them for the next time. It would be advisable to practise another exercise before repeating the Directed Retrieve again, now that you're working with all three of the gloves.

When Buddy can do all this satisfactorily, lay one side of the chute flat, then the other side, before removing it completely. You may enlist the help of a friend or a member of the family at practically any point in training for this exercise. It will not only save you steps, it will also introduce conditions that more nearly resemble the ring procedure. But *please,* don't get serious and forget that you and your pal are having FUN! Vary your practise procedures: omit your *sit* in front and/or the finish every once in a while; tell him what a good guy he is as he's bringing the glove back to you; toss it out for a "fun" retrieve after he gives it to you; and let him know just how much *you* enjoy it.

Teaching Down signal from in front, on lead

Teaching Recall signal, on lead

Looking at signals from dog's point of view

Signal Exercise

The Signal Exercise, if you think of it with the proper perspective, can be of very practical use in addition to fulfilling the requirements of entering into a show in the Utility Class. Your pal will learn to obey you, either close by or at a distance, just by watching your hand and arm and without depending upon your voice. He already knows signals (if both of you have learned your lessons well) for Heel, Stand, Stay, Wait, Down, Come and Finish. Some of these were dealt with at the last of the Open training, as a lead-in to Utility and to give some variety to your training. Perhaps you already have used them in your day-to-day association with your pal. Maybe you have even saved his life or prevented a serious accident by controlling his actions from a distance, e.g. signalling him to Down from across the street and keeping him from getting into the path of an oncoming vehicle. This has actually happened, as verified by many dog owners. Signals also prove very useful when an older dog becomes deaf, and they can also be taught to a dog who is already deaf.

Teaching Sit from the Down, beginning of signal, on lead

Sit

Your first step to add to your list of signals is to teach the "Sit", using the oral command and the signal together at first, teaching Buddy to respond from any position and at various distances away from you. Let us again employ the chute, even though the first work will be on lead. Set it up so one end is blocked, e.g., against a wall, a fence, an upturned table or similar obstacle and do your basic training at that end. This signal may be given with either your right or your left hand, depending only upon your personal preference.

In giving this signal, you must try to imagine what it will look like to your dog, from his viewpoint, from *his* eye level, and make it just as visible as possible to him. You may even find a mirror helpful for practising before you try it out on your pal. With your arm slightly away from your body and the palm of your hand toward your pal for the entire signal, bring your arm forward toward him, stopping it before you reach

Sit signal

Sit signal, from Down

waist level. Check to see that the palm is *still* facing your dog. As you practise this swing, put a little "zip" into it and stop it the same way. (See illustration.) You will be doing this with no body motion, other than your arm and hand, and no moving of the feet, so check yourself on this.

Now, with Buddy on lead and (of course) using the dead ring, put him in a Stand-Stay at the end of the chute, leave him and turn to face him about a half lead's length away from him. With the lead in one hand, shortened by folding it out of the way, come through with your signal with the other hand and give the command "Sit!" at the same time. As the swing of your signal comes forward, and in front of your dog, end it in a light slap under and against the lead held in the other hand. Vary the teaching by leaving him in a Down position also. Do not increase your distance, not even to the end of the lead, until Buddy responds well to both postions to the voice command and the signal for Sit, each one used singly, by itself. When he will do this with no extra help from you, then you may start to increase your distance away from him very gradually (using your lead in a "tuck-through" position in the collar to remind him of his attention on you), each time you are ready to leave him. Do not go beyond controlling distance of your dog when you are teaching something new. If you should be puzzled about why you are teaching the Sit from a Stand, as well as from a Down, just think of the many times it could come in handy around your home. In addition to this, the Sit on command, as your dog is moving (thus, in a standing position), is a most important part of the Directed Jumping Exercise in Utility.

Stand

While the signal for the Stand, given to your pal as he is in motion—heeling beside you—is a simple one, it also must be one that is not confusing. It has to mean one thing to him and only one thing, simply to Stand and hold that position until he is released by another command.

To teach this, put Buddy on lead (on the dead ring) and adjust the lead across and behind your body, just as we did in earlier training to correct a forging dog. Working in the chute, use your signal for Heeling and move forward three to five steps. As you come to a halt, give the command to Stand-Stay and give your signal at the same time. We have found that one of the easiest signals for the dog to learn, least confusing with others already learned, is a motion from in front of your waist with your left hand and arm, palm toward the floor, swinging out in a horizontal plane, until your hand is above and ahead of your dog's head,

Teaching Stand-Stay signal, on lead

in his full view. Hesitate a few seconds before returning your arm to the normal position beside your body as Buddy takes up any slack in the lead. Be careful that you don't tighten the lead with any body motion as he might confuse this and think you are correcting him for not *sitting.* Let him remain in the Stand for a few seconds, your tone of voice indicating your appreciation of how well he is doing, and then signal him to Heel again and repeat the exercise. Each time you do this, allow him to stand a bit longer until he's really steady, before you try it off lead. Even then, make the transition via the "tuck-through" of the lead to remind him to give you attention. Don't let any of this get boring or monotonous to him. Intersperse it with other parts of the Signal exercise and vary the training with other completely different exercises.

When you are ready to try the complete exercise off lead, work in the chute and *still* only about a lead's length away. At this distance you remain in control, in case anything happens that calls for a correction or for more guiding or showing. Don't worry about your regular Heeling

Signal for Stand, from Sit at Heel

practise at this time, let us check to find out how Buddy's reactions are to the other signals. Start with the signal to Heel, then give him the Stand signal when you have gone about a half dozen steps. Wait a few seconds and give him the Wait or Stay signal and leave him, turning to face him when you are about a lead's length away. Remember to avoid glaring at him when you are in this position—look over him and you'll still be able to see everything he does. Concentrate before giving each signal and be ready to refresh his memory if you see the slightest hesitation. But under *no* circumstances allow it to be a correction. You are still teaching and he is still learning! Signal for the Down, leave him in that postion for a few seconds, then follow with the Sit signal, then the Recall, and after several seconds, signal for the Finish. You may increase your distance away from him as he becomes steadier and more sure of himself, but do it very slowly and be ready to back up in your training at any point if you see Buddy is confused at all. Vary the time that you keep him in the different positions so that he does not develop a "habit pattern" of performance. As in teaching previous exercises, do not let it become boring; alternate with other parts of your training.

Naturally, it is of the utmost importance for you to have "dog attention" at all times when you are teaching and giving signals. It is just that simple —if he is not watching you, *how* can he see your signal?

Directed Jumping

Directed Jumping could almost merit a whole chapter, for we actually break it down into five separate parts to be learned and not to be put together until each of the five has been mastered. Again, remember: do not repeat any of the work more than three to five times; avoid the formality of ring procedure while you are teaching; and bring as much variety as you can into your training sessions and have fun together.

1—Turn and Sit: In teaching this, put Buddy on lead, on the dead ring, as you not only want him under control, you also will need the lead as an aid to show him what you want him to do and when. This way, we allow no room for mistakes to get started. Heel him forward five or six steps, the lead folded in your left hand. Call his name and back up *only* far enough for him to turn completely toward you and immediately give the command to "Sit", along with the Sit signal with your right hand. Naturally, if you are accustomed to signalling with your left hand just reverse the signal hand. If it is necessary to refresh his memory about the Sit, you can always come up with your signal hand under the lead and give it a tap. Be sure you reward him with praise each time, but PLEASE wait until *you* have reached him before you lay the praise on! If you but think for a moment, the reason is all too obvious. It is *your* mistake if you tell him what a good guy he is and he starts to come to you, breaking the Sit you put him in, and starting a bad habit that would mean corrections. And he would not understand *why.* You may even find it wise to use the command Stay at this point, until you're in position to praise him without his moving. Repeat this exercise a few times until, upon calling his name, he turns to you and will sit upon the verbal command only. You may then try the same thing off lead, still going no further away than the length of the lead.

If you still have a good response thus far, you may now begin to gradually increase your distance control on the Turn and Sit. We have found that a most satisfactory setup for teaching this is to plan to work against a wall (such as the garage or the side of your house) or against a fence. Put the lead thru Buddy's collar and, as you approach this barrier, use the lead for attention and draw it out, giving him a command to Stand, then Wait. Turn and leave him, going about a lead's length behind him, turning toward him as you come to a halt. After a few seconds, call his

Teaching "Turn and Sit," on lead, first phase of Directed Jumping.

#1

#2

#3

#4

name and give the command "Sit!" as he turns toward you. It should not be necessary to include the signal here, but do not hesitate to use it at any time if you detect any slowness or confusion in his response. Aim to drop it, however, as soon as you get him on the right track without it. As he sits, return to him and praise him there. Try the next repeat without the tuck-through of the lead, staying at the same distance. When this is satisfactory, you may start to increase the distance, but no more than three to six feet at a time.

It is extremely important that you get an immediate Sit as soon as Buddy turns toward you and hears the command. If any confusion or uncertainty on his part should develop, work it out before you increase the distance. Your ultimate goal should be control of him at least 50 feet away. Be overly careful of your tone of voice in your command. Bring authority into it without any resemblance to a correction. If you, yourself, get a bit perturbed over something and can't avoid letting it show, let the whole thing go for the time being. Tell him he's a good boy and that will be all for now. Then go back to it when you've calmed down and cooled off. When you achieve this distance control, you will be surprised how often it may pay off in your day to day living, perhaps (as already stated) even to the point of saving his life some day.

No doubt, when you start reaching for distance, you will go too fast. Most of us do, it's just human nature. One very obvious sign to look for is that of unsteadiness on the part of your dog, such as moving toward you when he should be staying in a Sit. This is particularly apt to occur later on when you start to put all the exercise together, more so if he gets excited over jumping. The answer? Go right back and work on the beginning of the Turn and Sit, on through again until you regain control at a distance.

2—Go Out: In teaching the Go Out, you will be schooling Buddy to leave you and go away in a direct line until you call him and give him a command to sit. This is why it is so important to teach the Turn and Sit first.

We should also exercise extreme caution and care in showing and teaching this part of the exercise so Buddy will not become confused or discouraged. After all, from his viewpoint, *why* should you be sending him away from you? Don't you want him by you any more? And you haven't even thrown anything for him to go get and bring back for you!

To begin with, we must first establish an incentive to make him *want* to go in a certain direction and a definite distance, determined by your command. It must be something that can easily be eliminated, done away with completely as the habit pattern is established and the distance accomplished, as Buddy learns just what you expect from him. We have found that the easiest thing to get, that answers the purpose, is just a plain paper towel.

Now, to get your pal's interest stirred up, wrinkle the towel a little and tease him with it. Heel him as you're teasing and wave it in front of his face. If he grabs for it, let him take it, and then have him release it to you. Your next step is to associate, with it, the command you are going to use to send him out. We will use "Go!" in our text. Other commands we have seen used are "Go Out", "Away", "Back" (avoid this one if you're also training for field trials or plan to), "Get Away", "Way Back", "Advance", "Way Out", "Run", etc.

At first, ball up the paper towel, heel Buddy with you and while both of you are in motion, toss it out in front and send him with "Go!". If you wish, give a signal in that direction. As he moves forward to pick it up, move up behind him. As he picks it up, or just before, call his name and tell him to Sit, using the signal with it if you feel it is necessary. As soon as he is sitting, go to him and heap on the praise. Repeat this simplified part of the exercise three or four times.

For your next step, the setup will be quite different. The "stage" will now have the necessary "props" in place so it will resemble a Utility ring as you see it at the shows for competition. In other words, put both the solid jump and the bar jump in place, on either side of "your ring" (only one 8 inch board in the solid, and the bar set at the same height). Plan where you want Buddy to end up, as you send him out, and that spot will be where you start to teach. In other words, instead of teaching him to go further away from *your* starting point, you will teach him to

Teaching Go Out

1—Placing incentive target

2—Teaching Go Out

3—Increasing distance on Go Out

4—Controlled Sit at a distance

go further by backing up more from the same spot you've sent him to. He will be going to the same spot each time, where the incentive will be. By setting up the jumps now, it will help you to gauge your progress and, at the same time, Buddy will get used to working between them.

Now set up the chute right down through the middle, leaving it wide enough for you both to work without being crowded. It should extend at least 40 feet, 20 feet either side of the midline between the jumps. Carrying the paper towel, heel Buddy down through the chute and back to make sure it doesn't seem strange to him.

Heel him back again, toward that spot you've picked out, halting about 6 feet before you reach the end of the chute. As he is sitting, tease him with the towel and drop it about 3 feet in front of him. Give him a command to Heel, do an About Turn and walk about 6 to 10 feet away. You may need to guide him a bit with his collar if he's too interested in the towel, but don't scold him, for you want to keep up that interest. Now turn and give him a signal, (pointed toward the towel) and give the command "Go!" If he should interpret your command for a retrieve, don't worry if he wants to pick up the paper towel and don't correct him for it. Just be ready with *your* part, most important at this point. As he reaches the target, call his name and get the Sit immediately. Return to him, receive the towel if he picked it up and lay on the praise. Give even more praise when you get the prompt Sit from him without his picking it up. Here you are getting through to him that the Sit is the thing you are after. Repeat this part two or three times and if you're happy with the results, then you may try a gradual increase in the distance. Remember, never go too fast and too far, as you *must* remain in control of your dog. If he becomes confused and unsure, back up in your training to a point where you can reassure him. It will pay off! He should never feel that he has to look back at you for a second command or extra help. Be careful you don't overdo on any of your practise sessions—don't let Buddy get tired of it or bored.

When you have reached a little distance on the Go Out, check yourself to make sure you are not calling his name and commanding him to Sit *before* he has reached the paper towel. If you stop and think, your aim is for him to go the full distance required (and even further in practise) and a command too soon from you will shorten that distance, possibly starting a serious fault in his performance.

When your dog is going out about 20 feet, you may start to decrease the size of the rumpled paper towel by tearing it in half. Another increase in distance will warrant decreasing the size again, so you're working with one quarter of what you started with. Roll this quarter towel into a small ball and increase your distance, using this, to about 40 or 45 feet. When you get excellent results at this point, tear it again and flatten it out so he can't see it at a distance. When he's working at this stage with enthusiasm and is under good control, you are ready for the "Big Finish"—the final step.

With this little piece of towel in your hand, heel Buddy to the far end of the chute as you have been doing. Come to a halt and show it to him, lay it down about 2 or 3 feet in front of you as before, but this time (instead of heeling him away) you will heel him and circle *around* the paper. Keep him in the proper position and as you come around it to face the opposite end of the chute, bend over and pick it up without drawing attention to the act. Get it out of sight immediately as you are heeling back, so that he knows nothing of its disappearance. Put it in a pocket, in your waistband, or anywhere to hide it. This time, shorten your distance again to no more than from 6 to 10 feet. When Buddy does this well, with no "target" to aim for as he goes out, you should be able to increase the distance gradually with no particular problems until he achieves about a 50 foot distance in the Go Out. You might have to back up once in a while to undo some confusion that conceivably might pop up, or even go back occasionally to vary the training and give both yourself and Buddy a bit of a refresher on the exercise.

Now, we have another important part of the Directed Jumping to learn before we start to put *any* of the parts together.

3—Directional Signal: In teaching Buddy to watch your signal for the Directional Jump and to respond correctly to it, we must look ahead a bit and get a picture of what it involves. He is going to learn to take a direction signal from you at a distance, one that will cue him as to which jump you wish him to go over, and one that may be given by you with either your left or your right hand and arm.

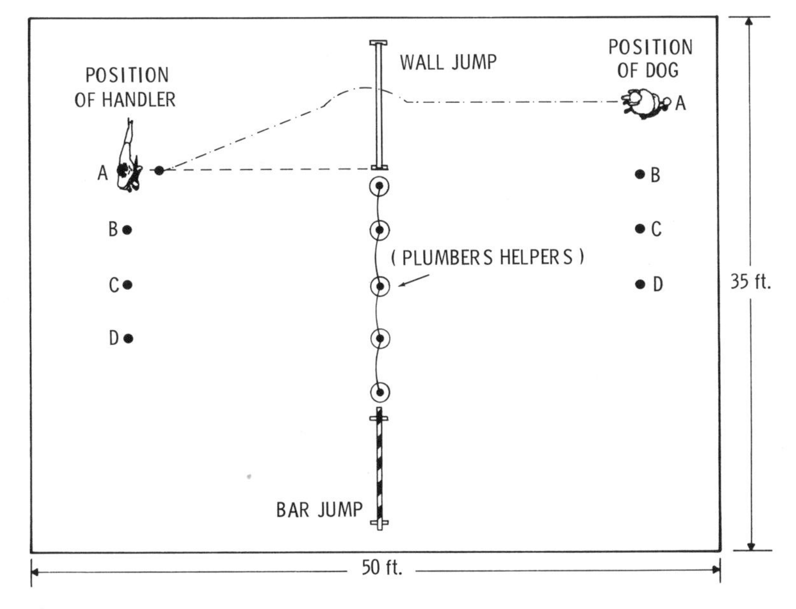

Plan for practise ring to teach direction on the jumps

To simplify things for him at the beginning, we will set up the solid jump only, (one 8-inch board in it), at one side of your training area, midway as in a ring. We will also use one section of the chute (one line of the plumber's helpers) and put it in line with that jump, extending it across the ring from the upright of the jump that is closer to the middle of the area. A look at the illustration will give you a clear picture of the setup. Space the plungers equi-distant from each other so you will be able to use them as your guide in this training. You will see what we mean as you progress by easy stages. This also acts as a deterrent in case Buddy gets the idea it is much easier to come straight to you, rather than going out of his way to go over a jump first.

Giving a signal to a dog to send it over the jump to the left

You will be working about 20 feet from each side of the jump, along an imaginary line parallel to the jump and the guide through the center. Put Buddy at this 20 foot distance, sitting and lined up with the center of the jump. Tell him to Wait, leave him and hop over the 8-inch jump, go 20 feet beyond it, turn and position yourself in line with the inside upright of the jump (thus making yourself 2 to 3 feet nearer the center of the ring than he is).

Before you get this far it would be best to practise the signal. Don't subject your pal to some type of flashing motion that he might not see, or, if he does see it, may not understand what you mean by it. Remember where his eyes are and try to make that signal as visible as possible to them at that level, as you have before, in teaching other signal commands. By trial and error over many years, we have found that the signal that attracts the best response is the one pictured here, keeping the palm of your hand toward your dog and raising your arm and hand in a plane parallel to the jump, reaching only to the height of your shoulder. The jump command should be given after the start of the arm motion, about midway up, to give the direction to Buddy's mind *before* you give him the stimulus to do the jumping.

Again, you have a choice of commands you may select for the jumping. We still prefer "Hup!", as we feel we can get a little more "lift" in our command with this word. Many people use "Jump", "Over", etc. Now are you ready to try it with your dog in position? Remember to raise your arm smoothly so he will have something to look at. If you were a clock, your signal would start near 6:00, the voice command would be given at 4:30, and the arm would stop at 3:00 on the face of the clock. Clearer?

Try it now with Buddy, remembering to get a pleasant tone of voice in your command and don't glare at him. As he jumps, turn slightly (the angle at this point is very small, but it will increase considerably as you progress) and receive him as in a Recall, being careful to look above him as he comes in on the Sit. Give him lots of praise, you can add the Heel Finish at any time. The thing you are working on here is the response to the Direction Signal, getting him to turn his head according to your signal and following through on the jump. *That* is what you are praising for.

Your next step will be to leave Buddy sitting, lined up with the inside upright (where you had finished), leaving and hopping over the jump, turning and facing him at a spot lined up with the first plunger toward the center from the jump. You have not only added slightly to the angle,

Signal for left jump

Dog over left jump

Signal for right jump

Dog over right jump

in relation to the jump, but you also have reversed your own position so that, this time, your signal will be given with the other arm. You may continue to progress this way, alternating your signal and direction and increasing the angle in relation to the jump, as Buddy's performance warrants. Any time that he is not sure of himself or seems a bit confused, check yourself and your commands and signals first, back up a bit in the steps and find out where the trouble lies. Remember, even though you are in advanced training, your pal deserves first consideration. You should still be following the guide of repeating an exercise no more than from three to five times. He needs variety and fun in his training, just as you do.

As you near the center of your "ring" in this training, you may find you have increased the distance too fast and he starts to come straight to you. After all, the straight return is the shortest distance between two points. Perhaps he's trying to demonstrate to you that he's a bit of a math expert, too? If you should see he is heading toward you instead of over the jumps, immediately take some steps toward the jump, keeping your arm extended in the direction signal, to remind him of what he's supposed to do. Back up to where you were as he jumps, receive him and heap on the praise again. Never increase beyond a point where you are encountering any difficulty until everything goes smoothly. Keep up the increases until you have reached a midline distance of about 20 or 25 feet in from the jump.

4—Bar Jump Combination: When this much has been accomplished, you will start back again as you did at first, but this time you will have added a striped bar above the solid 8-inch board. The only additional equipment you will need will be a pair of brackets that fit over the board, or on the uprights, and a bar that will fit between the uprights. This will allow practise in both directions and the bar can fall off on either side, just in case Buddy might hit it as he goes over. We wouldn't want it anchored solidly, as we know of instances that resulted in traumatic experiences that have set the dog back for long periods of time. The mental recovery from something like this can be more serious and of longer duration than the physical recovery. Let us avoid it if we can. The reason for using the combination bar and solid jump is so your dog will still have the familiar solid jump, along with the new striped bar. (If you did your Open work thoroughly, he already has had the initial introduction to the bar and he is only experiencing "newness" in relation to the way you have set it up to practise this exercise.)

Start as you did in the beginning of teaching the Directional Signal and Command for the solid jump—putting your dog on a line with the center of the jump and taking your position in line with the inside upright—and progress exactly as you did before, step by step. When you have reached 20 to 25 feet in from the jump, you may start to raise the bar a bit above the board, bringing more "daylight" between the two. Leave the solid board in place for a while, as a reminder. If your dog is a small Toy, however, you won't have much leeway here. *Don't* ask him to jump higher than he is required to. Also, don't expect your larger dogs to jump maximum height until all steps have been thoroughly learned and the pieces have been assembled into one complete exercise.

5—Bar Jump without Combination: When you are ready to try the bar, no solid board with it, set up the jump at the end of the "plumber's helpers," across the ring from the solid jump. Work with the shorter bar so it can fall either way and keep it at the same height (or even lower, if warranted) as the solid jump. Again work from the bar jump gradually toward the center line of your ring, first one direction, and then the other.

Now that you have both jumps in place, be especially careful that Buddy is responding to the *direction* of your signal. If he should become confused and get mixed up (try to take the wrong jump), don't scold or punish. Simply get your second line of "plumber's helpers" and set them up at right angles to those already in place, extending them from the center to the end of the training area. Your practise, while you are using this as a correction guide, will be limited to the one side of the area where it has been set up. But it will help to straighten out Buddy's thinking pattern, without any corrections which might serve only to add to his confusion. Before you take this section away, after you think it has served its purpose, just lay it flat on the ground (or floor). Also, when you feel you have accomplished everything in this part of the exercise, you may try laying the center section of the chute flat, the one which has connected the two jumps, and then remove it completely when all goes smoothly. Don't hesitate to return to these training aids at any time, for the effort of putting them in place more than pays off in the results you get.

6—Putting it Together: Now that you and Buddy have learned to do all the "pieces" of the exercise, you will try the complete Directed Jump exercise and will see how well the pieces fit together to make a whole complete picture. Your practise ring should be set up to simulate, as nearly as possible, a regular Utility ring as specified by AKC, no training aids even in sight.

Rather than to make the big jump right into the show routine, let us inject one more step leading to the finished product. Heel Buddy to the spot at the end of the area where you would want him to go in the Go Out, tell him to Wait, and go to the opposite end. Turn to face him and, with no body movements on your part other than your arm signal, give him that signal and the jump command. As he follows through on your direction, turn toward him to receive him. Try to practise your own timing to make your small turn as he is in the air. Give him plenty of praise to let him know he's done it right! Repeat placing him and leaving him, this time changing the signal to direct him over the other jump. Vary your routine in practise to keep his attention. Don't be afraid to make it two or three times over the same jump, then once over the other, etc. This can also be an excellent opportunity to begin a gradual (2 to 4 inches at a time) raising of the height of each jump, eventually reaching the maximum that is required for your dog. At this point, both of you are more free to concentrate on two or three things, before you put it all together.

In preparation for this final assembling, first review the text so that it is all clear in your own mind. Next, police the area for any leftovers from yesterday's picnic, children's dropped toys or balls, or anything that might prove to be an unnecessary distraction. Then do a little "fun" heeling around to let him know there still are other things than jumping, and at the same time letting him see that the jumps are in place.

Ready? OK—Put him in position at Heel beside you. Send him, let him get all the way out, call his name and tell him to Sit. Give him the Direction Signal and the command to Jump. Turn and receive him, finish and then PRAISE! Again, in proper position, repeat as above and direct him over the other jump. More PRAISE! "Voila!" There you have it, all the pieces assembled and a happy pair, you and Buddy.

Remember, I can't stress this too strongly, whenever you and your pal hit a snag of any kind, no matter how large or small, return to the beginning and work it out. Don't try to force him through. You will only cause greater trouble and further confusion, making your path back even more difficult.

Group Stand For Examination

The Group Stand for Examination is more or less a combination of the Novice Stand for Examination and the Group Stays, with a slightly different twist that qualifies it to be catalogued in the advanced work. It is, as the name implies, done in a group with other dogs present. The examination itself is much more involved, and the distance between you and your dog has been increased. When you put all these factors together, you have the Utility version of the exercise, but, as you have already learned in teaching previously presented exercises, you must learn to "creep before you can walk."

If you are attending a training class where you can work with a group, this is fine, provided you are aware of some pitfalls that might befall you before you are ready to be a part of that group. Most of your preparation work and a lot of your practise must make up your homework, just as in the rest of your training. So, your first training will be some solo work in your backyard, or wherever you do your practising.

Your Novice Stand for Examination was done "at least 6 feet away" from your dog. Now you will be, on the average, from 15 to 25 feet away from him. This increase is to be done gradually, of course. It would be a good idea, as a refresher, to start your practise with the "tuck-thru" of the lead, to make sure you have his attention. Get him used to the increased distance, reassuring him of your return as in the Stays, before you add the examination. Vary your distance away from him, also the length of time, so he doesn't get a stop watch built into his sense of timing. In competition, the time involved can vary terrifically. The only rules governing it say that it shall be a minimum of 3 minutes, but nowhere is anything mentioned of a maximum. Be sure, as you face him, that you avoid a direct meeting of your eyes with his—no staring or glaring at him.

When you have Buddy's complete confidence in waiting for your return, you may start getting him used to the more thorough examining, "going over the dog with his (the judge's) hands as in dog show judging." In doing this, use as much imagination as you can, without startling him at any time. To begin with, always make your approach from in front, but vary the way you come in to him, from various distances, sometimes slowly, sometimes fast, and occasionally in quite a normal pace. When he is steady in these situations, start to introduce some of the more extreme things that we have seen happen, or that could conceivably happen. It is difficult to picture ahead of time, when you have entered a show, just how a certain judge is going to approach your dog to examine him.

"Going over a dog with your hands, as in the breed ring" allows limitless interpretations. For example:

The front feet might be lifted, one at a time.

The mouth might be opened to check the teeth and the bite.

Examination might be made from both sides and the rear.

The tail (if you have a breed that has an evident one) might be raised to check the backline.

The judge might squat down quickly to get a close look.

He might lean over the dog to check the legs.

He might stand in front and lean over to check the tail.

He might approach your dog very quickly or, just the opposite, extremely slow.

He might reach toward your dog's head very quickly.

He might glare at your dog, as though he doesn't trust him.

A very frequent sight is that of a judge examining a dog with one hand while holding a clipboard in the other.

Once in a while you find a judge that walks around to the rear of a dog and begins the examination from there.

Sometimes the judges have rain gear on, maybe a long coat, a large hat, dark glasses, etc.

With this list and probably a few more that you may come up with, you can do a good job of setting up situations similar to what Buddy might come up against later on. Make sure that you get him used to them gradually. Don't take the chance of startling him, as this could easily set him back.

When your pal is accepting the many types of approach and examination, you may introduce the examination by a stranger. Make sure your stand-in for the judge is not afraid of your dog and that he is well schooled in the part he is to play. When he first starts, make sure you are no more than from 6 to 10 feet away from your dog. When you see that he freely accepts a normal examination from the stranger, let your "judge" try some of the more extreme approaches. Don't "throw the book" at him, though, and expect to get a finished, steady performance! Give him time to get used to different types of examination, a little at a time. When you have no further worry on this score, it is time to get into some group work.

This group practise is really important, for Buddy will have to get used to seeing dogs on either side of him, standing, being examined by somebody, and must realize that it is his job to Stay in that Stand position, no matter what goes on around him. Here is one place where participation in an obedience training class can be invaluable. A substitute for the class can be some group practise with your friends who are also training. In fact, it would be a good idea to take turns going to each other's homes so the training areas would offer a change of scenery for all of you.

With the knowledge you have gained thus far, you should be able to pretty well evaluate the methods of training of any instructor and form your own opinion of just how much you want to go along with. You may be one of the fortunate ones and get the right kind of help and cooperation all the way. Otherwise, do a bit of sifting and take only what you believe in, what you know will help both you and Buddy in the most effective way.

If you need to at first, if you feel your pal is a bit confused by having the other dogs around him, go back to the "tuck-thru" of the lead for attention, just before you give him the command to Stand-Stay. Don't be hasty when making a correction or letting somebody else correct him. *If* it is necessary, be sure it is done properly. Many times a break from position, or even a slight move, is caused by a dog on either side of yours. Sometimes it is a little snarl or growl from his neighbor, sometimes the neighbor will even break and come over to pay a friendly visit, or to do a little sniffing (a definite No-No!), or make an *un*friendly visit (still worse!). If the handler of the trouble-causing dog or the instructor will not correct him, or the instructor will not allow you to move Buddy to a different spot, this is your cue to change classes and instructor. If none are available, go to working with your own little group of friends, as suggested above. *No* dog should show nastiness toward another dog if he has been trained properly and completely up to and into the Utility work, nor should he show nastiness toward a person, or unsteadiness in this group exercise.

We are constantly pleading for a show of good sportsmanship in this doggy hobby of ours, but disappointingly, so many times there is an absence of it. I guess, as long as people are being born, we're going to have to face the fact that not all who are training their dogs in obedience are doing it for the pleasure and companionship it affords. We have even seen instances (I hate to admit it) where, as in the Group Stand for Examination, a handler would get a charge out of his dog going over and causing another to break, or even being responsible for starting a fight. It seems to furnish him with a new "conversation piece." May you have the good fortune of not having to meet up with characters in this category.

ADVANCED EXERCISES

As in previous chapters, we have presented some advanced exercises to practise and break up the monotony, as well as to lead into the work required for your next title. Here we cannot offer anything for another title, as there is no U.D.X. But, we do have some fine suggestions that will bear fruit in steadying Buddy and giving him even more confidence in himself and in you. He will give you still greater attention and become an even closer companion in your everyday life. He also will be more reliable if you participate in any demonstrations and exhibitions, by yourself or as part of a group. He will become an even greater joy to you than he has ever been, up to this point, in your training and companionship, even though you may question my sanity in making such a statement. You may believe that he already has reached the ultimate and nothing could enchance the relationship between the two of you beyond what you already are experiencing.

Advanced Heeling: In a dog show ring, the only Heeling has been done in the presence of a judge and two, or occasionally three, stewards. Now we'd like to set the stage for some Heeling that is considerably more involved and taxing upon your dog's attention to you, and involving the participation of several friends, neighbors, or members of your training class. You will start with only three to five people, at first, that will make up this *milling* group. Appropriately, they will be referred to as "Millers."

Have the Millers move around the ring or training area, laughing, talking to each other. At no time should they try to avoid crowding you or interfering with where you want to go. Have them speak to you and answer them. You can maneuver in any direction you wish to carry yourself and Buddy through to your "destination." They may even reach out and pet him as you go by, as long as there are no unnecessary moves toward him and nobody tries to "play smart" and deliberately make an effort to scare him. We can get along very nicely without that kind of people in our world. As you are walking around, don't be afraid to let your dog know how pleased you are with the attention he's giving you. Remember how valuable your tone of voice has always been and how your pal has always responded to the praise and love you've given him. Use it.

When this small group does not phase him and you have his complete attention, you may increase the number of your helpers. Make sure, also, that you have a variety in this group, some men, some women, and even some children, provided they behave themselves. Don't you wish, at times, that the majority of children were as obedient as the majority of dogs?

While going through this Heeling, do all the things included in a regular Heeling exercise—the changes of pace and all the various turns. If Buddy should show a bit of confusion, go back to the "tuck-thru" of the lead to reassure him. No corrections. Get his attention, then try it off lead again. Do not attempt the next exercise until you have worked, happily, with at least eight or ten Millers.

The College Stand: Buddy has now been introduced and has reacted favorably to the milling group, giving you his full attention and responding to your commands, in spite of distractions. For this new exercise, you will again use from three to five Millers at the beginning. As they are milling around, talking and laughing, heel your pal into the middle of the group. Signal him to Stand, then to Stay or Wait and walk about 10 feet away and face him. As the group is moving around, let the Millers, (one at a time) come to the front of Buddy, circle around him to Heel position, halt, praise with the left hand once or twice, and walk away. Your dog should continue to give you his attention and not be diverted by any of these Millers.

When this has been accomplished, you may increase the number of the group to as many as you wish. Be careful that they do not block you from Buddy's view for any prolonged length of time. You don't want to chance undoing all that you have accomplished so far. Any time you wish, return to him and reward him with praise, then heel him a bit and repeat the Stand as before. When he is steady on the Stand, go into the examination; at first with only one at a time; and then with two or three at a time, each one concentrating on a different section of his body (head and teeth—bite, feet, backline and tail, etc.). When you start the examining by one of the Millers, go no further away than about 6 feet, staying within controlling distance of your dog. This is mainly to reassure him as he may really need it, with such unusual things going on. Steady him by degrees and build his confidence gradually. Have your Millers go into a thorough examination, lifting the front paws one at a time, examining his teeth to check the bite, looking at the coat texture, walking completely around him, touching him here and there—but all of this with no sudden moves or lurches to spook him. If you feel you are losing his attention at any time during this, let your voice reassure him that all is well. Do not proceed to having two or three people examining at the same time until Buddy is perfectly at ease with having just one do it. Always reward with lots of praise, each time you return, with both your voice and your "praise hand."

Search and Find: This exercise could be likened to an advanced version of the old Utility Seek Back. It does have a practical purpose and is under conditions that you might expect to find on almost any street or at a busy shopping center. Again, you will need your group of Millers. You will also need a key case, a wallet and a glove, these to be used one at a time.

Buddy should be familiar with the people milling around by now. To start, Heel him around through the group as they are moving and talking. Drop one of the articles (you will carry all three and alternate from one to another, so he doesn't get into the habit of always looking for a certain one.) Have one of the Millers drop an article, also. It can even be the same type of article, as long as your scent has not been put on it. Drop the articles near the center of the traffic area so he will not get the idea of circling the outskirts for the "find". Encourage him to enter the area without regard as to where the Millers are walking. Also, from one time to another, change the position from where you send him. Before you ask him to find your "lost" article, do a little acting for his benefit. Be *shocked* when you find your wallet gone, upset, and enlist his help to find it for you. Your scent, naturally, will lead him to it and you will be overjoyed with its recovery, thanks to your pal!

Don't be perturbed if Buddy stops to smell the other articles as he's searching for yours; just let him go and be patient. When he starts to smell your article, remember you are teaching and come in with the magic word "G-o-o-o-d!" After this stage is successful, you may add distracting drops by two or three, or more, of the Millers. One bit of caution: Don't allow any member of the family to make any of these drops. Each one of the family has a scent that is just as well known and attractive to Buddy as your own. Be fair to him and don't expect too much from him. Also, don't treat this training lightly or as a joke. If you have this attitude, you might better forget it, as you would be doing your companion a great injustice. Have fun *with* him, but don't make fun of him!

Crowded Recall: For this exercise, you will vary the Recall in that sometimes you will call Buddy from a Sit and, at other times, you will call from a Stand. It also will be done so that he must come as directly as possible to you, going through the group of laughing, talking Millers. His desire to be with you, coupled with the sound of your voice, will bring him to you with no trouble. Perhaps he will need some extra encouragement at first, so that he isn't distracted along the way. After all, negotiating the route through all those moving legs, especially if you are not in full view of him could appear as quite a challenging task.

Some suggestions for you as you go through this exercise: Do a little heeling, and, at no particular spot, give the command to Sit or Stand, then Stay or Wait. Leave him and, on the way across, stop to chat a bit with one of the Millers, and then continue on to the distance you plan to work from. Turn and face in the direction of your dog, being ready to use a bit stronger (*not* harsher) tone in your command if he cannot see you.

Call his name and give the command "Come!" As he nears you, let him know how terrific he is. Forget the Finish to Heel most of the time, only throwing it in occasionally as a refresher. You are not performing for a judge now, worrying about what score you're going to get. If Buddy should smell the ground on the way across, don't worry about it. He might be just reassuring himself that you did go *that* way. Your job is to see that he keeps coming and is justly rewarded with praise and love as he gets to you. Some individual dogs (not any particular breeds) much prefer to depend more on their scenting ability than their seeing ability. All will use their ears, so don't hesitate to use your voice to help him concentrate on you, if you think he needs it. One reason for practising this from a Stand, in addition to the Sit, is simply a matter of weather. There are many times when you would much prefer to leave him standing, so he wouldn't get wet or muddy or cold. (He will appreciate it, too!)

You may increase the distance of these Recalls as you see fit, going back to using only two or three people when you go further away. Also, try to get the Sit after Buddy has started to you, in the middle of the Recall. You may add more Millers and greater distance as you progress. You may either return to him after the Sit or give him another Recall command, anything to make it interesting and more enjoyable for both.

Food Refusal: Teaching Food Refusal might well be the means of saving your pal's life some day. There are many different ways of doing this, but for our purposes here, we will concentrate only on teaching

Buddy that it is wrong to pick up anything from the ground or floor. This is usually where any poisoned food or other undesirable items are located and they could be very attractive to our pal's undiscerning appetite. Some of our dogs seem to particularly relish what they shouldn't have or what they can steal.

You will most likely find that about the greatest temptation for him will be pieces of hot dog dropped around the area. One big thing for you to remember, *don't ever* give your pal a tidbit while training. It is all right for you to reward him with something *after* your practise session is over, but *never* pick up anything from the floor and give it to him. Don't undo the very thing that you are trying to impress upon him is wrong, that of eating anything from the ground or floor. Rather stupid, right?

Your approach to this will be without the distraction of Millers, with tempting tidbits dropped around casually. You will be heeling Buddy around, past and over the tempting pieces. Have him *on lead,* or at least with the lead tucked through the collar, so your correction (if you need one) will be well timed and most effective. Watch his head and ears, for they will forecast his intention. As he *starts* to tip his head toward a tasty morsel, get your lead correction in at that point, a sharp snap and immediate release with a firm call of his name and put him to work right away. Do some more heeling or anything to divert his attention and bring it back to you again. If you wait until he picks up the piece, or almost reaches it, your correction will have lost its punch; it will have been administered too late, reflecting poor timing on your part.

When you think your teaching has sunk in properly and your dog pays no attention to the food and makes no move to show interest in it, you can consider yourself ready for a big test. Start with a completely clean area, well policed to be rid of formerly dropped food. Have the Millers in at this point, moving around and eating (or pretending they are), dropping some bits of food as they go. Don't go overboard with the amount dropped, but have an ample amount for distraction. While this is going on, heel Buddy through the group, off lead. Be sure you have his attention the entire time. If he still should be swayed by the temptation, then your teaching was done too rapidly and you must then return to do more practising on lead.

After he has become dependable on this much, you may then combine any of the other exercises with the practise for Food Refusal. Try a Recall straight through the Millers and the food. Remember, this is the first time he is doing this on his own. If he should slow down or act as if he might be tempted, call his name right away in a commanding tone, and bring his attention back to you, pronto! Repeat the magic praise, "G-o-o-o-o-d!"

You may progress to further combinations, the Stand for Examination, the Sit part way through the Recall, etc., all with the Millers and bits of food. If you feel particularly confident in Buddy's resistance to temptation and want to find out what a really good job you've done, try the Search and Find exercise with the same setup, and just a few tidbits around. Make sure you handle only the article you're going to send him for. Don't ask for the impossible and don't expect the possible too soon.

As anyone can readily see, any one of these exercises or all of them, can be done by *all* trained dogs, from the smallest to the largest, with the same amount of enjoyment on their part and with the pride of accomplishment by their owners.

Good Luck!

PROBLEMS IN UTILITY TRAINING

Scent Discrimination

Dog understands the scent discrimination but seems afraid to leave the handler to go out to the articles.

Return to your training "in motion" to get your dog fired up and anxious to go out to the articles. If you have been using a signal with your command, try dropping it and use only the voice command. He may be paying too much attention to the movement of your arm, especially your return movement, and be confusing it with a Recall signal. Think about it from *his* viewpoint. When he is responding to working in motion, start to decrease the amount gradually until you can return to sending him from a Sit position at Heel. Never forget your own enthusiasm in your practise.

Dog goes out to the articles and stands there, confused, as though he doesn't understand what is expected of him.

This has probably been the result of your trying to move too fast, pushing too hard. The only sensible thing to do in this case is to start from the beginning, with just plain retrieves of one article at varying distances. Don't let your dog dilly dally over it. He must understand that when a command is given, it is to be carried out. Work the articles next with the article mat inside the chute, keeping within controlling distance. Increase the distance only as the dog understands what is wanted of him.

Dog goes to the articles and circles them, will not work through them.

Return to working with the article mat in the chute, keeping the sections of the chute no further apart than the width of the mat. Introduce your dog to the mat and the articles again by heeling him through them, *on lead.* Don't let him jump over them as though they are something to be avoided. Walk slowly and encourage him with your assuring tone of voice. Be sure the articles have been spaced far enough apart to allow him to find sufficient space to put his feet down without their interference.

Dog starts licking his nose and sneezing on the way out to the articles.

You probably have been "loading" your dog's nose with your scent before sending him out, by holding your hand over or in front of his nose. It is difficult for us to comprehend the complexity of a dog's nose and the really uncanny ability he has of using it as it functions to serve him. Actually, when you "give him your scent", you are doing him a great disfavor and putting unnecessary obstacles in his way. He knows this, he also knows your scent exceedingly well and needs *no* reminder (having lived with you for some time and spent much of his time around things you have handled). If he did not attempt to clear out his nose on the way out to the articles, due to the lingering of the scent you put there, *all* of them would smell the same way. Just give the command for him to find your article and don't put your hand anywhere near his nose.

Dog retrieves everything well except metal, which seems very distasteful to him. He spits it out when he does pick it up, then will have nothing further to do with any of the metal articles.

Under average conditions, metal has a cold feeling and, of course, a very hard surface as one touches it. This, no doubt, is magnified in intensity to most dog's sensitive mouths, especially when their teeth come in contact with it, thus causing the reaction of spitting it out.

One good way to condition your dog to metal, before you start working with the scent articles, is to give your dog a tidbit or treat once in awhile (and aren't we all guilty of doing this for our pal?) via a metal spoon. The idea, of course, is to present the metal to him along with a "pleasant" association, avoiding any resentment later on.

Another way to counteract his feeling toward carrying the metal article is to take one of the metal articles (and keep this one for your practise article), and spray the mouthpiece, two coats, with clear plastic. This is available in pressure-type cans and is easy to use. Be sure it is thoroughly dry before you start to use it. Give it to him to hold so he will realize it is no longer distasteful, and do a few simple retrieves on the flat while *in motion.* Then follow by going into the regular, complete exercise, always using this same article. With continued use, you will find the plastic coating will be wearing off and your pal will be getting used to the bare metal gradually. Do not go to another, untreated, metal article until you are sure the plastic is worn off and his teeth are on the bare metal when he is holding it. Naturally, your praise and a good tone of voice go along with your practise, as in all of your training.

Dog retrieves articles and other items, as well, but upon delivery to handler he turns his head as though there is something wrong with his handler's hands.

With a dog's nose being as sensitive as it is, it could well be that he has detected something quite distasteful (or just plain "smelly"!) on his owner's hands. It could be a heavy tobacco smell, perhaps an item in the cosmetic line, such as perfume, hand cream, hair tonic, nail polish, etc. Check your dog's reaction by wearing a pair of light, close-fitting gloves. Look at the situation from your pal's point of view, and try to eliminate the troublemaker.

Dog does not use his nose, but just grabs any article in order to bring back "something".

No doubt but what the teaching has been at fault here and the dog believes he is doing what he is supposed to—that is, to retrieve an object. He *must* understand the difference between a retrieve and a searching for a certain article with a special scent on it. The best and most effective way to get this across to him is by using the article mat (described in the text) so there is an obvious association with the particular scent and the correct article.

Dog knows the exercise, but once in a while will try to pick up another article along with the right one.

Natural scent has a tendency to be a little "heavy" and may lay like a blanket, not only on the scented article but on others nearby, depending on the slightest carry of air currents on the floor or the ground. Experimenting, and, perhaps some habit changing, is called for here. If the articles you use are the open type (two or three bar) or dumbell type, be careful to scent them only *between* the ends, not *on* the ends, keeping it more or less "boxed in" so it will not drift easily to nearby articles. If your articles are solid pieces, try using the count method so you will know how much scent to put on them without confusing your dog. Let *him* be the judge and the guide for you.

Dog knows the exercise but approaches the articles very slowly and returns the same way, after picking up the right one. He acts as though he has been beaten. This is the only exercise in all the obedience training where he reacts like this.

This will be what could be called a calculated guess, determining the cause of this condition, based on the training experience we had years ago before we came up with the idea of the article mat. The only difference the dog could see between this and the regular flat retrieve, which he already knew, was the fact that there were *several* articles put out for him to bring back instead of *one* being thrown out, and that he was corrected and scolded and had it yanked out of his mouth when he did bring one back (the wrong one, of course!). Naturally, after a few corrections, he's going to lose whatever display of spirit he had when he started to work on this exercise. If you were in his place, how long would *you* stay happy and speedy? He's afraid he's going to make a mistake again and afraid he's going to be punished when he brings it back, so why be glad about it and anxious to do it?

For the remedy, forget the extra articles and take just one article of each material. Do some plain retrieving with each one, throwing and sending him while both of you are in motion. Get his spirit built up so that it is actually fun and he is running out to get it and running back to give it to you. When you have accomplished this, go to the very beginning of the step by step progression, using the article mat (see text) and making sure you take advantage of the magic word "G-o-o-o-d". If you are sincere in your efforts to undo your previous mistakes and show enjoyment yourself, you should encounter no further problems.

Dog will find the right article but will then leave it and go on over all the others, at times repeating the process two or three times before picking up the correct one and bringing it back.

Scent and its effect on the dog's nose is a very elusive thing to study, for we can't see it or touch it. We have a long way to go to understand it and possibly never will, completely. However, we have really learned a lot over the past several years and it has been the dogs, themselves, that have taught us the most.

In fact, the way we look at this situation is that very likely the scent is too strong for this particular dog's sensitive nose, so it is distasteful to him. The best way for him to handle this is to let the offensive scent have time enough to "cool off", disseminate into the air, or otherwise tone down, so that he doesn't resent it. Here is where it pays off to check your own dog's reactions by using the count method in scenting the articles, finding out how much scenting he needs for doing a good job.

Signal Exercise

On the signal to Heel, the dog starts forging and continues to forge.

No doubt this condition has existed in both the Novice and Open training, but now you've really become aware of it because you find your dog too far ahead of you as you attempt to teach him the Stand on Signal.

Return to on-lead practising, positioning the lead across *behind* you. Adjust it so that it allows no forging ahead while he is heeling at your side, yet is not tight enough for him to feel that you are pulling him toward you. Take up the slack in your right hand as it rests on your hip. If you are in the habit of giving the signal with your right hand then position your left hand across the front of your body and hold the lead with that. Do not try to make a correction with the lead. As you stop, your dog will take up what little slack there may be, and will still be in the proper position for the Stand signal, with his shoulder even with your left leg. Establish this habit pattern and the rest will come easy, including an improvement in *all* your Heeling exercises.

Large dog responds very slowly to the signal for Heeling.

Many people, and handlers of large dogs seem to be guilty of this more than others, make an inexcusable mistake in the type of signal they use. They start the signal from behind the dog's head and bring it past the side of his head. If you were the dog, how much of this signal could you see? The dogs don't have eyes in the back of their heads, any more than we do in ours.

The handler usually starts moving at the beginning of his signal, as he gives it to his dog. The dog starts to move when he starts to see this signal out in *front* of his eyes (unless he is alert and responds to the motion of your foot instead). Whatever style of signal you give, think about where your dog's eyes are located and make it one that is visible to him from beginning to end, the complete sweep, so he can respond to it immediately. (See section on Signals for further description and illustrations).

On the signal to Stay or Wait, the dog turns his head away or blinks his eyes, and he always starts to move as the handler leaves him.

Once again, here is evidence of a dog's reaction to a poorly given signal and, as usual, the dog is taking the blame. So many people use a signal that is a fast sweeping motion, with either the left or right hand, directly toward the dog's face and stopping (if lucky) just before the hand touches the nose. The dog is not sure, when the hand sweeps down toward him, whether or not it is going to stop before actually touching him, so, naturally, he ducks it to avoid the anticipated contact and blinks his eyes. He doesn't know just where that sweep is going to stop. Let somebody do it to you and see how *you* react! This confusion and uncertainty in interpreting the signal to Wait or Stay could very well carry through in the dog's mind when the handler leaves, causing him to feel that he needs to stay with him for reassurance or further instruction and guiding. No doubt the signal was quite lacking in finality and perhaps the dog is not that advanced but what he still needs some oral commands along with the signals.

Dog goes down on the Drop signal, starts to sit on the Sit signal, then goes right back down again.

This is probably caused by a lack of clear differentiation, from the dog's viewpoint and at his eye-level, looking first at the Drop signal and then the Sit signal. From his level, looking up toward your own shoulder level, the two signals might appear similar enough to be confusing to him. This may sound crazy but try a little experiment to double check it. Have somebody who is interested, as you are (otherwise they will think you have blown your top) help you, and assume a position that will bring their eyes about the same height from the floor as that of your dog (lie *prone* in the case of some Toy breeds or a Dachsie!). Then give the signals to him as you have been giving them to your dog. Make sure he is truthful about his impression of your signals and whether or not the two might seem nearly the same to your dog. You might even reverse the procedure, if your friend would give the same type of signal that you use, and *you* be the dog, to see what it looks like from down there. Quite a difference!

Now to further study your signal, stand in front of a mirror and look at first, the signal to Drop. Is it just a flash? Is it in full view, from your dog's level? Does it stop at a point most effective to your dog? Then study your signal to Sit. Check this signal the same way and then compare the two for similarities and differences. Study how you can improve them for your dog, practise them, and be sure the one signal is different enough from the other that there will be no further risk of mistaking one for the other.

Dog knows all the voice commands but does not respond to the signals.

There are two distinct possibilities here as to causes behind such a situation. One is that you are very likely trying to push too fast, not making sure that one type of signal is learned before presenting another one. Each signal should be taught *on lead,* associated with the command and the dog should be responding well before the command and the lead are dropped.

The other possibility could be faulty or impaired vision. The only way to determine this is through the service of a reliable veterinarian. You can do some checking on this yourself by observing the dog's reaction to motion at close distances, then gradually increasing the distance. Use a signal that he knows well and see if he "loses it" at a certain distance. Be careful that you don't mistake a lack of attention for inability to see.

Dog knows and obeys all the signals but often anticipates the next part of the exercise, before receiving the signal.

This problem goes all the way back to Basic and Novice training. It is a result of habit patterns in behavior that have appeared because your practise sessions have always followed a set routine, so the blame is entirely at your own feet. If your dog gets used to *always* going to Heel, following a Recall, he will start to anticipate it. If a Sit signal *always* follows a Drop signal, then he will start a habit of sitting from the down position before the signal is given. Vary the time between signals, and also change the order of the signals in the exercise. You will have a much sharper performance and a more attentive dog, for he is not going to be able to tell for certain just what is going to come next and will wait for your signal.

Directional Retrieve

Dog does not wait for direction line and signal or command, rushing out to retrieve glove upon slightest movement of handler.

About the easiest way to keep control of your dog in teaching this exercise, and also in correcting the habit of anticipating (as in this case), is to take hold of the collar with the right hand, putting the left hand over the right and placing it in position alongside the right side of the dog's face, and pointing the finger tips toward the glove for a proper "line". Hold this for a few seconds until the dog has steadied down. Then gently take the right hand off the collar, and after another few seconds, give the command and send him for the indicated glove. You will be able to tell by the dog's reactions how long it will be necessary to practise this way before he realizes what you want of him, as well as how often you should revert to this for a refresher. Some dogs need a review more frequently than others, just as some human students need tutors and special classes.

On changing position to face either the glove to the right or to the left, the dog breaks and goes for a glove at the slightest sound or movement.

First, be sure you control yourself when this happens and make no corrections, no yelling, stamping your feet, etc. This only adds to the confusion already in the dog's mind. Go back to training with the leash and collar, with the leash in the "tuck-through" position so you are still in control. Put the gloves in position, then start pivoting or turning, both to the left and right. Do this several times before sending him for a glove. Follow this procedure in your regular practise sessions until he realizes that he must give you his attention and wait until he gets the direction and command from you. He will learn that he cannot outguess you.

Dog retrieves any of the three gloves, regardless of where the fingers are pointing for the directional line.

Again, a caution against any correction here, for the dog believes he is performing as you wish him to, just bringing something back to you. Back up in your training and start all over again, using only one glove at a time. Follow the text carefully, step by step, right from the beginning of teaching this exercise. Don't get anxious and try to jump ahead too fast or the dog will never get things straightened out in his mind. Patience, praise and understanding really pay off in this situation.

When dog picks up the right glove, he proceeds to shake it violently, apparently aiming to "kill it". Then he drops it and stands looking at his handler, seeming to be very pleased with himself.

This has been "allowed" to happen and nothing has been done to prevent it. There has been too much distance between dog and handler to offer any control. To put an end to this, and to do it without any unpleasant corrections, send him out for the glove and *follow* him. As he picks it up, clap your hands to get his attention on you, call him with a pleasant tone of voice and receive the glove, giving him plenty of praise. Repeat this procedure in your practise, gradually decreasing the distance you follow him until it is no longer necessary for you to move out at all. Continue the hand clapping and extra praise for as long as he needs the extra diversion to take his mind off "killing" the glove and putting his attention on you. Gradually eliminate this diversion as justified by his performance.

The dog takes the direction line well, picks up the indicated glove, but then goes to one of the other gloves, drops the first one and picks up the other one, and returns to the handler.

There is no doubt this has happened because the exercise has been taught too fast and show routine has been introduced too soon. It is very important to teach this by concentrating on *just one glove at a time,* making sure there is no problem with one glove before introducing the second glove. In other words, the correction can be accomplished only through the elimination of the confusion in the dog's mind and that must be done by backtracking in the training to the beginning. Let the dog indicate the amount of learning he can handle and still enjoy; learn to read him and adjust your teaching accordingly.

When the dog is sent for a glove, he tries his best to bring back all three of them, paying no attention to the handler and his commands.

Evidently the dog has had retrieving impressed upon him so much that when he gets the command for the glove it is the only thing he thinks about. This, again, is a result of teaching too fast, creating confusion. Don't make things worse with corrections. Get out the training chute, the plumber's helpers, and set up your practise area so that your gloves are separated by them from each other, thus preventing the dog from going from one to another. This will break his habit pattern. By using your best tone of voice, you should be able to get the idea across to him that he is to bring the glove right back to you as soon as he picks it up. Don't be too quick to dispense with the chute in your practise; give the dog ample time to get his mind straightened out. After all, we need time to straighten our own minds out occasionally!

Dog goes to the proper glove but won't pick it up, then goes to another glove.

This, too, could have been caused by rushing the training and the training chute can be used to advantage here, just as in the previous problem. There is also quite a possibility that the dog is very sensitive to motion and is influenced by the last glove dropped, even though he goes to the indicated glove first. Check to find out if he is following this pattern, then change the order in which they are dropped. Be sure to use the chute in practising so the dog will retrieve the proper glove and forget about which one was dropped last. Concentrate on changing the order frequently.

When pivoting or turning to face the glove, the dog goes to Heel position by circling around behind the handler.

This happens when a dog has been trained to go to Heel position around the back and the handler has neglected to teach it to finish to the left, using a different command. *Don't* blame the dog! First and foremost, you must choose a completely new command. Then work on teaching this part of the exercise, just as elementary a process as teaching the Heel command in Basic Novice. To begin the teaching of taking position as the pivot or turn to the left is taken, show the dog how to "back up" for just a few inches (refer to this section in the text), always accompanying the action with the new word and much encouragement. Use the lead in the "tuck-through" position; control it close up to the collar with the left hand and, if necessary, show him what you want by a gentle pressure against his chest with the right hand. Soon you will have him performing a regular dance routine with you and both of you will be having fun.

The pivot or turn to the right is even easier, for the dog only has to step forward a few inches to get into position. Be sure to keep control with the lead, in order to check the habit of circling completely around. When the dog has learned both, put variety in your practise so that he never knows in which direction he's going to be asked to move. Off lead work can be tried *after* the new command has been learned.

Directed Jump

The dog will not go the required distance beyond the jump on the Out Command. He wants to turn and sit when he gets in line with the jumps, about halfway out.

This is a problem seen very frequently in the Utility work and has its origin in faulty Open training, in the Retrieving training. It is easy to get into a habit without realizing what adverse effects can show up later as a result. What we refer to here is the distance you usually threw the dumbbell for the retrieve, giving your dog the idea that he was only supposed to go away from you that far, *no* further.

To counteract this idea in his mind, return to plain, unadulterated dumbbell Retrieving on the Flat. Throw it about 15 feet one time, then heave it 50 to 75 feet the next (provided you have that much oomph!). Try, anyway. If you find the dog hesitating to leave you on the more distant throws, start by heeling him with you and throw it out while you are *in motion.* As he reaches a good distance with no trouble, reduce your motion to just a step forward to get him moving, then eliminate the step completely. But keep the variety in the distance of the Retrieve in your practise.

Dog does not go out in a straight line, but always angles over one side or the other and ends up in line with either the solid or the bar jump on the Sit.

It is easy to get into a routine in practising for this exercise and it doesn't take long for a dog to get into a habit of anticipating a certain jump—so that is what he is heading for. It is necessary for you to break *your* habit pattern before you can expect to correct his. In your training area and at school, change the position of your jumps from one time to another, varying it even in *one* practise session. Be careful: if the bar jump can be knocked off in only one direction, see that it is changed and set up in accordance with the direction you are working in at the moment, in case it might be bumped accidentally.

It would also be advisable to set up the training chute through the center and backtrack to using the paper towel, dumbbell, toy or whatever, as a target to place for him to head toward. Place it well beyond the chute so he will go past the ends before you call for the Sit. Aim for a long straight Go Out, before even trying to combine it with the jumping. Retrace your beginning training on this; it will pay off.

The dog, on the way out, always jumps the high jump, then expectantly waits to be told what he is supposed to do.

This dog is just confused and has not separated, as yet, the Open Jump from the Utility Directional Jump in his mind. He probably thinks that whenever he sees a solid jump it means just one thing, *jump* it. Return first to do some Heeling on Lead, involving the jump. Heel past it, close to it, and then right up to it, giving a Heel command and doing a right turn before he has a chance to jump. Vary it with left turns and about turns. In other words, teach him (as should have been done in Open training) that he never should jump unless he gets a command to. When you feel he understands, try it *off lead.* Vary it still further by sending him over the jump now and then, and you go past it; then continue on in the Heeling. Occasionally send him over to retrieve the dumbbell. Do a straight Recall past the end of the jump. Then, finally, practise the Go Out with the aid of the training chute. Don't be in too much of a hurry to accomplish all of this and to get back to show routine.

Dog goes out straight and turns on command but doesn't sit; then anticipates the command and direction to jump instead of waiting for it.

This apparently is the result of an overanxious handler, wanting to get his dog through the exercise as fast as possible, and not having sense enough to give "time" between commands. The best thing to do here is to go back to the text and follow, carefully and *slowly,* the first two parts in teaching this exercise, the Turn and Sit and the Go Out. Make sure he is in good control before you start to work with the jumps set up again. When you do start again, set the jumps at minimum height. A high jump, it seems, acts like a particular challenge, a magnet to many dogs. Increase the height very slowly as you progress in practise, paying strict attention to giving your dog enough time to get calm and settle down from one command before you throw another at him. Be ready to retrace your training at any time you see evidence of the old habits popping up. It is the *only* way to eliminate confusion.

Dog goes out fine, responds to the Turn and Sit, but does not move on being given the signal for either jump.

This confusion has apparently stemmed from the type of signal being used for designating the proper jump. It may be a carry-over from force training on the signal to Down in the Open work. If force was used to teach this, and there is any similarity in the signals for that and the jumping, there could easily be a bad association here, causing him to fear the consequences if he should move. Return to working on lead and "showing" him what you want of him, with absolutely no hint of any kind of force. It will take time, but both of you will be happier for the time you spend to work things out. Be sure the lead is attached to the non-working ring of the collar, and study the tone of voice you are using in giving commands. In addition, put yourself in front of a good-sized mirror and go through your signals. See if there is a similarity between the Down and the Direction signal for the jump. Try to imagine what they look like from your dog's eye level. If you can't check this by yourself, get a friend or another member of the family to help you. Then go to work on improving the type of signal you are giving.

Dog takes signal for the Solid Jump but comes to a halt as he approaches it, seems confused, and refuses the jump. However, he has no trouble with the Bar Jump.

It seems obvious here that the reason is connected with the dog's inability to see where he is going beyond the Solid Jump, as he has no trouble going over the Bar Jump where everything is wide open for him to see. It might be that sometime, during previous training or practising, he hit something there that was not visible to him and was hurt, physically. Things like this are a very traumatic experience and remain in a dog's mind for a long time.

This will have to be done slowly and with much patience. You don't restore a dog's confidence in a day, and that is what is needed. You must go back to working with a minimum height jump, raising it very slowly as your dog indicates to you that he is ready for the next height. In addition, vary the location of the jump, putting it in the center of the training area, on different sides, near a wall or a bush, etc., but keeping it low for some time. Be sure your voice is reassuring to him and give him plenty of praise. You are sure to have him responding happily and confidently if you, yourself, are understanding and work accordingly.

Dog knows the exercise but has particular difficulty with the bar, knocking it off sometimes with his chest, sometimes kicking it, and occasionally even going under. However, he always makes the effort in order to try to please the handler.

It seems here that the dog is working from fear, or pressure, desperately trying to do what is asked of him, even though he is not thoroughly schooled for it. It may also be that he has been frightened by the noise created from knocking the bar off when it first happened.

It would be advisable to start back from scratch. But first, get yourself a different bar to practise with. Go to a store that sells carpeting and ask for one of the heavy cardboard tubes that carpeting is rolled on from the factory. Cut it to the length needed for your jump and mark the black stripes on it with paint, or stripe it by using black plastic tape. Starting back at the minimum height, practise by doing a dumbbell retrieve over the jump. This will divert his mind from the bar as he is jumping. As you raise the height gradually, if he should bump the bar off he will not be frightened, for there will be no loud noise as the new bar hits the floor. Reduce the height of the jump again and keep working this way until his confidence is rebuilt, and you reach the height required for show routine with no trouble, before you go back to using the solid wood bar.

Group Stand for Examination

Dog acts like a copycat, doing the same as the dog next in line, whether it breaks position, moves away, sits or lies down.

This must have developed from the class training in the Stays in the Novice and the Open work, or perhaps also in the Utility class work, where all dogs in the class were required to do the same thing at the same time. We have found that one of the best exercises to develop steadiness in the Stays, all of them, is to vary the positions in which the dogs are left, going down the line with one in a Sit, one in a Stand, next one in a Down, etc. Then let the handlers move around when they have left their dogs, getting the dogs used to seeing people move around while they are on a Stay. Another variation is to line the dogs up, down through the center of the training hall or ring and alternate the direction in which the dogs are facing. Here, after the handlers have left the dogs, they will turn (all to the left or all to the right) and will go forward, circling the entire group of dogs, close enough so that each handler will touch the head of each dog facing him as he passes by. Repeat this exercise in each of the three positions, Sit, Down and Stand, before going back to try the show routine. In this set-up, the dogs get used to commotion and movement all around them.

If the dog is anywhere except last in line, he will sit after the examination is completed and remain in place until the exercise is finished.

The best thing to do here is to practise the exercise and to change the position of the dog each time, bringing the time up gradually, as when it was first being taught. Follow with the same procedure practise as in the previous problem.

The dog had no problem in the individual Novice Stand for Examination, but now, in the Group Stand, will break position when the examiner comes close while going over the dog next to him, sometimes when they bend toward the other dog and the clothing brushes (or nearly touches) him. He doesn't resent a direct approach, as when he submits to the examination.

Again use the type of class formation suggested in the first ("copycat") problem. Vary it this time by having the handlers weave in and out between the dogs, right down the line, in serpentine fashion. Have the handlers bend over, and exaggerate their body motions, without actually touching the dogs. It may be necessary, at the beginning, for the handler working on this problem to stay close to his dog until he sees the confidence being restored. Don't expect results too quickly; build up to it gradually.

The dog responds to the Stay signal very well but is extremely sensitive to any kind of body motion from the handler and will go down. While he is standing, he also acts cowed and afraid.

Correction for this calls for a little imagination and group participation in a sort of "game". You may have to stay with your dog at first, even on lead, until he steadies down. The balance of the group, after they have left their dogs and before any examination has started, should begin to move around, shake hands with each other, talk and laugh. This will convey to the dog the idea that there can be motion around and that he should not be affected by it. When he steadies with other people moving, then the handler joins the group, being ready to assure his dog if necessary that everything is OK. This will teach him that his handler does not necessarily have to look like a statue.

As for his acting afraid and cowed when he is standing for this exercise, this could very well come from your staring at the dog while facing him. It is amazing how most dogs react to this, and what improved performances result when direct eye to eye contact is avoided. You can still watch your dog by looking above him or a bit to the side of him.

OBEDIENCE TRIAL CHAMPION

Should you aim to add O. T. Ch. to your dog's name, first carefully read the requirements for this title as described in detail in chapter 6 of the Regulations for AKC Obedience Trials, at the back of this book. It involves no changes in the Obedience classes. So we just offer a few reminders that may be of help in achieving the necessary 100 points and in making you and your dog a better team.

1. Complete dog attention is needed at all times.
2. Dog's position must be consistently correct.
3. Work must represent a smooth, happy rhythm of team.
4. All turns must be smooth, proper, show team unison.
5. Handler's body motions must be kept to a minimum.
6. Keep your head up and eyes looking ahead.
7. Make your starts and halts smooth and consistent.
8. Change smoothly from one pace to another.
9. Do not make direct eye contact or glare at your dog.
10. Receive dumbbell and scent articles properly, no jerking.
11. Use signals visible from beginning to end by your dog.
12. Avoid anticipation of the judge's commands.
13. Scent your articles at the shows as in practice.
14. Remember to praise by body contact or voice when allowed.
15. Smile when you give commands, it shows in your voice.

You know your dog — work WITH him. Don't confuse him with sudden drastic changes. Avoid resentment as well. Practice — take nothing for granted.

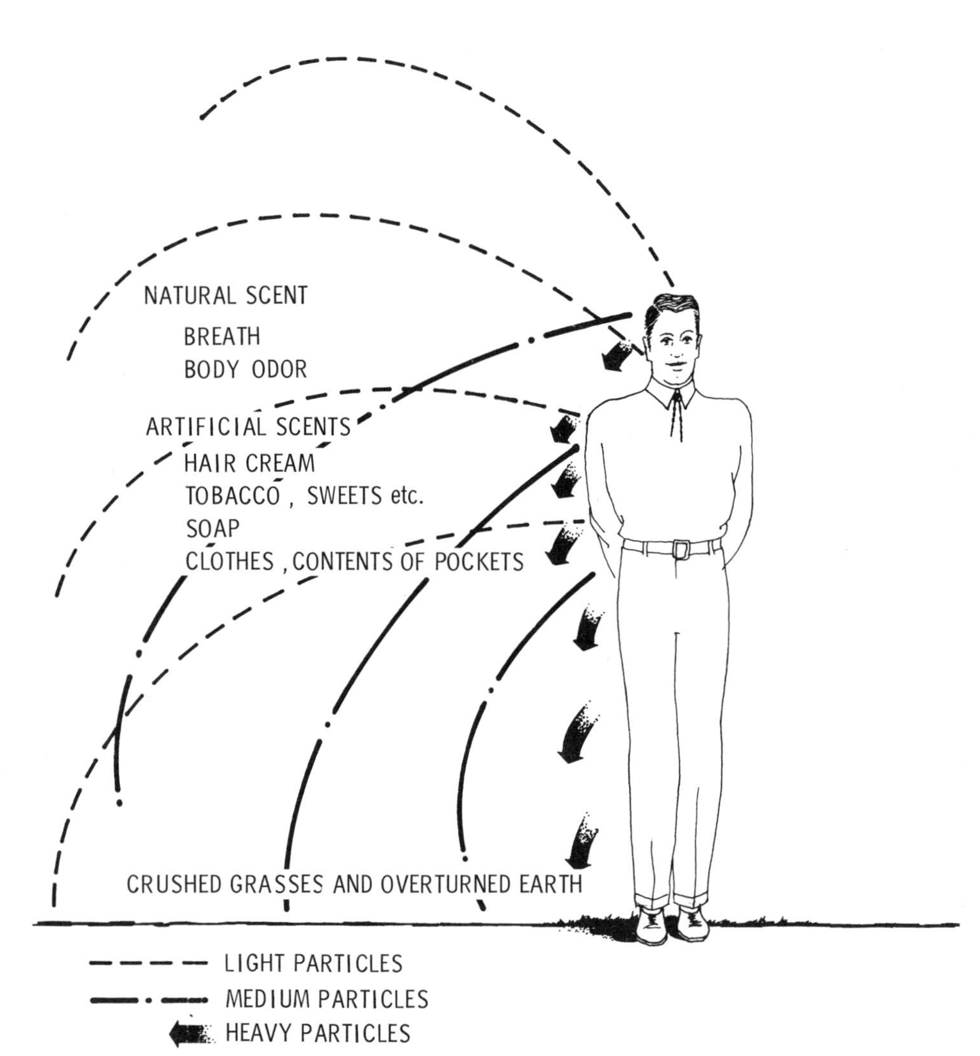

Illustrating a breakdown of the types of scent

Tracking

BEFORE going into the subject of teaching you to teach your dog to track, there are some related topics to be taken into consideration. One is scent—a layman's view of it, and the detection and/or identification of it by the dog. Another is topography of the land where tracking is likely to occur in a test, in practise, or in actual serious use. A third is weather—cold, heat, humidity, rain, snow, wind, air currents, etc. A fourth is equipment.

As should be obvious, all of these items (or a combination of them) are factors which should be considered and understood as thoroughly as possible because they affect the performance of every dog that Tracks. Understanding them, before you and Buddy get started, can also mean the difference in your getting across to him at the beginning just what you want him to do for you. This knowledge is a vital thing for you to have as it will mean a stronger communication between you. You will be able to "read" him as he is working out ahead of you, and you'll know, from his indications, whether he is actually working or just taking you for a stroll in the beautiful outdoors.

Scent

Much has been written on the research that has been done on scent, both by chemical analysis of its composition and qualities and in actual controlled testing on both humans and dogs (as well as many insects, fish and other marine and animal life). The Encyclopedia Britannica quotes that H. Henning, after conducting many tests, concluded that there were six main odor qualities: fruity, flowery, resinous, spicy, foul and burnt, (this, from the human viewpoint).

Further related statements, from the same source:

> To be odorous, a substance must be slightly volatile so that the molecules can be given off and carried into the nostrils by air currents. . . . The unique chemical or physical property that causes odor remains to be defined . . . Most odorous substances are organic compounds in which both the arrangement and structure of the molecule, as well as the presence of particular chemical groups within the molecule, influence odor.

Quoting from *"The Senses of Man"* by Joan Steen Wilentz, Chap. VI, "Your Nose is a Camera", we find some more interesting observations on this subject. She says:

> Not everything in life smells. Whatever smells has to be broadcast. The source must be volatile—evaporating molecules into the atmosphere. This automatically eliminates iron, steel, and many other common materials (provided they are clean), because at room temperature they are not volatile. . . . Heating, of course, increases the rate of evaporation. This is one reason why cabbage cooked is smellier than cabbage cold. . . .
>
> The molecules must to some extent be soluble in the saltwatery mucus that lines the nose . . . they probably also need to be dissolvable in the fat and watery solution that makes up the lining of the olfactory cells.

There has been still more effort put forth in chemical research on smells in attempts to analyze and catalog them, but they are most elusive. As Joan Steen Wilentz observes "Smells just don't lend themselves to the neat analytic measurements that sound and light do. There are no smellicycles or smellivolts." She also states that "a long-lasting continuously smelled odor may stimulate the cells to fire for a while at a steady rate, but then dwindle down to nothing. Adaptation has taken place." It is quite likely that this is what has happened within the canine smelling machinery when we say they are suffering from nose fatigue.

One of the best descriptions of the smelling construction of noses, in words easily understood by the average layman, I found in "The Sense of Smell" by Roy Bedichek. He says:

> The more efficient mammalian noses . . . are equipped each with a patch of membrane secluded in an upper corridor from which emerge hairlike processes, or cilia, submerged in mucus and undulating like threads of algae in a stream. These receptors are ever on the alert to select from the scrambled mass of odor broadcasts any message possibly affecting the welfare of the creature which is carrying around his neatly built-in odor set.

In other words, we can liken the system to radio or telephone, the cilia in the nose being the microphones that receive the messages and send them to the brain where they are interpreted. Perhaps they are stored there for later use, perhaps they are acted upon immediately, depending upon the circumstances.

In trying to classify and describe some of the properties and characteristics of certain odors, we are again groping in the dark. The scientists are still not in agreement on their various observations. But we can rely upon some of their conclusions and they do give us more insight into the subject of Tracking. Natural scent from the human body can be described as "heavy". That is, it can be imagined as falling to the ground. Each person's scent is individual, due to the molecular components in it and is identifiable from another's by the amazing ability of a dog's keen nose. He can actually "sort out" odors or combinations of odors and remember them. A statement made by Fernand Mery in "The Life, History and Magic of the Dog" emphasizes the canine gift thus: "The olfactometer, which is in use today, shows that the dog's sense of smell is in fact a million times superior to our own." Please bear this in mind and remember it when you and your pal are out in the middle of a field, all alone, and you get the idea that *you* know where the track is and he doesn't! He can smell better than *you* can, provided you have done a good job in teaching him which smell he is to pursue, and have also created in him the desire to follow a specific task, on command.

There are other odors that we classify as "artificial" and they are, in general, "light" (as opposed to "heavy"). In other words, they are more volatile and rise up, disseminating more quickly. In general, we think of them as perfumes, deodorants, cosmetics as a whole, hair sprays, tobacco, soap, gasoline, etc. These are more elusive and disappear faster than the heavy odors and yet they play a very definite part in making up the particular combination of smells that a dog follows in Tracking.

A third type of odor that also plays a part in the makeup of a track for your dog to follow is that created by the physical act of walking on the ground. When a person walks across a field or into the woods or brush, he actually crushes under his feet the grass and other vegetation he steps on. He also, usually, overturns some gravel, soil, dirt as he walks along. We believe that this forms a certain combination with the heavy and the light odors to become an especial individual scent for a dog to follow. Of course, this scent is affected and influenced by several factors that we know for sure, one of which is: Topography.

Topography

Topography is the description of the surface features of the earth, e.g. the hills, valleys, how steep they are, or how gentle in grade, etc. It is important to study how the "lay of the land" can affect a track, in addition to humidity and wind, sun and rain. Wind and air currents in general are definitely influenced to a great degree by the topography. We have tested "just run" tracks with smoke bombs for our own information and education, and have taken pictures in sequence of the results. It is difficult to believe what happens to air currents, even with no measureable wind and no lapse of time. And if these things happen to just the *air,* we must conclude that it also happens to scent, for we do know that a great deal of it is air-borne. Thus, the importance of observation and study out in the field when you and Buddy start working. And remember, no matter how much you know and understand at the beginning, you will always be able to learn more through your own experiences and that of others.

Weather: This, in itself, is a subject that could fill volumes, but we'll try to limit the discussion here to the most important aspects as they affect Tracking and the efficiency of our pal's nose.

About the first thing we think of when weather is mentioned is *temperature.* No imagination or guesswork is needed here, as facts are very much accepted as to its influence. Both the ground and the air have measureable temperatures and their effect on each other at ground level, where they meet (*and* where the track is, basically), will influence the scent of the track. Nature works to equalize, or bring together, these two temperatures when they differ, and they usually do vary, especially in the early mornings and the evening.

An ordinary indoor-outdoor thermometer can be used very easily to get an accurate reading, so your assessment of the conditions can help you foretell what your dog may be doing, how far he might be from the actual footsteps and yet be working. Set the thermometer up in the general area where you're going to work, three or four feet above the ground, then stick the thermocouple *into* the ground. Leave it for 15 or 20 minutes and take the readings. Your "indoor" reading will be the air, and the "outdoor" will be the ground temperature. If you find the ground colder, it would tend to suck the heat into itself to try to equalize the condition. Thus, the scents of the track would lie more or less in the area (excluding a factor of wind).

Using the indoor-outdoor thermometer, wind velocity meter, wind direction indicator, and hygrometer

Conversely, if the ground were warmer than the air, the heat would be rising and pushing *up* the cold air. Here you would have a natural rising of the scents, carried by thermals of the air, without regard to any other factor influencing the air currents. In such a case, you could expect your dog to be working on the particular scent and yet be much further away from the actual track as it was made.

Now, let us add some wind to the picture. It is quite obvious that the second of the two situations, with the warmer ground, will show a much wider distribution of scent with a little wind *or* a lot of wind, than where you have the cold ground-warm air condition. Consequently, Buddy could be working much further away from where the foot track was made and still be right and following the scent. We judged a dog once who did a terrific job at a Tracking Test, even though the two legs of the track which were at right angles to the wind direction were worked at least 30 feet downwind and parallel to the plotted track. In cases like this, we must also consider the individual dog and his "nose ability". Each dog is going to work a track where the scent is most comfortable to him; that is, where he gets the most efficient messages sent to his brain from his own microphones.

We have touched on temperature and wind to some extent. Now, how about rain and snow? Don't forget, if you are going to be serious about teaching your dog to track, you will be working in *all* kinds of weather, fair and foul. Tests are not postponed on account of weather, except in extreme emergencies. (We've known of only two such occasions. One was following a blizzard when there was too much snow on the ground. The other was a situation of a severe storm causing flash floods, washouts of roads and bridges, practically prohibiting all access to the site). In addition to preparing for Tracking Tests and a "T" title, hopefully your dog's accomplishments will become great enough that you and he might be relied upon to help out in emergencies, like looking for a lost child. And believe me, *no* child is going to get lost purposely just when the weather is most ideal for you and Buddy to get out and track him! Thus, you can readily see how important it is for you to work under different weather conditions and know more or less what to expect, depending on what they are.

Water is known as a good conductor. And the odorous molecules in smells, as we are told, are soluble in watery fluids. Here, as you can see, we have an ideal union to make a track *more* "followable" than over dry ground. Morning dew is very good; high humidity and a drizzle type rain, too, are excellent for holding the scent for easier following. Only when you encounter a real downpour are you likely to run into trouble. This is actually because the scent is disseminated and spread out thinly over a much larger area, making it extremely difficult for Buddy to confine it to one direction and work it as a "track".

Snow, of course, is just another form of water, but one beautiful quality of it is that it is not running downhill or over the countryside as water does. It blankets the smell of a track and holds it in place. Even when a track has been laid and snow has fallen covering it up, it is very easy for a dog to follow it. We're all familiar with the reputation of the St. Bernards in their search and rescue work in the Alps. We've also observed the excellent results in the way dogs have worked in many of our tracking classes, as well as what we've seen in Tracking Tests. Don't be afraid to get your boots on and other necessary comfortable clothing and get out in some of that white stuff. Buddy will enjoy it, too. It's right down his alley.

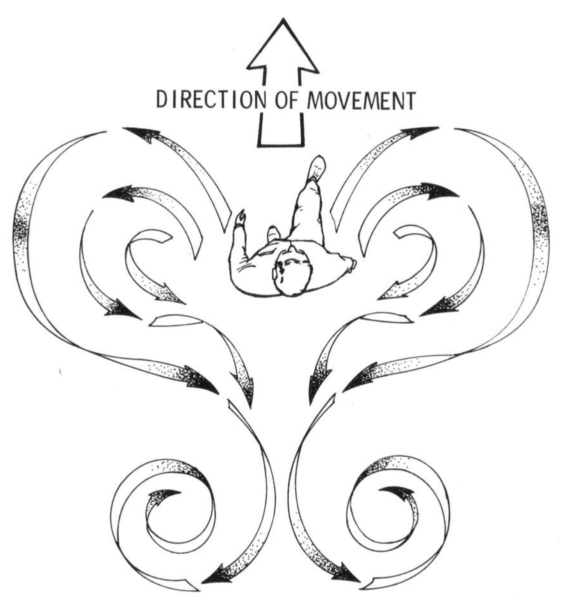

A simplified diagram illustrating how eddy currents of the air can be created and set in motion by a person walking

The next factor to discuss is air currents. If we had some fabulous Superman type of vision so that we could actually see these air currents, many of our questions would be answered. Some currents are strong enough, when they become breeze or wind, that we can feel them. But we know, from the work with the smoke bombs, that air is "on the move" constantly, even though we are not conscious of it. We have also found that it moves in many directions, horizontally, vertically, obliquely and in circular patterns. Sometimes it even seems to separate, one part rising and clearing the tops of bushes and trees while a lower layer seems to drop and hug the ground, especially when there is a depression in the terrain. It will even hug bushes and vertical sides of buildings.

We also know that bodies moving through it, including human beings and other animals, will set it in motion. As a person moves, he pushes the air and it starts a formation of eddy currents. If he is walking forward, these currents circle away from him toward both sides and return behind him to take the place of the displaced air. Thus, it is easy for us to picture the scent being deposited *both upwind and downwind* of a track. Naturally, the more concentrated area of the scent will be downwind, depending on how strong the wind is blowing and what the terrain and weather are. Just *where* the particular dog is going to work this track is an altogether different matter for it just might be that he may be blessed with an overly sensitive nose. In that case, he may prefer to work a more diluted scent, where it is easier for him to sort out the odors that make it up. From this, you can see how very important it is for you to know your own dog and draw your own conclusions from the way he works. Permit me to emphasize, at this point, that "breeds" as such do not even enter the picture. Each individual dog of a breed differs from the others of the same breed, even from its own littermates. Because you have a Bloodhound is no assurance that he is going to be a better tracker than your friend's little Pomeranian, or any other breed you might name.

Equipment

The subject of equipment for Tracking is also extremely important for successful and happy work, both for you and for your dog.

We must still consider the dog's viewpoint here, as his comfort should come first. The Harness (a collar is *not* used for tracking) should be of a size, pattern and weight that is comfortable on the dog and does not interfere with the action of his legs. It should be wide enough material that it will not cut into him (as a rope or cord would), yet light in weight, depending upon the size of the dog. We prefer the pattern that allows the "pull" to be exerted across the chest, the lead attached at a point at the top of the shoulders (pictured P. 278.) For the larger breeds, we like to see a chest plate in the design and have it lined with a soft material, e.g. sheepskin. It doesn't take long for your Buddy to recognize the harness and lead when you take it out and he will jump for joy, provided he has had a happy association with it at the beginning.

The Tracking lead, as specified for a Tracking Test, should be from 20 to 40 feet in length. We recommend the full 40 feet (you'll learn why later) and with a marker, such as a loop or a change of color, placed at 20 feet so you will know when your dog is working that far in front of you. We personally like a lightweight webbing, as it is easy to handle and to keep from snarling. Naturally, a lighter weight material, such as nylon or venetian blind cord, must be selected for the small breeds.

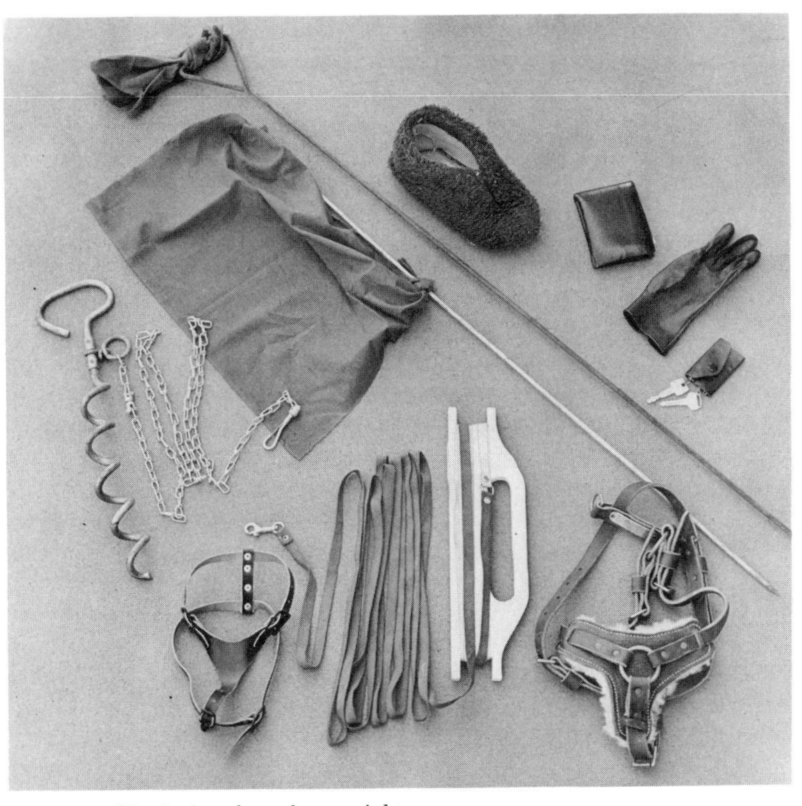

Clockwise, from lower right:
Harness for large dog
Tracking lead on holder rack (20 feet of one color, 20 feet of another color)
Harness for small dog
Tie-out stake
Starting flag
Turn stake
Assortment of articles (slipper, wallet, glove, key case)

Vizsla with tracking harness and lead

Other "auxiliary" equipment for training includes: two starting flags; several turn stakes; a tie-out stake (this spirals into the ground); a collar and a chain lead for use with the tie-out; several articles, such as an inconspicuous dark glove, wallet, key case, shoe, slipper, etc.; a weighted glove; an indoor-outdoor thermometer; a wind gauge (helpful, but not an absolute necessity); a pan and some fresh cold water in a thermos jug; and something to act as a drag at the end of the lead for testing the dog on his willingness to "pull".

For the two starting flags, we like to see the waving flag part made of a bright material and about 12 to 15 inches square, the rods about 30 to 36 inches above the ground, flags flying at the top. The rods, or stakes, can be of wood, bamboo, metal, fiber glass or any available material that will serve the purpose. The length of the turn stakes should be around 6 or 7 feet, and marked at the tops to be visible against outdoor backgrounds, using a bright colored material or paint (such as a fluorescent orange or red) on the top 10 inches or so. To avoid letting a dog become "flag conscious" (and we have seen it happen!), we advise *no* flapping flags on the turn stakes. These will only be used as field markers for your convenience and help.

A tie-out stake is of a metal corkscrew type of construction with an eye at the top. You can insert it into the ground close to the first starting flag, and use it to tether your dog via a collar and chain lead fastened to it. It is very convenient when you have no helper to aid in holding your dog while you are laying a track out in front of him, especially if he is not as "steady as a rock" on a Stay command (the *only* obedience command, by the way, that we use when working on tracking).

The different articles suggested are to be used for drops on the tracks, giving the dog a variety to look for, and to provide more than a single article on one track as you progress in your training. At a Tracking Test your dog is required to find and identify one article left by the tracklayer and it is supposed to be a glove or wallet, inconspicuous and dark in color. However, if when you and your dog should be trying to track a lost child and a shoe or sock or sweater is found, your dog thinks his job is done with just one item found and refuses to go on further, you are not going to be of much help! This is why we work up to a point where the dogs are able to locate four or five articles on a full track.

We have already discussed the value of an indoor-outdoor thermometer and how you can benefit from its information. A wind gauge, such as those used by sailing craft (available from marine supplies), can also contribute to your understanding of weather effects on Tracking. Most of us, though, can judge well enough as to how strong a wind is blowing and whether or not it will have much bearing on carrying the scent away from the track. Much of this knowledge will be gained from actual experience as you go along.

There are several different things you can use on the end of your lead to test your dog's willingness *or* reluctance to pull when in harness. Again, your dog's size is a determining factor. One dog might refuse to pull even a small branch, where another might not be fazed a bit by an automobile tire. But you wouldn't think of trying the Pom with the auto tire, and you'd definitely expect a Shepherd to drag more than a little branch. The purpose of this testing, before you start the teaching, is so that you, as the handler and trainer, will know how best to handle your lead. With the dog who will pull without a second thought about it, your lead handling will be much simpler. If you have a dog who won't pull, it is going to be up to you to keep that lead loose. If not, he is going to quit, right at the beginning, and usually will return to the handler. In many cases, as the dog progresses, his enthusiasm will take over and he will develop a love for the Tracking. As a result, he will forget his first feelings about it and will start to pull, making it easier for you to "read" him as he is working.

Dachshund dragging piece of plastic pipe on a "pull" test

Before we leave the subject of equipment, we should consider "people equipment." By this, I am referring particularly to wearing apparel. Your chief guide in choosing the items you will be putting on for your tracking practice is *comfort.* It is just as important for you to not be distracted from the job at hand, as for Buddy. If your clothes are too tight, too warm or not warm enough, if your shoes have gotten wet or you are wearing new shoes or boots before you've broken them in, or you don't have anything on your head and it starts to storm or the sun is too hot for you, your misery and discomfort are going to reflect in Buddy's work, for you won't be able to concentrate on what he is doing. It most certainly is not necessary for you to get a new wardrobe just because you're going into something new. Believe me, old clothes are more comfortable and you won't have to worry about a new pair of slacks or shirt getting snagged or torn as you climb over a fence or stone wall or pass too close to a gate with a nail sticking out of a board. You can't enjoy a day in the outdoors with a dog if you have to be concerned about your "fashion-plate" appearance.

Out in the Field

When you have collected your equipment, and picked a day and a time to start Tracking, your first task will be to find a property that is available, suitable, and within reach, travelwise. If you own such a piece of land or have an understanding relative or friend who does, you are most fortunate and to be envied by the great majority of tracking enthusiasts. The most desirable piece of land for a beginning tracker would be clear of most trees and bushes, fairly level, long enough for a straight track out of at least 150 to 200 yards. The ground cover, ideally, should be rather short for around 50 yards, then changing to a higher growth. To set up for your first practise, put the two starting stakes in, about 30 yards apart. If any breeze is blowing, plan the stakes so you will be working with the wind coming toward you. Only one turn stake is needed here, straight out beyond both of the starting stakes. If you are working alone, be very careful that you walk in a straight line (*not* easy for most people) and return in that same straight line.

Now we are ready for the first lesson.

Let us first understand that we are not going to try to teach Buddy to smell, for he was born with that gift and is already well aware of what *you* smell like. And at the beginning, it will be you that he will be smelling. It is our job, at the start, to create in him the desire to do the job that you want done and to have fun doing it. There should be a lot of enthusiasm and spirit on your part, in order to give him encouragement and let him know what a good time you can have together.

Some people are reticent about starting a young puppy to track, but it has been done very successfully by a number of people. Naturally, the work periods would have to be shorter than with a mature dog and one must be very patient and understanding with a youngster. There is no requirement of any Obedience title to be earned before a Tracking Test. A dog can carry a T.D. (Tracking Dog) after his name as soon as he earns it, at 6 months of age or over (see Appendix for A.K.C. regulations for certification by a Tracking Judge, etc.). We judged an English Springer Spaniel puppy not too long ago, that was 6-months-old on the day of the test. He had been certified, we learned later, when he was 4-months-old. He passed on the track, 440 yards, in about 3½ minutes, no trouble at all! Of course, this was an exceptional case. We're not all that lucky. Some people, on the other hand, prefer to wait until their dog has completed the Utility title. I feel this is a matter of personal convenience, and of available time for practise, more than anything else.

In addition, some people do not have confidence in their ability to separate Tracking from whatever other phase of training they happen to be in.

If a dog has already been taught to retrieve, even in play (as a puppy), the beginning teaching of Tracking is easier. But it *is not* a requirement. Even at a Tracking Test, a dog is only required to find the article and it may be picked up by the dog or the handler. Naturally, if the dog picks it up, the judging decision is much easier to make.

We advise working in tracking no more than twice a week, and find that once a week is usually adequate. Don't try to see how much you can accomplish in each session or try to keep up with somebody else who may be working with you. Be careful, too, that your Buddy doesn't tire of the new game on account of being pressed too far, or too fast, or for too long a time. Give him a rest after working a bit, also a nice drink of cool fresh water.

Recommended procedure at first starting flag:

> Put the harness on here not before—this is where the Tracking association with the equipment has its beginning.
>
> Take the time here to lay out your lead behind you, disentangling it if necessary.
>
> Any time consumed at this point will benefit Buddy, as any scent left here by the tracklayer will have time to register through the delicate membranes of his nose.

To start, take Buddy up to the first starting stake, put on his harness and the long lead. Lay it out behind you so there'll be no snags, and remove any other collars. The *only* obedience command you will use, if you need it, will be a "Stay" when you start away from him to drop the glove. But at first you will be using the heavier, weighted glove and you will be tossing it straight out toward the second stake for a visual retrieve. This is where you will introduce a new command for the new work. You may find it necessary, for just a few times, to use it along with the command to retrieve if he's familiar with that. Then you can drop it (retrieve command) as soon as you see he has the idea.

As to what word is best to use, it is entirely up to you to make the selection. Just be cautious in your choice and try to settle on one that does not sound like an obedience command you are presently using or plan to use later. Personally, we like the word "Track". Others we've heard are: "Glove", "Find", "Seek", "Sook" (phonetic for the German word to Seek), "Search", "Look for It", etc. There are no regulations

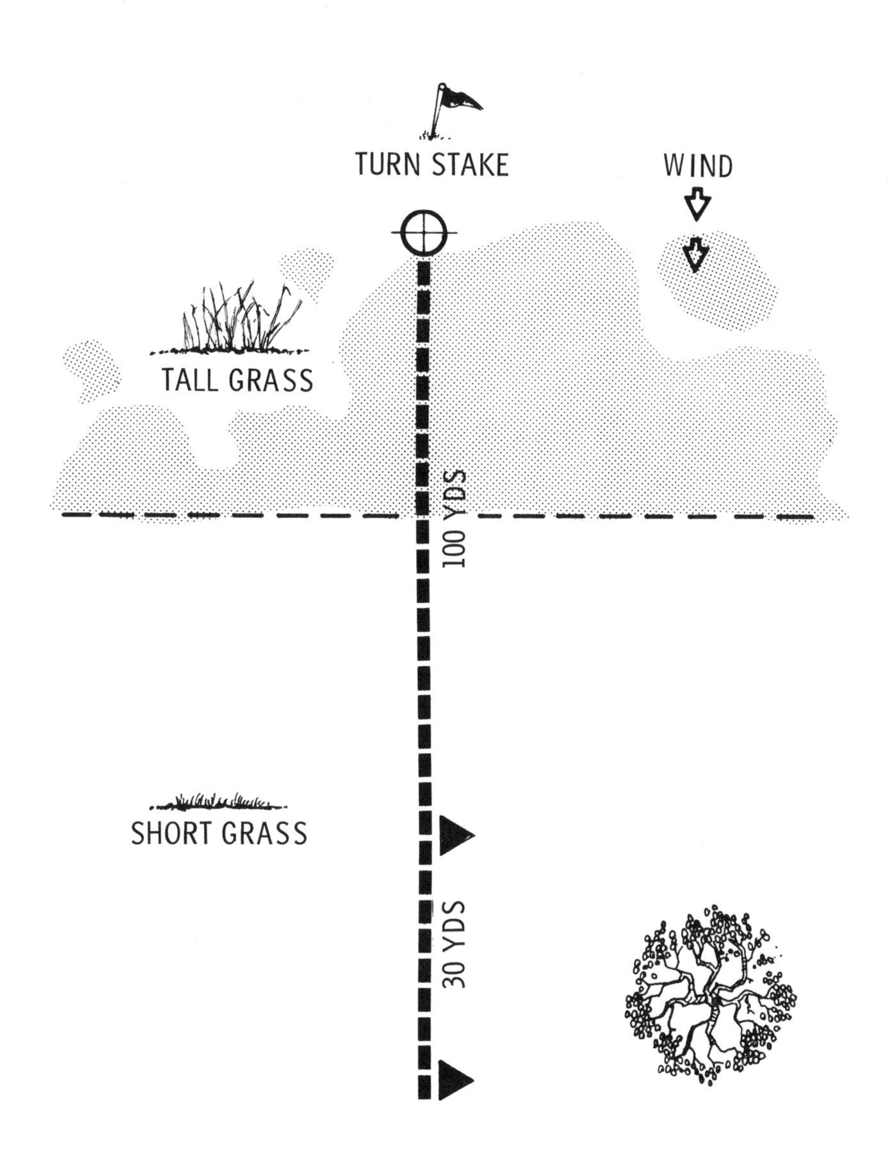

GUIDE FOR BEGINNING TRACK LAYOUT OF FIELD

governing or restricting your use of commands on the track, but BEWARE: Study the reaction of your own dog, and if you find your voice is distracting him and diverting his attention back to you, rather than keeping it on the job in front of him, cut it down to a minimum. Some dogs benefit by encouragement from behind them, others can concentrate better without it. One very important thing to remember is to *never* use your dog's name when he is out front working a track. This is a definite diversion of his attention, right back to you.

Hopefully, you have been able to plan your start with the first two flags and the turn stake set out so as to take advantage of the wind direction, blowing toward you and Buddy. Thus, the scent will be wafted in his direction and it will be easier for him to associate it with the new command. If any grass has had to be mowed, it should be done a few days before using the field. Freshly cut grass has such an odor that we humans smell it, so why confound our dog's overly-sensitive nose by making it overwork, sorting through extra odors to select the ones we want him to search for? Let's make it as easy as possible for him.

With the first stake at your left (your dog will then be closer to the track and its smell as you build it up), toss the weighted glove toward the second stake. Let him go out for it immediately, accompanied by the new "Track!" command. Show him how pleased you are—really go overboard with your praise. If you have to go out with him to help, be very aware of that straight line between the two flags and return on the same line each time. You will be making a more obvious track of your scent as you go over it each time, building it up. Don't worry if Buddy goes away from it slightly; just don't confuse him by having *your* scent spread out in several directions. Return to the starting point again, rearrange the lead out behind you, and then repeat the glove toss, adding a little more distance this time. Be sure you give your "Track!" command just as soon as the glove hits the ground, building up your pal's enthusiasm for the new game. Remember, too, how important the right tone of voice is in your training. Don't pull on the lead as he goes out; just let it slide through your fingers as he takes it out with him to make the retrieve. *Never* use the harness or lead to pull or correct him while Tracking. You may "snub" the lead if you have to, but use your voice and coax him back to you if it should be necessary.

When you have reached the furthest distance you can with a *straight* toss of the glove, your next step will be to tell Buddy to "Stay" at the starting stake, walk out a few feet further than the last toss, turn toward your dog, raise your hand high so he can see it, and let the glove drop to the ground *in front* of you. Return in the same straight line, pick up

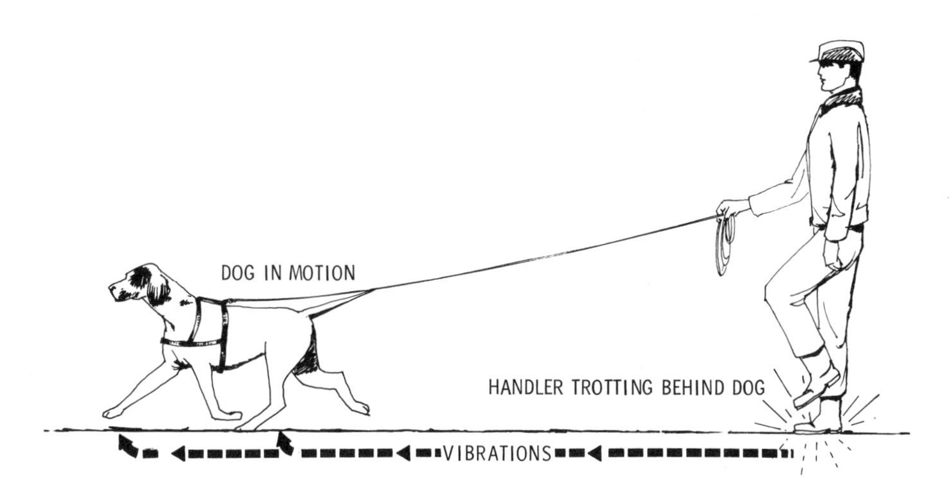

the lead, give him some praise and a happy command to "Track!" and off you go. Let him take the initiative to lead out away from you; encourage him to get out there on his own. Follow along so he'll know you're with him in the new game, but try to gradually increase the distance between you as you progress in the practise sessions. If he acts hesitant about going out by himself, make believe you're trotting a bit as you follow behind. He can hear your footsteps and feel the ground vibrations and will react much better as a result. When he gets the glove, squat down to receive it from him and lay on the praise. A point of advice to you, that will pay off later: Start right now to form the habit of raising your arm high in the air to show that you have the glove, even though there may be no other person within sight of you! This gesture is unmistakable at a Tracking Test and can be seen by the judges at a distance, so make it a habit now.

Still working back and forth in the same straight line, repeat as above, increasing the distance a few feet at a time (depending upon the individual dog's ability and eagerness) until you have reached the second stake, 30 yards away. Never increase distance on a drop if your dog found the last one difficult. In such a case, repeat at the same spot, or make the drop even closer, before reaching for more distance. Remember to watch your dog for tiring signs, and give him a rest when you think he should have it (I said give your *dog* a rest, not *you*!)

The next drop will be slightly different, for you won't be facing him so he can watch it. Go about 5 or 10 feet beyond where the last drop was, drop the glove in front of you, step on it and take another step or two, turn around, and step on it again as you retrace your steps back to the start. Buddy may be a bit slower this time in starting out as he didn't *see* anything to go for, but, from his past efforts, he knows there must be something there or you wouldn't be giving him that new command. So he'll "give it a go", as long as you say so. If you get some real reluctance and a lack of interest here, guide him out all the way to the glove and act as though he'd done it all by himself. If you did have to help him at this point, be sure to repeat until he has done it on his own, even though it may have to wait until another practise session. At this next session, start out again with a visual retrieve and build up gradually to the drop that he cannot see.

Extend the distance until you reach the edge of the taller grass, and then make the next drop just *into* the taller growth. When Buddy goes out this time, he won't see the glove out in front of him, saying "Here I am, pick me up!" This is where you will see a really rewarding sight, for he will show you just how he can put that smelling machine of his to work to do the job at hand. You won't even have to be reminded to praise him—it will be an automatic response of happiness and pride on your part.

This stage of training also gives you the opportunity of starting to "read" your dog so you will begin to know how he acts when he is working a scent, when he gets near the article, etc. Watch the carry of his head (high or low), the angle of his ears, the action of his tail (unless he doesn't have one, of course), the wiggle of his body, and the variation in his speed of travel. He can tell you a whole story, as plainly as though you were reading it from a printed page, if you will only learn to observe and interpret his actions.

On the next drop, increase the distance so you penetrate about 15 feet into the tall grass. Here you will really see the nose go to work as he can see nothing to retrieve at the point of his last find. He may need some extra encouragement here. Give it to him. Let him work it out, and heap on the praise again when his nose has led him to his quarry. Be careful at this point that you yourself don't become overenthusiastic and give your dog too much work, now that you've seen him use his nose and you know he *can* do it. Remember his nose can get very tired and he may need a rest before you do. He may be able to go out on the track five times in a day without tiring. But then the following week he may get tired on the third time out. Watch for this. Dogs have their good days and bad days, just as you and I do. Don't allow any confusion to develop if you can possibly avoid it.

Get accustomed to looking for your turn stake and guiding toward it in a direct line, even though you are *not* ready yet to make a turn. It is so important for you to remain in that straight track and build up your scent on it, and a distant marker is absolutely essential. If you have a sporting dog or a Poodle, and are not familiar with their instinctive work pattern in the field, do not be alarmed if you see him weaving back and forth across the track. This is a natural inherited style of working and is called *"quartering the field."* Occasionally we see it in individuals of other breeds, also. If your Buddy works this way, you might possibly have to curtail the distance somewhat and encourage him to concentrate a bit closer to the track. He could conceivably get into the habit of working too far off the track. You can check his forays by gently snubbing the lead before he gets too far, encouraging him as necessary.

First Turn

If your field is ample in size, continue this procedure of straight out, drop, return to your dog, "Track!", praise, until you have no problems doing a straight track of about 200 yards. When you can do this, it is time to start planning your first turn. And to be successful, *it must be planned ahead.* Your field should be laid out a few days ahead if you have no helpers working with you. If two or more of you can practise together, you can plot the area where you will be working for each other. This way, you can take advantage of the wind direction and lay it so your first turn will be heading against the wind, bringing the scent *toward* Buddy to make him realize you "went that-a-way!" If you have to do it by yourself, plan ahead for the prevailing wind direction and hope it "prevails."

From now on you will not be doing an about turn to return to Buddy. The turn stakes which you will be using as guides should not have your own scent on them, for this could make for more confusion in the field. This is why a helper is so important. It is also good practise to plot the area on paper, indicating any obvious markers in addition to the stakes (they could disappear) and also the approximate distances. The simplest pattern is an inverted "U," making a complete "box" as you come back to the starting stake. Refer to the diagram for a suggested plot. This does not involve a great deal of area and a combination of both right and left turns is not important right now. A plot with all right turns or all left is perfectly OK. Be sure that there is at least 50 to 75 yards between the "legs" of the track so that the wind will not be likely to carry a scent across to Buddy strong enough to confuse him as to the location of the track. Before you actually make your first turn, do one straight

TURN STAKE

FIRST TURN AND RETURN

100 YDS

ARTICLE

TURN STAKE

100 YDS

WIND

30 YDS

END

GUIDE FOR LAYOUT OF TRACK AFTER FIRST TURN

practise drop, going about the same distance as your last time out. This serves as a bit of a refresher and is a good policy to follow each time you start a practise session.

To make your first turn, track with the first turn stake ahead as your guide. Go *no closer* to it than 10 or 15 feet. Remember, we don't want Buddy to start associating the stakes with the track and the turns. We call it getting "stake-happy." They are out there for your use and your use only! Make your turn as near a 90° turn as possible, then scuff the ground good (really *dig in*) before you take any steps. In case you may wonder why we direct you to scuff *after* you turn, we have found that the dogs react much quicker and easier if this procedure is followed. The only logical explanation we have for this is to say that we believe that scent has "direction." How else can you account for a good hunting dog being able to immediately follow game in the right direction when he comes upon a track? Surely, by no stretch of the imagination can we claim, even allowing for the wonderful scenting power of a dog's nose, that he can smell the difference in freshness between the tracks of the front and the hind feet of a rabbit!

After scuffing at the turn, slide your feet a bit as you walk for no more than 10 or 15 feet, drop the article in front of you, step on it, and walk toward your second turn stake. Here you must plan where your next turn will be, as you will be going over this same track each time. Again, turn about 10 or 15 feet before you reach the stake, head for the last stake and come back to Buddy at the first starting flag, approaching him from the *rear.* This will avoid any inclination on his part to start off on your fresher track; and we thus keep any bad habit of backtracking from developing.

You may, if you wish, sit down and rest a few minutes before starting out on the track. You will be accomplishing two things here. One, you will feel better and more ready to tackle the next trip around. Secondly, the track will be starting to age just a little, even by a few minutes. At a Tracking Test a track must be at least a half hour old, no more than two hours, so we must build toward this gradually. As you progress to the aged track, you will still want to vary his work and give him a fresher track occasionally. You may even observe a difference in the way he works an older track, compared to a freshly laid track. Keep your eyes open and your thinking-cap on, *all* the time.

Now you are ready to get going, starting just as you have been doing on the straight tracks. As you see Buddy getting near where you made the turn, be especially careful of your lead handling and *very* observant of his actions. It is also important to be able to "read" him as he works

Handling the lead, slack between the hands

out a turn. He *could* go right on past, even past the turn stake, but don't allow him to go that far. He could go past the turn a few feet, then start circling to the right and to the left in an effort to pick up the scent he has run out of. The word used to describe this is *cast.* He is "casting" at a turn to locate the track. Or he also could make a beautiful turn immediately, just as though there were a direction sign posted there just for his benefit (lucky you!).

In discussing lead handling, I will try to describe what we have found is the easiest way to hold a lead while working. If you are left-handed, just reverse the directions. Take hold of your lead with your right hand about as far back as you usually work behind your dog. Leave a slightly slack loop in it, and grasp it further on, maybe 3 or 4 feet of lead between the two hands. Hold firmly with your left hand and let the rest of the lead drag out behind you. This way, if the lead in the rear should snag or get tangled, you can snap it and pull it free, but it will not have a chance to distract Buddy and cause him to forget why he is out in the field. Get in the habit of holding the lead this way and you will avoid many problems that could have been caused by your thoughtlessness.

If you find that he has rushed right on through, it is very likely that he may still be relying more upon his vision than his nose. If you do not have a satisfactory reaction from him just by checking him before he gets as far as the turn stake (snubbing the lead) and encouraging him, then you most assuredly have gone too far before he was ready for the turn. As in other problem training, back up. Do more straight tracks into the tall growth, where he *must* use his nose to find the article. Make sure that *you* can see him working. Go overboard with the praise when he locates it. Do not try the turn until this much is accomplished. It is necessary for you to see what signs he gives as he uses his nose on a straight track in order for you to be able to tell whether or not he has located the track in making a turn. You must be able to "read" him.

If you have the dog who starts to cast to try to relocate the missing scent at a turn (and the majority of trackers fall into this class), learn to *stand still* yourself at this point and remain facing in the same direction as in that part of the track on which you have just been going. You may play out the extra length of your lead here, the whole 40 feet if your dogs needs it to work with. He may cast just once in each direction and make up his mind as to where he should go to pursue the scent, or he may cast three or four times before he is sure. He may even circle all the way back to a point behind you, reworking that part of the track for a refresher. Remember, don't change your own position or direction; learn to "stay put" until he has definitely settled on his course. You may have to raise your feet up to keep from becoming entangled in the lead, but keep it free so he doesn't get the idea he's being corrected or that you want him to return to you. Try to avoid any extra arm motion in handling the lead, so that should he watch you once in a while, he won't confuse this with any signals he may have learned. Don't get into the habit of pointing a direction for him to follow as he may get into the habit of depending upon you for it, rather than his own nose ability. And where would that leave the two of you when you get out on a "blind track," one that you have no idea as to where the tracklayer went?

Once Buddy has made up his mind where the track is (and you know he is right), and he has given you the signs you're watching for, then follow him, making sure *you* turn where you did in making the track (for you shall pass this way again!). Lay on the praise, of course, as he finds the article. He will be mighty proud of his accomplishment and you will, too, needless to say. Continue on around, back to the starting flag, as you did when you laid the track.

If you have a dog that makes the turn with no extra work and you want to reassure yourself that he knows what he is doing, that it wasn't just a lucky accident, check him lightly with a snubbing of the lead. If he insists on the turn at that point, and it is in the general direction of where you went, let him go and follow him, even though he may not be in your footsteps. Remember our earlier discussion about the individual dog's ability and his comfort zone for his own nose, as well as the variance that may be caused by weather and wind conditions. Learn to rely upon his assessment of where he can best follow the scent.

Try to remember all you have learned on this most important first turn. Learn to apply it to all later work as you progress. Learn to take a correct perspective, and to make an unbiased evaluation of your work as you go along, trying to come up with some logical solutions to whatever problems may arise. Also, try to forget the existence of the turn stakes as you and Buddy are working. Make believe they have been whisked away without your knowledge and try reading him as though you had no idea where the track is. Does he tip his head lower to find the track? Does he raise it higher? Does he slow down? Do his ears or his tail change position? Does his tail stop its enthusiastic wagging? Look and THINK!

Now that you have the glove (and have raised it high above your head) after the first turn, continue on around the balance of the track as you did before, returning to the first starting flag from behind it. Your next step will be to go out as before, but this time make the drop about 20 feet beyond the last spot. When Buddy can find the article 30 feet or more beyond the first turn with *no* assistance from you, it is time to think about planning for some future work. This can actually start before you try a second turn.

Even though your only interest in this phase of training is to achieve a "Tracking Dog" title from the American Kennel Club, the next paragraph should still be considered as an important step in your *practical* training. It will be the means of giving you the satisfaction of knowing that your dog will be capable of locating a lost youngster, some other person, or another's pet dog, when you have completed his training and have gone beyond the AKC requirements. The foundation for this should be planned right now.

A most important thing to teach is that when you say "Track!" it means there is something out there to be found, even though Buddy may have just located a glove. Looking ahead, suppose a youngster had lost a shoe and you were looking for him. If your dog found the shoe and had the idea that his job was finished at that point, he wouldn't be of much help, would he? Now, if we start to use a second article in laying a track and he gets the idea that there is something else out there to look for as long as you say so, it will carry right on through his training.

For the second article, use something that he will retrieve, such as your wallet (empty, of course!), key case, one of your old shoes or an old slipper. Drop the new article about halfway between the second flag and the first turn stake, making sure you can tell the location of it when you're working behind your dog. Drop the other article you've been working with between the first and second turn at the same spot at which he made his last find. As he works the track and makes the first find, you may discover he needs some extra encouragement to continue on. When he does get to the second article, let him know what a splendid job he has done. He will get your meaning fast and will know that as long as you give him that command that he still has a job to do out there.

You may add still more articles as the two of you become more sure of yourselves and are more advanced in training. In fact, a good formula for you to follow is to add an article every time you add another turn. Be sure you change the location of the articles from one time to another so he doesn't start looking for one each time around at certain spots. When you are ready for your second turn, plan it ahead, just as you did the first turn, and each *new* turn as you make them. Remember, if there is any breeze blowing, use it to your dog's advantage for each new turn you work on, so that the scent is being carried toward him from the article you have dropped. Give him every benefit you can as you are training.

Assuming that everything has worked out satisfactorily up to this point, you are now ready to make your tracks more interesting, with more variety in their plotting, longer tracks, a change in ground cover and terrain (if it is available), and a bit more aging. Start by planning a track (to be laid out with the stakes a day or so ahead of time by your co-worker) so that it includes both right and left turns. As you work from one time to another, change the number of turns and their direction. Also, change the distances from the flags to the first turn and between the turns. Once in a while, for variety, plot the first turn right at the second starting flag. This has actually occurred, although rarely, at some Tracking Tests and has been known to "throw the dog for a loop," as they had never experienced such a thing before and the dog-handler team were not that sure of themselves that they could cope with it.

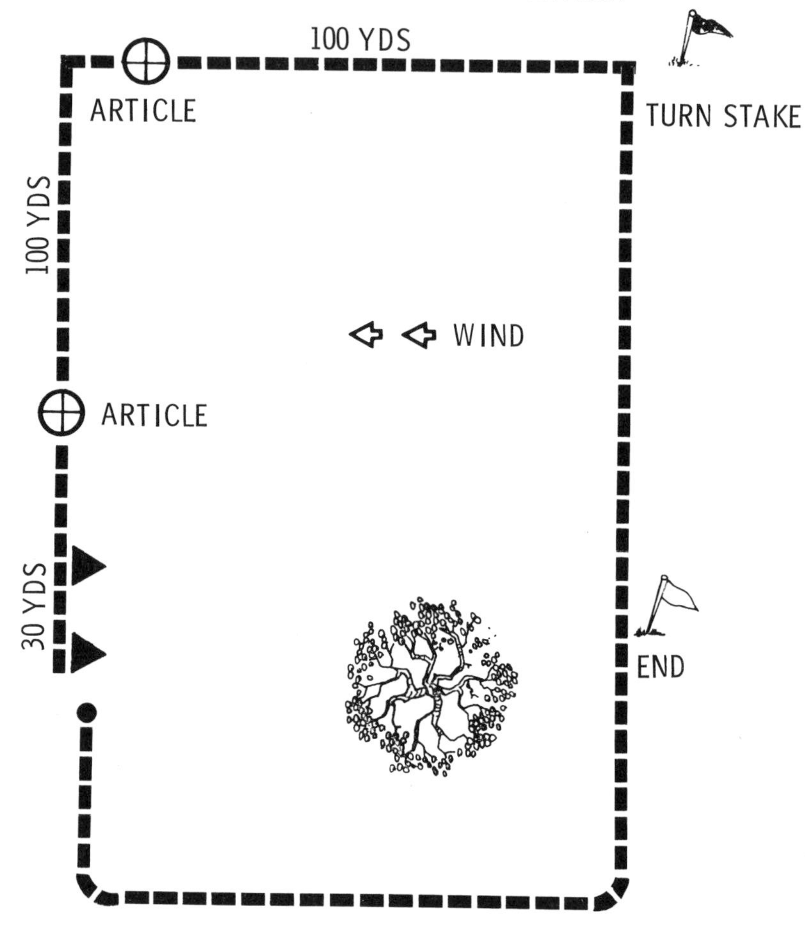

PATTERN FOR FIRST DROP OF
TWO ARTICLES

Tracking the Stranger

Now that you and Buddy are well along in tracking your own scent, you will prepare for the next big step. By well along, we mean you have no trouble working a track over 440 yards long (this is one quarter of a mile!) and tracks that have up to five turns in them. Now, do you really qualify so you can go ahead to something different without confusing your pal and upsetting all the work you've done before?

Introducing him to a stranger's scent to follow is a horse of a different color. First and foremost, no member of your family or anyone living in your household can be termed a "stranger," for he knows their scent as well as he knows your own. It must be someone who is not well known to him, but it is perfectly all right for a friend, someone in the neighborhood, a training (or tracking) class member, or a relative that is not around him frequently, to become your transfer agent. Your co-worker who has been putting in the stakes for you can be a very likely candidate for the job. Make sure he (she) is in good health and not down in the dumps, in pain or all doctored up, as this might present an offensive odor to your dog, and he may not want to break in on such a scent. Let's make the job as pleasant as we can for him and give him a natural body odor for his first strange scent to track.

Plan your simple "U" track, as you did at the beginning. If you can work from short grass into taller cover, excellent. Your procedure will be similar to that of your beginning, except that you will continue around the complete track, right from the first. To lay the track, both of you will go on it at the same time, you leading the way and he following about 6 to 10 feet behind you, carrying your glove, walking in the same path. Make sure your helper understands his role well, and what he is to do before you start out. If you believe your dog is catching on to the work fast enough that it warrants skipping a small step here, you can try having your assistant carry one of his own gloves, rather than the one you've been carrying.

The first drop by the transfer agent should be somewhere between the second flag and the first turn, but don't have him tell you where it is. Before you start, make sure he understands what to do and that he remains back away from Buddy at the starting flag, after completing the track with you. It would be a good idea if he went in the opposite direction from where you're working, perhaps over to sit in the car while the two of you are out in the field.

Before you start out, let us first try to creep into Buddy's mind and imagine his thoughts if he could express himself in our language. When he starts out, as you give him the command, he is aware of a strange scent mixed in with your familiar scent. Now he's wondering just why it's there and what it has to do with his game of finding your glove, so it slows him down a bit as he tries to figure it out. But your smell is still there, so he goes ahead on the strength of the familiarity of that, as well as from the encouragement in your enthusiastic tone of voice. As he goes along and continues to please you, he begins to realize that he's doing the job as you want him to. If you try to put yourself in his place in this manner, it will be easier to understand any hesitation or slowdown from his usual style of attack.

Encourage him as he is working through the other scent. Even do a bit of exaggerated trotting behind him if you think it might help him. When he reaches the glove, you might even see some hesitation on picking it up with the strange scent on it. Remember the old magic praise word "G-o-o-d!" as he comes to it; let him know how right he is and how happy you are.

After maneuvering successfully to find, for the first time, an article that has introduced a strange scent along with your own, you're ready to do a drop and add one turn to the track. Lay the track in the same manner as you just did. Make the turn just as you did your first one *except* that you only walk—the transfer agent does the scuffing and digging in after he turns and he drops the glove somewhere between the first and second turns, not telling you where it is. From this point on, proceed as you did before, adding one more article each time you add another turn, varying the location of the drops, the location of the fields where you practise, the terrain (if possible) and the weather conditions.

When Buddy has been able to do a 500-yard track with several turns in it, with your assistant and you working together to lay the track, you are ready to try a track *without* your own scent on it. For this you will want a completely clean field, one that you haven't worked in for at least a week. You will also want to use the same helper who has been working with you on the transfer. Looking at it from Buddy's point of view, as he starts the track, he might be thinking "This is not my master's scent but this scent is the same one that was mixed with my master's, so it must be OK to work on this one." Once this is firmly established in his mind, you have a big hurdle behind you.

At this stage, it should be obvious that you will require a third party, one who can put out the stakes for you. If you get somebody who will

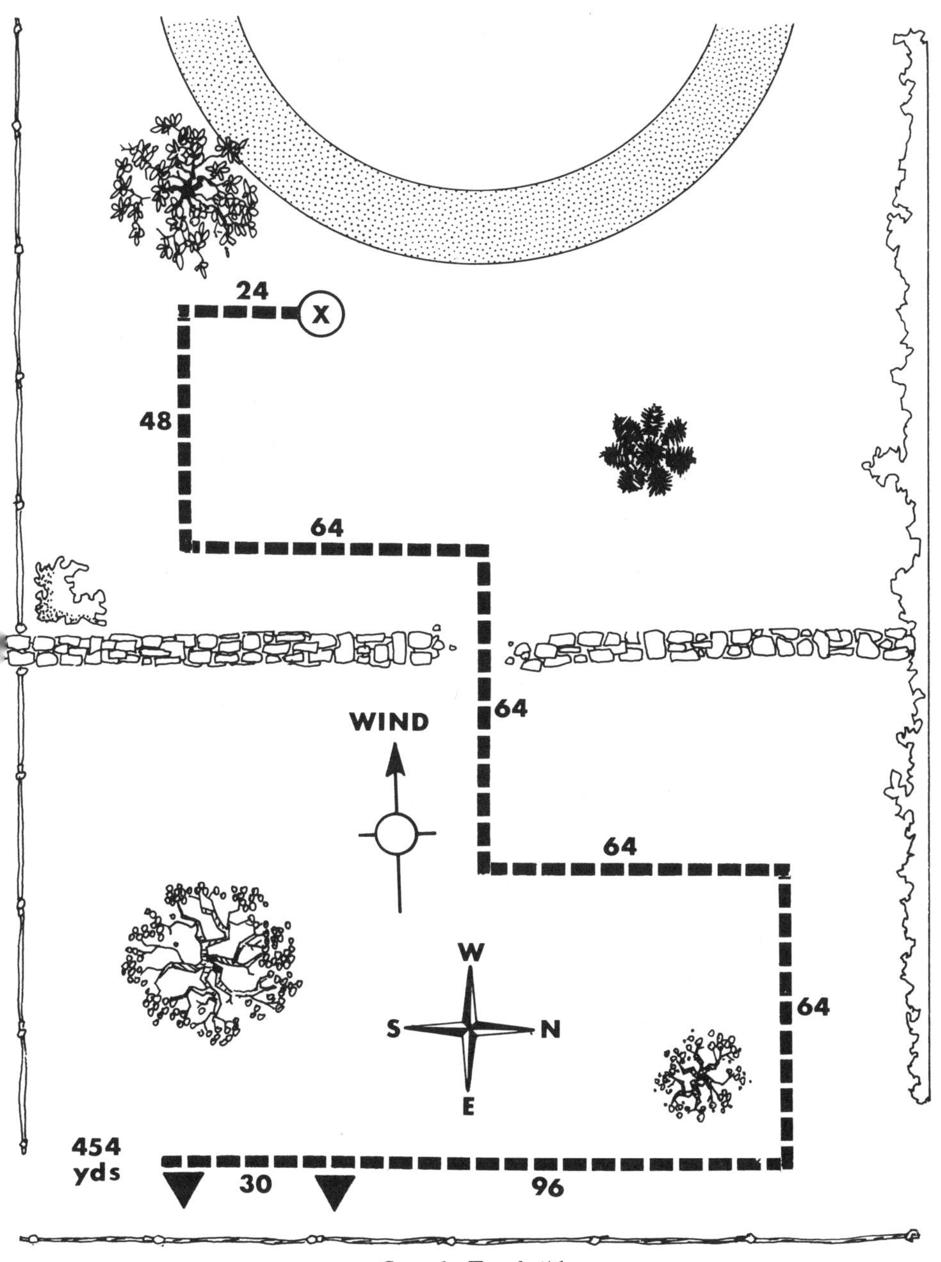

Sample Track #1

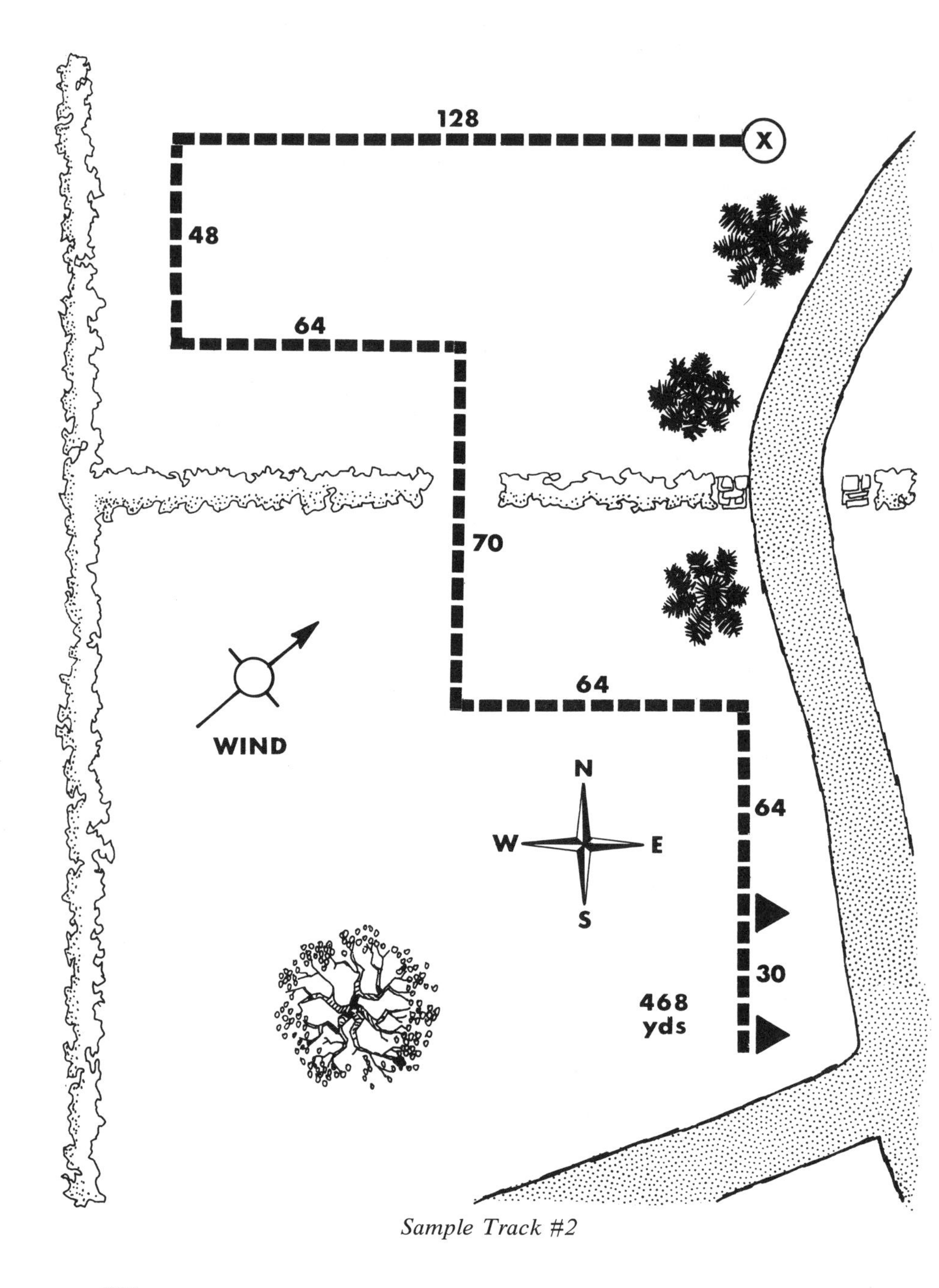

Sample Track #2

be able to perform as your next "strange" tracklayer, fine and dandy. To expand Buddy's tracking experience from here on, try to get as much variety as possible in your tracklayers, using both men and women, young people and people of varying weights. From now on, you should be able to do all your practising with "strange" tracks. You might very likely find Buddy slowing down somewhat on these new tracks, perhaps more on some people than on others. We can't ask him *why,* for he can't tell us in so many words. We can only guess. Maybe it is because he doesn't feel anxious to work today. Maybe the tracklayer's scent is not too attractive to him: it could be that it is too strong for him, or not strong enough. Perhaps there are too many different elements in its composition, making it hard for him to sort out the distinctive features to follow. Sometimes it takes longer for the message to get to the brain and register that "This is it."

This will also differ greatly from one dog to another and is something to watch out for if you're working in a group, especially if you are instructing or even just helping. We saw a very vivid example of this at a Tracking Clinic we conducted not too long ago. It happened that we were working with two German Shepherd Dogs that presented some problems. During the course of working out the problems we saw very definite evidence that one dog was getting his message from the scent of the track at about 20 yards from the first flag. The other dog was taking a good 45 yards, 15 yards beyond the second flag, before the message got through and registered and he was able to take off and work with any self assurance.

We have also found out through our experimental work that, in some cases, the success or failure of a dog working on a track can depend upon the attitude of the tracklayer and his self-confidence, or lack of it. You may think that this is getting a bit "far out," but we have seen it. A tracklayer should be very positive about what he is doing, understand what is required of him, and be able to carry out the instructions with no hesitation once he has started in the field. We can only guess why this is so, but believe it is quite likely that a much heavier scent is being dropped from the body when there is apprehension or fear present, or a loss of confidence, and this confuses the dog and he needs a much longer time to work out of the more heavily scented area. This is particularly noticeable on turns where the track layer wasn't sure as to when to make the turn, or in which direction he was to head next. Also, some dogs will work faster when they hit a fear scent, it being heavier and easier to pick up the message. But this can work adversely at turns for they might be going too fast and overshoot the turn too far, making it difficult to retrace and pick up again.

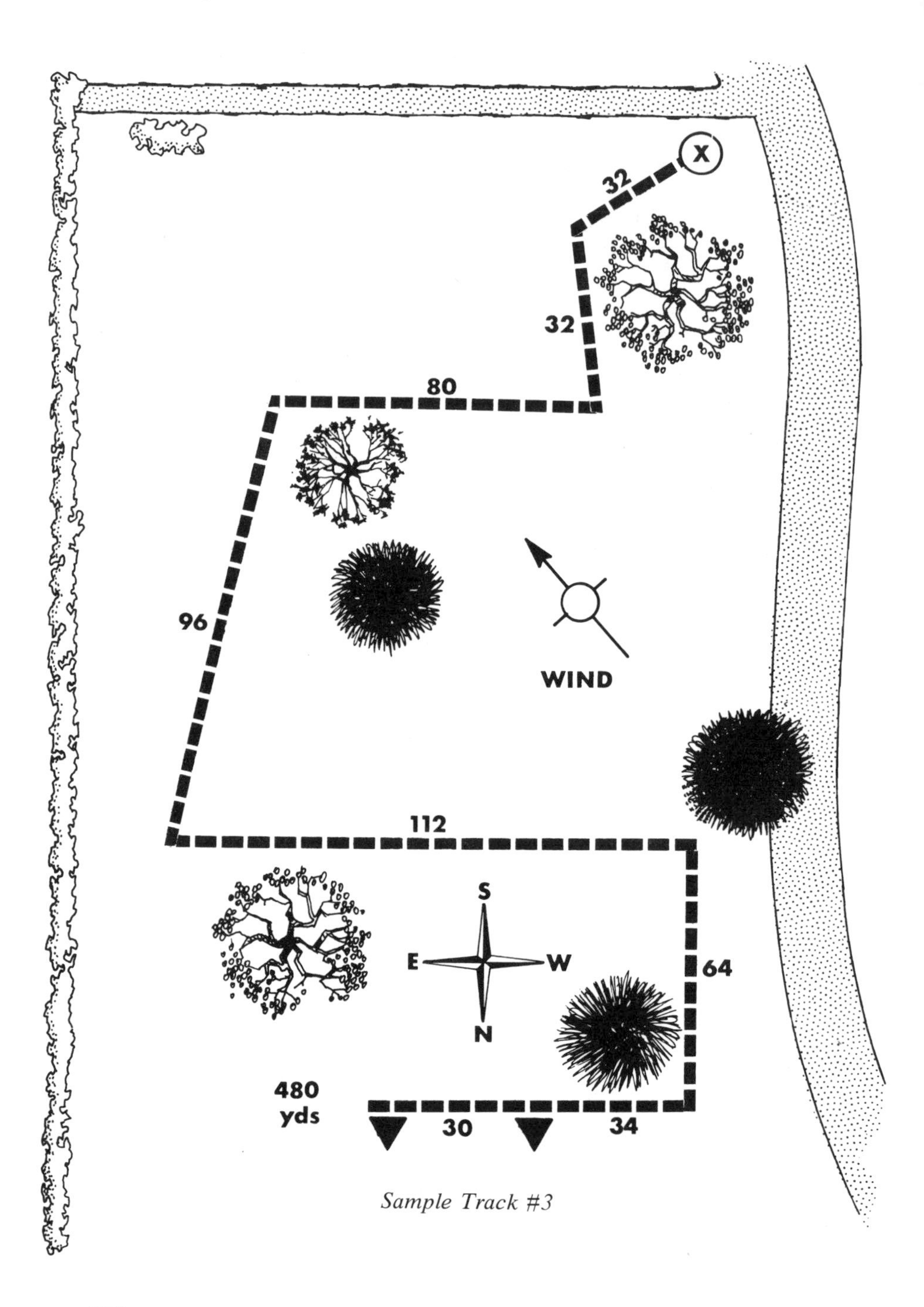

Sample Track #3

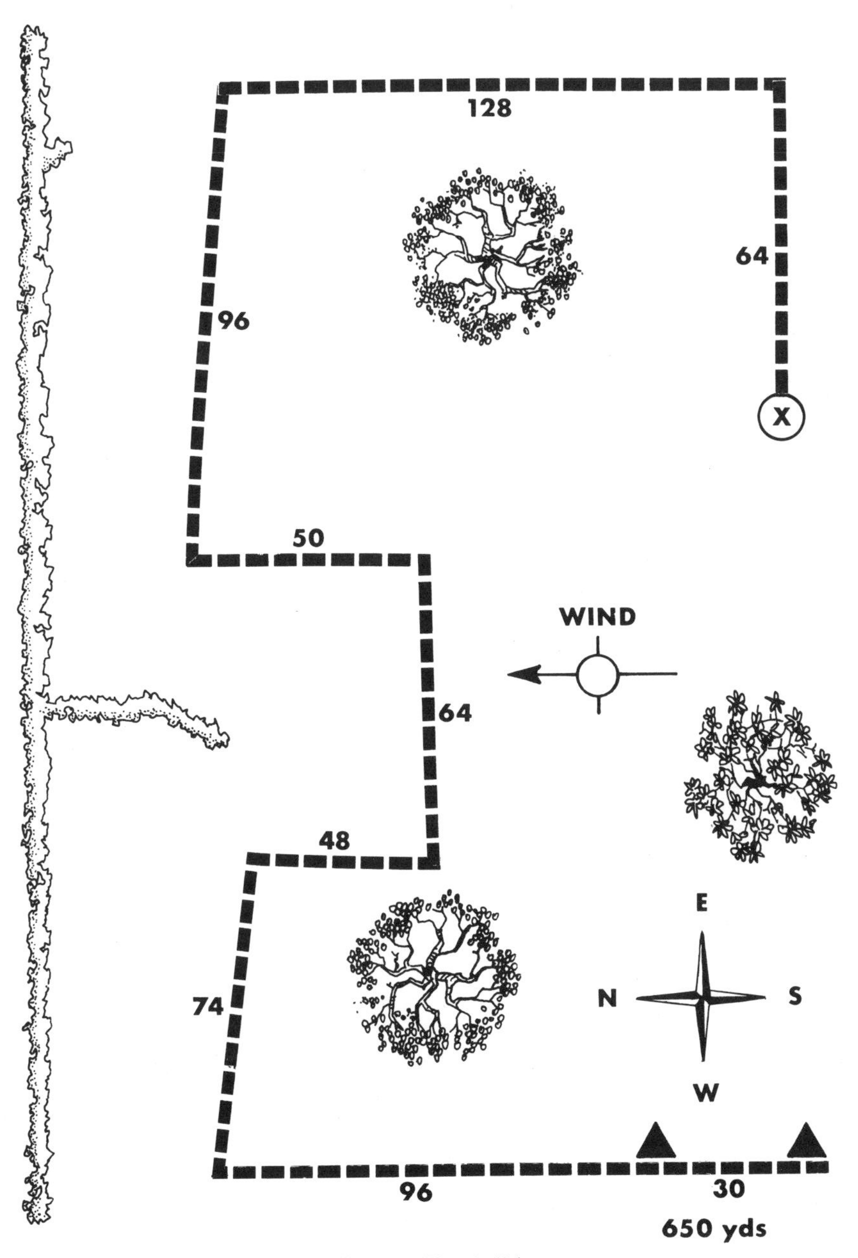

Sample Track #4

Now that you are working all your tracks on strange scent, you are ready for your next series of steps. You will begin to test your own ability now, finding out if you can really read your dog. The first step will be for your tracklayer to eliminate the first turn stake. Watch Buddy closely for his indication to you that there is a turn and he must search for it. Stay put in your tracks, facing forward as you were (for you know he was on the track and going the right direction when he passed over the ground where you are now standing), then go with him when he gives you a really positive sign that he has found the right scent again and is ready to move. As you progress and become confident in yourself, gradually remove the other turn stakes one by one.

When you start working the entire track "blind," with only the two starting flags, not knowing where the turns are or how many articles are on the track, make sure your tracklayer doesn't get any crazy idea of throwing in something different to try to "test" Buddy. We want *no* confusing situations here for either of you! Be sure you and your various tracklayers are familiar with the plotting regulations as set forth by the AKC in the Obedience Regulations and be content with a regulation track until you have that coveted "T." Also, work in as varied weather conditions as possible, and over as different locations as you can find, without violating recommended stipulations.

Certification

When you have completed several sessions of tracks such as these with satisfactory results (for *both* you and Buddy), you may be ready for certification by a tracking judge. This is necessary before you try your luck at a Tracking Test, as the signed and dated certification *must* accompany your entry. As many tests are limited to 10 or 12 entries (a full day's job for two judges to plot in preparation for a test), it is best to plan ahead as far as possible and send in your entry as soon as the test is announced if you can.

If you do not have a tracking judge in your area, or within driving distance, you might be able to take advantage of one who is scheduled to come to judge at a nearby show. No matter what the situation is, be sure you show him (or her) the courtesy of asking ahead and making the arrangement at the convenience of that judge. It usually means a full day invested by the judge, considering traveling and all that is involved. You should expect to be given a regulation track, just as you would get at an AKC Tracking Test, the only difference being that one judge,

THIS IS TO CERTIFY THAT I HAVE OBSERVED THE WORK IN TRACKING OF THE

Labrador Retriever	Missy Findaglove
Breed	Name of Dog

SZ 100100 OWNED BY John Doe, 1589 Merrymaker Lane,
AKC # Name and Address of Owner

Hometown, USA 00000 TODAY AND CONSIDER THE PERFORMANCE OF A QUALITY

FOR ENTRY IN AN A.K.C. TRACKING TEST.

February 29, 1972 — Margaret E. Pearsall
Date — Tracking Judge

Sample of a typical certification for entry into a Tracking Test

instead of two, passes upon your performance. A judge who is easy on you and does not require a regular track is not being fair to you or to other judges, and is only giving you a false impression of the performance by yourself and Buddy if he certifies you. Be sure you can do a satisfactory job before you even consider asking for a certification.

This little signed piece of paper is good for six months. If you should not pass the first test (within that 6-month period), you will need to be certified again for another entry, and each entry until you do pass. After you earn that great big "T," and we guarantee you it will be a bigger thrill than any of the other Obedience titles or even a Best in Show, you don't need anything other than a regular entry blank for entry in any future tests. We have known people who loved Tracking so much that they have piled up records of passing as many as 16 tests with one dog. That is real dedication, love and also stamina on the part of the handler. Working in the great outdoors, next to nature and your dog's own inborn ability, can't be matched in any other field of canine training. Enjoy it while you can!

AMERICAN KENNEL CLUB COPY

Dog's Catalog No. 000

N

Chart the track in solid line on graph below in two judges' books. Each judge will then be given a book and will chart the dog's course in a broken line.

Track #3

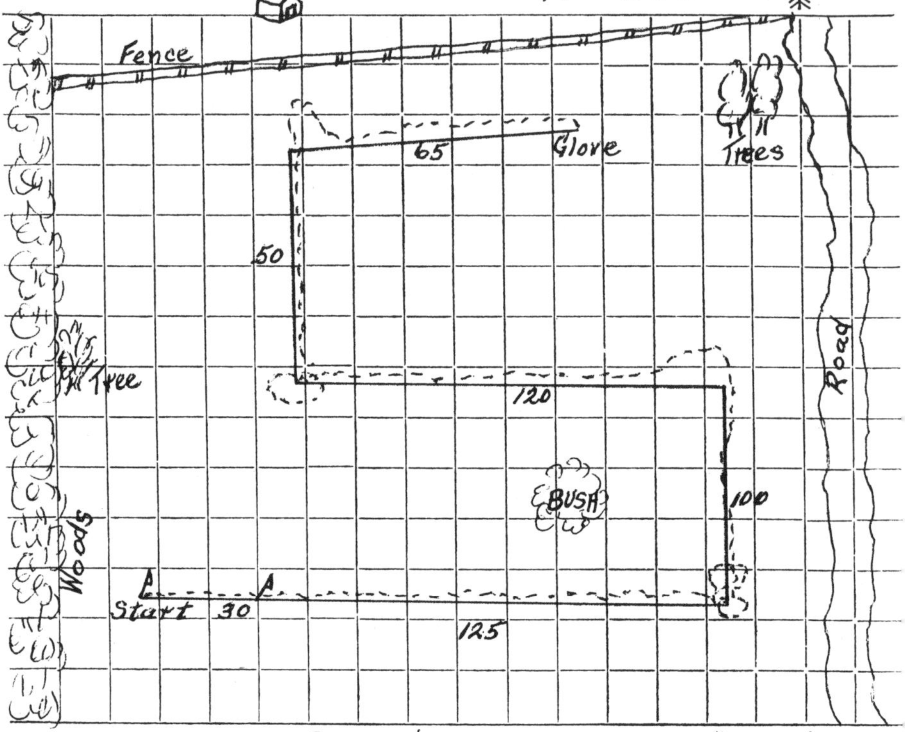

490 yds.

Passed or failed Passed

Time tracklayer started 9:00 a.m.

Dog's starting time 9:45 a.m.

Dog's finishing time 9:51 a.m.

Ground conditions Damp

Weather conditions Cool, overcast

Wind direction From South, light

If this dog is absent, mark "absent" on this page.

I hereby certify that I have judged the above dog after having read the instructions on the cover of this book and followed them out to the best of my ability.

Margaret E. Pearsall
Judge's Signature.

Sample of a worked track as submitted by judge to AKC

PROBLEMS IN TRAINING FOR TRACKING

Dog keeps looking back at handler instead of concentrating on working the track.

Refrain from using the dog's name. Limit any talking, other than what is actually needed, to a very minimum. Never point at the track or wave your arms as this is distracting to the dog; let him follow the dictates of his nose.

Dog refuses to pull on the lead. When handler tries to make him pull, he simply quits working.

Not all dogs will pull, apparently feeling that a tight lead is a correction. Some dogs really enjoy pulling when in a harness. Follow the instructions in the text for testing as to pulling; then learn to handle the lead and work behind the dog so there is no tension on the lead.

Dog only goes a certain distance, then quits if he hasn't found the glove.

This is probably due to a poor beginning, either working too short a track for too long, or increasing the distance from one drop to the next by too much, before he realized just what was wanted of him and to what extent his nose could work for him. Back up in the training and progress gradually, being sure to use the wind direction coming *from* the glove *to* the dog for invaluable natural help.

Dog refuses to retrieve any article.

To teach the dog to retrieve (although, as explained in the text, it is not a requirement in Tracking), refer to the latter part of the Novice chapter and to the Open chapter, where it is dealt with fully. The dog is only required to "find" the article. However, if you wish to make sure your dog will retrieve the articles you will be using, make the training absolutely separate from your Tracking. Let there be no association with the harness or working out in the field on a track.

Dog will retrieve the article as long as he can see it, but refuses to use his nose in searching for it when he can't see it.

The best method we have found to encourage the dog to use his nose is to find an area (as explained in the text) where there is short grass for the visual retrieve; then work into the longer grass beyond where the glove is not obvious, using the wind direction so that it is to his advantage and increasing the distance from one drop to the next very slowly, always giving much praise as he gets to the glove.

Dog loves to track but seems to lose interest on any strange scent.

Perhaps the introduction to a number of strange scents has been done carelessly or too impatiently. Remember, a dog needs a certain amount of time for the right messages to register and give him the proper clues or guides to go by. Too, each individual dog can be as different as day and night. Study more closely the section "Tracking the Stranger", dealing with the transfer to the scent of another person.

At a Tracking Test, dog is more interested in watching the judges, spectators, other dogs, etc., than he is in tracking.

Apparently, this dog and handler have done most of their practising and learning by themselves, perhaps with one other person helping as tracklayer and putting out stakes. The thing to do here is to back up in your training, rather than try to push on through with hope that you *might* strike it lucky at one of the Tracking Tests and get your "T". Go back to short straight tracks, but add some distractions, like two or three people moving around out in the field. Or add a couple of dogs once in awhile, too. Above all, make the work interesting to him. It is up to you to instill in him the desire to follow any particular scent, on which you have directed him to follow.

Dog will track and find the article, then continue on where the tracklayer went. Sometimes this happens so fast that the handler is unaware of the find, even though the dog picked it up and carries it on with him.

There are different ways to overcome this but the training should not be done out in a tracking field or while the dog is wearing the harness. The best way is to teach him that in *all* retrieves, regardless of the article you are using, he *must* return to you with it. If he does not retrieve, then teach him that he must SIT when he gets to an article and wait for you to come to him.

Dog is a large, fast worker that loves to track, but handler cannot keep pace with him, and if handler jerks on the lead, the dog quits.

Even though a fast working dog is a thrill to watch and a job to own, the pace can be detrimental to both dog and handler. Some people are not in condition physically to follow a fast dog. In addition, it adds to the likeliness of a dog overshooting a turn to an extent where he will reach the so-called "point of no return".

It is obvious that the dog must be slowed down, but it has to be done with a great deal of caution. He must not be allowed to get the idea that he is being corrected. Start out in short grass so the glove can be seen as he approaches it, working at fairly short distances. Tie the loop end of the lead with a *non-slip* knot, making a circle of it large enough to go around your waist. As you send him out, lay into the lead gradually, *no* jerking or sudden stops, and get him used to the rate of speed which is comfortable for *you* to travel. There is no time element involved at a Tracking Test, as long as the dog continues to work. I once observed a Pomeranian work a track in Massachusetts that took *one hour* to complete the track successfully, and earn its "T".

Dog loves to track but w.ll not keep in a straight line between the two starting flags.

The two starting flags are primarily placed for the handler's benefit, to assure him that the tracklayer did walk in a straight line between those points and that the particular scent in that area is what the dog is supposed to track. If you have trained him carefully and have learned to read him, you will be able to tell whether or not your dog has the scent, and whether he is working or goofing off. If he should be working, and was able to pick up the scent fast at the start, he may find that he can work it best by *not* following the footsteps, going either downwind or, in some cases, even upwind. Remember all the factors that influence scent of a track (temperature, humidity, weather in general, wind velocity, topography of the land, physical condition of the dog, of the track-layer, etc.) and then trust your dog. Don't try to force a foot track performance, as *you* may cancel completely your dog's desire to track.

Dog becomes confused very quickly when out on a track, yet "knows how" to track. Handler tries to help by pointing the direction for him to go and by trying to encourage him on by talking.

It would be difficult to imagine a worse situation, from the dog's viewpoint, than having this on the "person end" of a tracking lead! To begin with, once a dog learns how to track and goes out on his job upon being given the command, the handler's chief purpose is to watch his dog, keep the lead free from entanglements, stand still while he works out a troublesome spot or a turn and go with him when he's "on track". The handler does not know, at this stage, where the track went so it would do no good to "point the direction". This only serves to make confusion and encourages the dog to rely upon the handler instead of himself. Just whose nose is supposed to be working here?

As for encouraging by talking, have you ever tried to read a book or newspaper and have someone talking to you at the same time? It is disconcerting, to say the least, especially if the someone speaks to you by name. Show your dog the same consideration of his concentration and the importance of his job that you like to have people show to you and your interests.

Dog ordinarily loves to work, but when it comes to Tracking he seems afraid of the harness as it is put on, doesn't want to move out with it on, and cannot concentrate on the work.

Apparently there is some bad association here with the harness itself. Perhaps it is too tight or doesn't allow free movement of the front legs. Maybe a correction was made with the harness on, or a sudden snagging of the lead which, in his mind, was the same thing. It might be that it is a type that is too heavy for this particular dog.

Introduction to equipment, harness and long lead, is most important before actually beginning the work in the field. Make sure the harness is a comfortable fit, not tight anywhere, and get the dog used to walking out in the fields with it on. Even play ball or any games with him while he's wearing it. When he is used to it, add the lead, again going for a walk with him, letting him drag it behind. After this, add something to the end of it to give just a bit more drag; increase the weight a bit more later on if you wish. *Easy* does it, lots of praise and a good pleasant tone of voice to encourage and give him confidence.

Dog acts startled when low, flapping flags are used as the starting stakes, even though he loves to track.

To get him used to this situation so that he will completely ignore them if encountered again, make up two stakes about 30 inches high and with the pennant part a good 15 inches square, and of a bright color. Even though dogs are supposedly color blind, we do know they react to high intensity of color, such as a brilliant red. Put these two flags out in your yard where your dog plays and exercises, and let him work out his own problem, getting used to them at his own speed. Don't try to force him up to the flag. You will be able to tell, just by watching his actions, whether or not they worry him any more. You might even fix a supply of several different colors and shapes, giving him a variety to get used to. If you have a male and see him using a stake as a substitute for the proverbial hydrant, destroy that one before he gets into a bad habit.

Dog tracks fine at home, but becomes confused and returns to handler before the end of the track at a Tracking Test.

This is obviously due to a scarcity of available *different* areas for tracking practise, or a lack of perseverance on the part of the handler in locating suitable areas. Dogs must be familiarized with various types of terrain in order to be ready to tackle any kind of track at a Tracking Test. The more variety, the better.

On receiving the command to Track, the dog moves so slowly that the handler is unable to read him, and is not sure whether or not he is tracking. The dog often "quits", seemingly rebelling against the handler.

We could make an almost endless list here of possible causes behind such a situation. A few of the guesses (from experience) are:

1. The lead and harness may have been jerked as a correction while tracking.
2. Handler may have been impatient, not realizing that this dog needed a longer time to receive the message from his nose to his brain.
3. If the slow action only shows on tracks of a strange person, then something must have been slipped up on in the transfer.
4. Maybe an attempt was made to slow down the dog for the handler's benefit and it was overdone.
5. Maybe the dog was worked when he was already suffering from nose fatigue.
6. Perhaps he was overworked when he was actually physically tired out.
7. The handler may have given no incentive to the dog to make it interesting and fun.
8. Handler might be overly quick to scold at the slightest indication of a mistake.
9. Dog may hesitate to lead out on a track because he has a fear of being corrected.
10. Perhaps the handler is altogether too serious and does not play with his dog or allow him to have any play time on his own.

For you and your dog to become a happy and successful working combination, you *must* look at things from his point of view. When you can do this, you can figure out how to TEACH and SHOW your dog what you want him to do, in a way that he will understand. Go slowly in studying the chapter, understand it as thoroughly as possible yourself before you "experiment" with your dog, avoid having to say: "If only I hadn't done—so and so—he would have been all right". Better to be safe than sorry, for it just means unhappiness and much time lost. Do it the positive way and everyone will benefit.

Before going into more advanced work, we'd like to draw your attention to a few things to remember right from the beginning:

If Buddy should get his lead wound around a bush or entangled in some way while working a track, simply drop your end of the lead, walk up to him and straighten it out; then give him another command and pay out the lead again as he gains some distance beyond where you are. This is also quite permissible at a Tracking Test.

Be very cautious about your rate of progress, and be sure you don't go on to one step when Buddy is not yet sure of the preceding step.

Remember that scent can be carried in many directions and can cling as though it were plastered all over bushes, trees, hills, buildings, stone fences, etc. Give him a chance to check it all out before he makes up his mind as to the track direction.

There are several types of field cover that you should avoid, especially in beginning training, as you don't want to make the work more difficult than necessary. Don't put obstacles there that you can get along without, as they might induce early nose fatigue. Avoid any freshly mowed areas, any fields thick with clover (especially in blossom), fields heavy with wild onion, fields that are extremely dry and dusty, freshly plowed, infested with cactus or wild mustard seed, or areas that are near animal barns or stables. It is too difficult for a beginner dog to work through an odor that a human can smell and sort out the scent combination he is supposed to follow. Try to look at it from Buddy's point of view.

Special Supplement

TRACKING DOG EXCELLENT TEST (T.D.X.)

It is advisable that you read the regulations for this advanced work as approved by The American Kennel Club (included in the Appendix) before you start to train for it, as you need to understand what will be ultimately required of you and your dog working as a team. Your goal will be a much more practical one in that it should qualify you to be of valuable assistance in cases of lost people, especially when children or elderly people are involved, and particularly if they are on essential medications and time is of the utmost importance. You might even be called on to find someone's beloved pet who has strayed.

For such a working team to be successful and dependable, there must be an unusually close association built up between the handler and his dog. The handler should be able to "read" his dog at all times without a doubt in his mind — knowing whether he is on track, is checking out a cross track, or has completely lost the track. It is not easy to accomplish all this but, if you take it sensibly, don't push, work step by step, it can be accomplished and will be more rewarding than anything you've ever done. Remember when you got that first "T"? Just imagine how much more thrilled you'll be when you get a T.D.X.!!

You are going to have to do plenty of thinking on your own while training for this, as we can't possibly describe details of every situation you might encounter. And you must make up your mind that the surest way to train for the "X" is to return to some basic exercises, even though you have your "T".

On the credit side, the equipment is still the same, the tracking harness and a 40 ft. lead. Your first goal is going to be lengthening the track. So far, your dog has been required to concentrate on one combination of scents for only 440 to 500 yards. There's a big difference between that and 800 to 1000 yards. In addition, he has been working on a track from 30 minutes to no more than 2 hours old, usually closer to the 30 minutes. Now it will be from 3 to 4 hours old. And he will be required to find four different articles along this track, with only the last one being a glove or wallet. Quite a contrast to what he did when he earned his "T".

And then there's getting used to following a track made by people using various kinds of footwear, going through all kinds of terrain and weather, and learning that only one (the original one at the start) track is to be followed, even though he encounters other human scent left by the cross trackers.

Let us begin by going back and having your dog follow your own scent. This will make it easier for him, for you know he loves to find you. Probably one of the most difficult tasks for you will be to find a suitable area to work in, one large enough to lay a 1000 yard track in, with at least three right angle turns and each leg of the track measuring between 200 and 300 yards. Plan your track and make a map of it, so you'll be familiar with what markers you use — certain trees, telephone poles, buildings in the distance, fences, etc. Until you have successfully covered the distances two or three times (not all in one session), use a second starting flag. This will help you at the beginning.

Put your dog at a tieout stake about 50 feet before the first flag so he can watch what you are doing. As you get to the first flag, stand still while you slowly count to 15 or 20 (scent is dropping around you so it will be heavier there), then walk your planned track at a normal pace, dropping an article at about 450 yards. Continue to travel the balance of the pre-planned track, returning to your dog without coming near any part of the track and approaching him from the rear. Follow the previously recommended procedure of starting your dog on a track from the first starting stake.

When he finds the article, tell him how good he is but keep him under control, walking him on the rest of the 1000 yard track you plotted. As you reach what will be the end of it, praise your dog as you stand there a few moments. A concentration of both your scent and his in this area will help you later. Return to the tieout stake via the same offbeat track you used before to return to him. Let him refresh himself with a drink of fresh, cool water.

For your next step you will need a second article. Proceed as you did before, dropping the first one, then the second one about another 50 to 100 yards beyond that. Return as before, being sure you follow the same route as previously, including the approach back to your dog from the rear.

Start your dog on the track as you did the first time. When he finds the first article, make a big fuss over him, receive the article and keep his attention on you, getting him to smell the article he just located. Let him hold it for a bit if he wishes to. Be sure you keep your own position on the track facing the right direction. When he's calmed down a bit, repeat your command to track, let him smell the article again and urge him on so he knows there's something else ahead for him to find. If necessary at this point, you can even point in the right direction and make believe you have thrown an article ahead. Encourage him as he catches on to the idea, repeating your command only as necessary. If he seems slow to get the idea, you can even resort to guiding him with the lead or harness until the light dawns on him that you've "lost" something else out there. Remember that you're still teaching your dog what you want him to do.

Watch him for signs he should be giving you as he comes nearer the second article, encourage him with your voice and repeat your praise when the find is made. Continue on the track to the end and return as before. If you've encountered no serious problems so far, it's time to plan for a start on a track emulating that of a regular test as described in the regulation. But leave it for your next time out.

You may use the same fields and track as before, but let three or four days pass. Now you need only one flag for the starting point and a third article. You may still leave your dog at the tieout stake so he can watch you leave. At the flag, face in the direction you're going to follow count to 10 or 15, drop one article, step on it, then walk the previously planned track, dropping the second article where you had left the first and dropping the third article where you had dropped the last one before. Return in your established pattern. From now on, you will also start to increase the aging time of the track. There should be no problem here as you know your dog is already trained to follow a track from 30 minutes to two hours old in order to have earned his "T". But don't make the mistake of increasing this too fast; judge by your dog's actions what he's ready for. Don't risk any confusion — progress gradually.

Take your dog up to the starting flag and the first article. let him pick it up if he wishes to. If not, you pick it up and give it to him. Have him hold it a few seconds so he gets a good whiff of it, then give him the command to track and proceed as before. If you see that your dog is not ready for this step back up and repeat your former pattern with two flags. If all is well, continue on in your training until your dog is finding all 4 articles on a full length track. Don't be afraid to back up to where he's doing a good job before increasing the difficulty.

Along with adding to the length and age of the track, get your dog used to tracking you with changes in your footwear. Wear rubber boots, sneakers, hunting boots, old dress shoes, sandals, etc. Your own scent will still be present but following the scent of the added different material might slow down his work a little. Be ready for this and give him some extra encouragement if you think he needs it.

Before you start working in other areas so you can get a variety of terrain and different kinds of obstacles along the track, make your transfer to a different tracklayer, beginning with a partial track as you did in preparing for your first tracking test. Let us say here that we have run across a few dogs who seem to lose interest in tracking their owners. A "different" scent from another person appears to be more attractive or more of a challenge to them, and offers more self-satisfaction and a real sense of accomplishment. If you think an earlier introduction to a stranger as the tracklayer might prove more of an incentive to your dog, by all means, try it. You might even be able to do all the preceding exercises with someone else laying the track. But be sure your dog is benefiting by this and is not being confused — read him well.

Now you should be ready to tackle a new area offering more changes in terrain, maybe some gulleys, fences or stone walls, different ground cover, a small stream, some brush and a sparsely wooded area. Study the situation well, the likely effect caused by the temperature, wind, and other weather conditions. Don't push your dog; give him time to work things out, especially when he gets near brush or is through a section of woods. Remember that the scent clings to anything with which it comes in contact so it will be more difficult for him to find the track through such areas.

Watch your dog's work carefully and be ready to help him if his lead should snag on a bush, tree, fence, etc; drop your end of the lead and go right to him to help him out of his predicament, then encourage him to continue on. The rules allow you to drop the lead in case it becomes entangled but you must retrieve it and your dog must be under control all the way and never led or guided by you just as in the regular tracking tests. To the judges, this is a definite indication that they shall mark the dog "Failed". In such a case, it is actually the handler who has failed. Learn to trust your dog, your own nose will never equal his!

Your next big hurdle is to introduce your dog to cross tracks of strangers and to teach him how insignificant they are and how important the original track is. Plotting this properly is very necessary, so study the diagram (page 315) of a typical possible track to become familiar with all the requirements.

Naturally, two more people are needed to make the cross tracks as indicated, walking side by side about four feet apart and crossing the track twice at the points indicated, one hour to an hour and a half after the trackayer started. When you're working track, watch for signs from your dog that he has come upon another human scent. Allow him to "check it out" but don't let him go any distance off the regular track. Stay on the

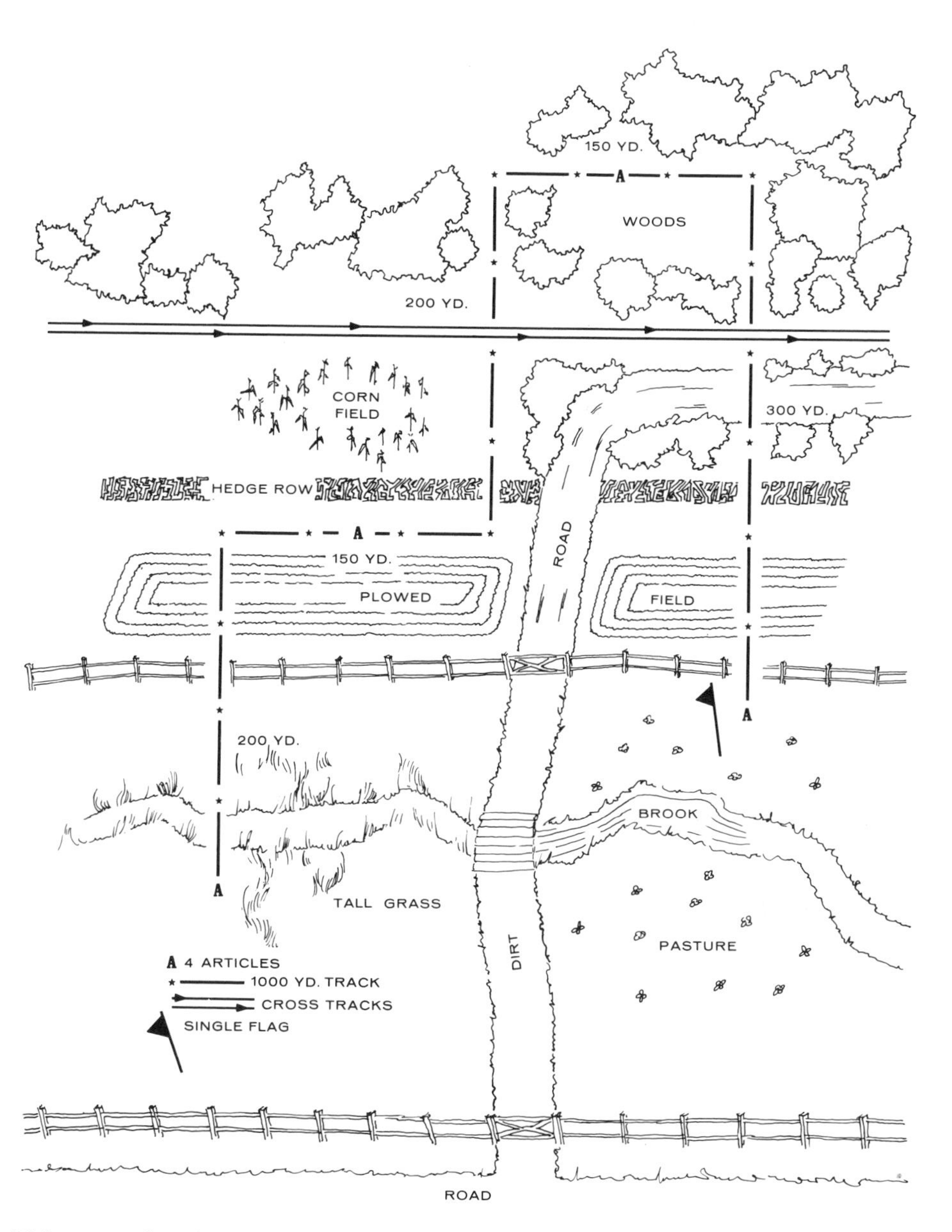

This example of a plotted T.D.X. track is not representative of an average track that one is likely to encounter. Rather, it is a hypothetical plot embodying practically all kinds of terrain, for showing what a dog should be able to accomplish in order to qualify for entry in a T.D.X. test.

track yourself and remain facing the direction the original tracklayer went. Control your dog and bring him back to the track; encourage him when you know he's in the right area and give him your track command again. Be sure *you* are right, however, and know where those cross tracks are. Don't let him check further than the length of your 40 foot lead, otherwise he'll be taking you off the track and then you're lost, too!

Repeating these experiences with different cross track people will teach you how to read your dog so you'll be ready to get judged at an AKC Sanctioned Tracking Dog Excellent Test.

In practice, use the required number of articles and remember that the last one is a glove or wallet. When your dog finds this one, always praise him and relieve him of the tension he's been under while working. Let him know "this is it" with an "OK" or similar word as you head back for the judges. Along the way, form the habit of raising each found article high above your head, especially the last one. This makes it much easier for the judges to make their decision. One last bit of caution, be sure you take everything slowly and progress step by step. Never ask your dog to do more than he's ready for and keep him eager to do the job by making it fun for him to please you with a good performance.

And now, to sum up some important things in general for you to remember:

1. Always be sure your tracking equipment is comfortable on your dog and is put on correctly.
2. Give your dog TIME at the starting flag before you ask him for a commitment on the direction of the track. (The message from the nose to the brain takes longer for some dogs than others).
3. Carry fresh, cool water and his drinking dish to each practice session and test.
4. Keep any frustration on your part out of your voice and mannerisms.
5. Don't hesitate to back up when your dog shows that he is confused.
6. Don't let your work sessions become too long or too frequent; keep them interesting.
7. Never correct your dog with his tracking equipment (lead and harness).

Good luck for success with your T.D.X. Test!

IN CLOSING this effort to try to bring you, through these pages, humane methods of training that we have endeavored to continually improve upon as we have taught and have conducted obedience training and tracking clinics and schools for instructors over more years than we care to count, I would like to leave a few thoughts with you that we consider most important:

- *Any time that you have a training problem, first check yourself and what you are doing, for 99 out of 100 times it is your fault.*

- *If your dog doesn't seem to be catching on to what you're trying to teach him, put on your thinking cap and analyze the situation from his point of view.*

- *If he is not enjoying the work, take a look at yourself in the mirror, then learn to SMILE and have fun. Give your commands with a SMILE on your face and a SMILE in your voice.*

- *Consider your dog FIRST, LAST and ALWAYS.*

- *Let your watchwords by which you train be the five P's:*
  PATIENCE
  PRAISE
  PERSEVERANCE
  PLAY
  and the PEARSALLS. Good Luck!

APPENDIX

How They Give the Commands in Other Lands:

ENGLISH	RUSSIAN	FRENCH	ITALIAN
Heel	Idiom	Allons	Sinistro
Sit	Syat,i	Assis	Siedi
Down	Lyag	Couche	Giu
Stand	Vstan	Place	In Piedi
Stay	Stoy	Reste	Fermo
Wait	Shdy	Attends	Aspetta
Come	Siuda	Viens	Vieni
Go	Idi	Vas	Va
Over	Nad Nim	Dessus	Salta
Hup	Hop	Hop	Salta
Jump	Prigay	Saute	Salta
Retrieve	Prinesi	Recupere	Portami
Take It	Vosmi	Prends	Prendi
Fetch	Hvati	Attrape	Portami
Bring	Prinesi	Apporte	Portami
Search	Ishchi	Cherch	Cerca
Find It	Naidi	Trouve	Trova
Seek	Dostan	Obtiens	Cerca
Hold It	Dershi	Tiens Le	Tieni
Give	Day	Donne	Dami
Out	Von	Dehors	Fuora
Swing	Vernis	Retourné	Gira
Back	Nasad	Arriere	Indietro
Track	Ishchi Sled	Traque	Pista

FLEMISH	DUTCH	GERMAN	SPANISH
Aan Voet	Naast	Fuss	Al pie
			Anda
			Vamos
Zitten	Zit	Sitz	Sientate
			Sentado
Liggen	Af	Platz	Echate
Recht	Sta	Steh	Parate
Staan or Biyven	Blyf	Bleib	Quieto
	Wacht	Warte	Espera
Kom	Kom	Komm	Ven or Aqui
	Ga	Geh	Ve
	Over	Ruber	. . . .
Springen	Hup	Hop	Aupa
	Spring	Spring	Salta
	Aport	Hols	Recoge
Pokop	Neem	Nimm	Cogelo
		Aport	Tomalo
	Haal	Hols	Trae
	Breng	Bring	Trae
	Zoek	Such	Busca
	Zoek	Such verloren	Buscalo
Zoek	Zoek	Such	Busca
	Houden	Halts	Sujetalo
	Geef	Gibs	Dame
			Entrega
	Uit	Los	Dame
	Los		
	Zwenk	Schwenk	Gira
Perug	Terug	Zuruck	Atras
	Speuren	Su-u-u-u-uch	Rastre-e-e-ea
			Pista

Regulations for American Kennel Club Licensed Obedience Trials

(As in effect March 1, 1980)

Purpose

Obedience trials are a sport and all participants should be guided by the principles of good sportsmanship both in and outside of the ring. The purpose of obedience trials is to demonstrate the usefulness of the pure-bred dog as a companion of man, not merely the dog's ability to follow specified routines in the obedience ring. While all contestants in a class are required to perform the same exercises in substantially the same way so that the relative quality of the various performances may be compared and scored, the basic objective of obedience trials is to produce dogs that have been trained and conditioned always to behave in the home, in public places, and in the presence of other dogs, in a manner that will reflect credit on the sport of obedience. The performances of dog and handler in the ring must be accurate and correct and must conform to the requirements of these regulations. However, it is also essential that the dog demonstrate willingness and enjoyment of its work, and that smoothness and naturalness on the part of the handler be given precedence over a performance based on military precision and peremptory commands.

CHAPTER 1
General Regulations

Section 1. **Obedience Clubs.** An obedience club that meets all the requirements of The American Kennel Club and wishes to hold an Obedience Trial at which qualifying scores toward an obedience title may be awarded, must make application to The American Kennel Club on the form provided for permission to hold such trial. Such a trial, if approved, may be held either in conjunction with a dog show or as a separate event. If the club is not a member of The American Kennel Club it shall pay a license fee for the privilege of holding such trial, the amount of which shall be determined by the Board of Directors of The American Kennel Club. If the club fails to hold its trial at the time and place which have been approved, the amount of the license fee paid will be returned.

Section 2. **Dog Show and Specialty Clubs.** A dog show club may be granted permission to hold a licensed or member obedience trial at its dog show, and a specialty club may also be granted permission to hold a licensed or member obedience trial if, in the opinion of the Board of Directors of The American Kennel Club, such clubs are qualified to do so.

Section 3. **Obedience Classes.** A licensed or member obedience trial need not include all of the regular obedience classes defined in these Regulations, but a club will be approved to hold Open classes only if it also holds Novice classes, and a club will be approved to hold a Utility class only if it also holds Novice and Open classes. A specialty club which has been approved to hold a licensed or member obedience trial, if qualified in the opinion of the Board of Directors of The American Kennel Club, or an obedience club which has been approved to hold a licensed or member obedience trial may, subject to the approval of

The American Kennel Club, offer additional nonregular classes for dogs not less than six months of age, provided a clear and complete description of the eligibility requirements and performance requirements for each such class appears in the premium list. However, the nonregular classes defined in these Regulations need not be described in the premium list. Pre-Novice classes will not be approved at licensed or member obedience trials.

Section 4. **Tracking and Tracking Dog Excellent Tests.** A club that has been approved to hold licensed or member obedience trials and that meets the requirements of The American Kennel Club, may also make application to hold a tracking test. A club may not hold a tracking test on the same day as its show or obedience trial, but the tracking test may be announced in the premium list for the show or trial, and the tracking test entries may be included in the show or obedience trial catalog. If the entries are not listed in the catalog for the show or obedience trial, the club must provide, at the tracking test, several copies of a sheet, which may be typewritten, giving all the information that would be contained in the catalog for each entered dog. If the tracking test is to be held within 7 days of the obedience trial the entries must be sent to the same person designated to receive the obedience trial entries, and the same closing date should apply. If the tracking test is not to held within 7 days of the obedience trial the club may name someone else in the premium list to receive the tracking test entries, and may specify a different closing date for entries at least 7 days before the tracking test.

The presence of a veterinarian shall not be required at a tracking test.

Section 5. **Obedience Trial Committee.** If an obedience trial is held by an obedience club, an Obedience Trial Committee must be appointed by the club, and this committee shall exercise all the authority vested in a dog show's Bench Show Committee. If an obedience club holds its obedience trial in conjunction with a dog show, then the Obedience Trial Committee shall have sole jurisdiction only over those dogs entered in the obedience trial and their handlers and owners; provided, however, that if any dog is entered in both obedience and breed classes, then the Obedience Trial Committee shall have jurisdiction over such dog, its owner, and its handler, only in matters pertaining to the Obedience Regulations, and the Bench Show Committee shall have jurisdiction over such dog, its owner and handler, in all other matters.

When an obedience trial is to be held in conjunction with a dog show by the club which has been granted permission to hold the show, the club's Bench Show Committee shall include one person designated as "Obedience Chairman." At such event the Bench Show Committee of the show-giving club shall have sole jurisdiction over all matters which may properly come before it, regardless of whether the matter has to do with the dog show or with the obedience trial.

Section 6. **Sanctioned Matches.** A club may hold an obedience match by obtaining the sanction of The American Kennel Club. Sanctioned obedience matches shall be governed by such regulations as may be adopted by the Board of Directors of The American Kennel Club. Scores awarded at such matches will not be entered in the records of The American Kennel Club nor count towards an obedience title.

All of these Obedience Regulations shall also apply to sanctioned matches except for those sections in which it is specified that the provisions apply to licensed or member trials, and except where specifically stated otherwise in the Regulations for Sanctioned Matches.

Section 7. **American Kennel Club Sanction.** American Kennel Club sanction must be obtained by any club that holds American Kennel Club obedience trials, for any type of match for which it solicits or accepts entries from non-members.

Section 8. **Dog Show Rules.** All the Dog Show Rules, where applicable, shall govern the conduct of obedience trials and tracking tests, and shall apply to all persons and dogs participating in them except as these Obedience Regulations may provide otherwise.

Section 9. **Identification.** No badges, club jackets, coats with kennel names thereon or ribbon prizes shall be worn or displayed, nor other visible means of identification used, by an individual when exhibiting a dog in the ring.

Section 10. **Immediate Family.** As used in this chapter, "immediate family" means husband, wife, father, mother, son, daughter, brother, or sister.

Section 11. **Pure-Bred Dogs Only.** As used in these Regulations the word "dog" refers to either sex but only to dogs that are pure-bred of a breed eligible for registration in The American Kennel Club stud book or for entry in the Miscellaneous Class at American Kennel Club dog shows, as only such dogs may compete in obedience trials, tracking tests, or sanctioned matches. A judge must report to The American Kennel Club after the trial or tracking test any dog shown under him which in his opinion appears not to be pure-bred.

Section 12. **Unregistered Dogs.** Chapter 16, Section 1 of the Dog Show Rules shall apply to entries in licensed or member obedience trials and tracking tests, except that an eligible unregistered dog for which an ILP number has been issued by The American Kennel Club may be entered indefinitely in such events provided the ILP number is shown on each entry form.

Section 13. **Dogs That May Not Compete.** No dog belonging wholly or in part to a judge or to a Show or Obedience Trial Secretary, Superintendent, or veterinarian, or to any member of such person's immediate family or household, shall be entered in any dog show, obedience trial, or tracking test at which such person officiates or is scheduled to officiate. This applies to both obedience and dog show judges when an obedience trial is held in conjuction with a dog show. However, a tracking test shall be considered a separate event for the purpose of this section.

No dogs shall be entered or shown under a judge at an obedience trial or tracking test if the dog has been owned, sold, held under lease, handled in the ring, boarded, or has been regularly trained or instructed, within one year prior to the date of the obedience trial or tracking test, by the judge or by any member of his immediate family or household, and no such dog shall be eligible to compete. "Trained or instructed" applies equally to judges who train professionally or as amateurs, and to judges who train individual dogs or who train or instruct dogs in classes with or through their handlers.

Section 14. **Qualifying Score.** A qualifying score shall be comprised of scores of more than 50% of the available points in each exercise and a final score of 170 or more points, earned in a single regular or nonregular class at a licensed or member obedience trial or sanctioned match.

Section 15. **When Titles Are Won.** Where any of the following sections of the Regulations exclude from a particular obedience class, dogs that have won a particular obedience title, eligibility to enter that class shall be determined as follows: a dog may continue to be shown in such a class after its handler has been notified by three different judges of regular classes in licensed or member trials, that it has received three qualifying scores for such title, but may not be entered or shown in such a class in any obedience trial of which the closing date for entries occurs after the owner has received official notification from The American Kennel Club that the dog has won the particular obedience title.

Where any of the following sections of the Regulations require that a dog shall have won a particular obedience title before competing in a particular obedience class, a dog may not be shown in such class at any obedience trial before the owner has received official notification from The American Kennel Club that the dog has won the required title.

Section 16. **Disqualification and Ineligibility.** A dog that is blind or deaf or that has been changed in appearance by artifical means (except for such changes as are customarily approved for its breed) may not compete in any obedience trial or tracking test and must be disqualified. Blind means having useful vision in neither eye. Deaf means without useful hearing.

When a judge finds any of these conditions in any dog he is judging, he shall disqualify the dog marking his book "Disqualified" and stating the reason. He shall not obtain the opinion of a veterinarian.

The judge must disqualify any dog that attempts to attack any person in the ring. He may excuse a dog that attacks another dog or that appears dangerous to other dogs in the ring. He shall mark the dog disqualified or excused and state the reason in his judge's book, and shall give the Superintendent or Show or Trial Secretary a brief report of the dog's actions which shall be submitted to AKC with the report of the show or trial.

When a dog has been disqualified under this section as being blind or deaf or having been changed in appearance by artificial means or for having attempted to attack a person in the ring, all awards made to the dog at the trial shall be cancelled by The American Kennel Club and the dog may not again compete unless and until, following application by the owner to The American Kennel Club, the owner has received official notification from The American Kennel Club that the dog's eligibility has been reinstated.

Spayed bitches, castrated dogs, monorchid or cryptorchid males, and dogs that have faults which would disqualify them under the standards for their breeds, may compete in obedience trials if otherwise eligible under these Regulations.

A dog that is lame in the ring at any obedience trial or at a tracking test may not compete and shall not receive any score at the trial. It shall be the judge's responsibility to determine whether a dog is lame. He shall not obtain the opinion of a veterinarian. If in the judge's opinion a dog in the ring is lame, he shall not score such dog, and shall promptly excuse it from the ring and mark his book "Excused—lame."

No dog shall be eligible to compete if it is taped or bandaged in any way or if it has anything attached to it for medical or corrective purposes. Such a dog must be immediately excused from the ring, and under no circumstances may it be returned later for judging after the tape, bandage or attachment has been removed.

With the exception of Maltese, Poodles, Shih Tzu and Yorkshire Terriers, which may be shown with the hair over the eyes tied back as they are normally shown in the breed ring, no dog shall be eligible to compete if it appears to have been dyed or colored in any way or if the coat shows evidence of chalk or powder, or if the dog has anything attached to it for protection or adornment. Such a dog may, at the judge's sole discretion, be judged at a later time if the offending condition has been corrected.

An obedience judge is not required to be familiar with the breed standards nor to scrutinize each dog as in dog show judging, but shall be alert for conditions which may require disqualification or exclusion under this section.

Section 17. **Disturbances.** Bitches in season are not permitted to compete. The judge of an obedience trial or tracking test must remove from competition any bitch in season, any dog which its handler cannot control, any handler who interferes willfully with another competitor or his dog, and any handler who abuses his dog in the ring, and may excuse from competition any dog which he considers unfit to compete, or any bitch which appears so attractive to males as to be a disturbing element. If a dog or handler is expelled or excused by a judge, the reason shall be stated in the judge's book or in a separate report.

Section 18. **Obedience Ribbons.** At licensed or member obedience trials the following colors shall be used for prize ribbons or rosettes in all regular classes and for the ribbon or rosette for Highest Scoring Dog in the Regular Classes:

First Prize .... Blue
Second Prize .... Red
Third Prize .... Yellow
Fourth Prize .... White
Qualifying Prize .... Dark Green
Highest Scoring Dog
in the Regular Classes .... Blue and Gold

and the following colors shall be used for Nonregular Classes:

First Prize .... Rose
Second Prize .... Brown
Third Prize .... Light Green
Fourth Prize .... Gray

Each ribbon or rosette shall be at least two inches wide and approximately eight inches long, and shall bear on its face a facsimile of the seal of The American Kennel Club, the words "Obedience Trial," the name of the prize, the name of the trial-giving club, the date of the trial, and the name of the city or town where the trial is given.

Section 19. **Match Ribbons.** If ribbons are given at sanctioned obedience matches they shall be of the following colors and shall have the words "Obedience Match" printed on them, but may be of any design or size:

First Prize .... Rose
Second Prize .... Brown
Third Prize .... Light Green
Fourth Prize .... Gray
Qualifying Prize .... Green with Pink edges

Section 20. **Ribbons and Prizes.** Ribbons for the four official placings and all prizes offered for competition within a single regular or nonregular class at licensed or member trials or at sanctioned matches shall be awarded only to dogs that earn qualifying scores.

Prizes for which dogs in one class compete against dogs in one or more other classes at licensed or member trials or at sanctioned matches shall be awarded only to dogs that earn qualifying scores.

Prizes at a licensed or member obedience trial must be offered to be won outright, with the exception that a prize which requires three wins by the same owner, not necessarily with the same dog, for permanent possession, may be offered for the dog with the highest qualifying score in one of the regular classes, or the dog with the highest qualifying score in the regular classes, or the dog with the highest combined qualifying scores in the Open B and Utility classes.

Subject to the provisions of paragraphs 1 and 2 of this section, prizes may be offered for the highest scoring dogs of the Groups as defined in Chapter 2 of the Dog Show Rules, or for the highest scoring dogs of any breeds, but not for a breed variety. Show varieties are not recognized for obedience. In accordance with Chapter 2, all Poodles are in the Non-Sporting Group and all Manchester Terriers in the Terrier Group

Prizes offered only to members of certain clubs or organizations will not be approved for publication in premium lists.

Section 21. **Highest Scoring Dog in the Regular Classes.** The dog receiving the highest qualifying score in the regular classes shall be awarded the ribbon and any prizes offered for this placement, after the announcement of final scores of the last regular class to be judged. The Superintendent or Show Trial Secretary shall mark the catalog to identify the dog receiving this award.

In case of a tie between dogs receiving the highest qualifying score in two or more regular classes, the dogs shall be tested again by having them perform at the same time some part or parts of the Heel Free exercise. The judge for the run-off shall be designated by the Bench Show or Obedience Trial Committee from among the judges of the obedience trial. When the run-off has been completed, the judge shall record the results on a special sheet which shall identify the dogs taking part in the run-off by catalog number, class and breed. When the judge has marked and signed the sheet, it shall be turned over to the Superintendent or Show or Trial Secretary who shall mark the catalog accordingly and forward the sheet to The American Kennel Club as part of the records of the trial.

Section 22. **Risk.** The owner or agent entering a dog in an obedience trial does so at his own risk and agrees to abide by the rules of The American Kennel Club and the Obedience Regulations.

Section 23. **Decisions.** At the trial the decisions of the judge shall be final in all matters affecting the scoring and the working of the dogs and their handlers. The Obedience Trial Committee, or the Bench Show Committee, if the trial is held by a show-giving club, shall decide all other matters arising at the trial, including protests against dogs made under Chapter 20 of the Dog Show Rules, subject, however, to the rules and regulations of The American Kennel Club.

Section 24. **Dogs Must Compete.** Any dog entered and received at a licensed or member obedience trial must compete in all exercises of all classes in which it is entered unless disqualified, expelled, or excused by the judge or by the Bench Show or Obedience Trial Committee. The judge must report to The American Kennel Club any dog that is not brought back for the Group exercises.

Section 25. **Judging Program.** Any club holding a licensed or member obedience trial must prepare, after the entries have closed, a program showing the time scheduled for the judging of each of the classes. A copy of this program shall be mailed to the owner of each entered dog and to each judge, and the program shall be printed in the catalog. This program shall be based on the judging of no more than 8 Novice entries, 7 Open entries, or

6 Utility entries, per hour during the time the show or trial will be open as published in the premium list, taking into consideration the starting hour for judging if published in the premium list, and the availability of rings. No judge shall be scheduled to exceed this rate of judging. In addition, one hour for rest or meals must be allowed if, under this formula, it will take more than five hours of actual judging to judge the dogs entered under him. No judge shall be assigned to judge for more than eight hours in one day under this formula, including any breed judging assignment if the obedience trial is held in conjunction with a dog show.

If any nonregular class is to be judged in the same ring as any regular class, or by the judge of any regular class, the nonregular class must be judged after the regular class.

Section 26. **Limitation of Entries.** If a club anticipates an entry in excess of its facilities for a licensed or member trial, it may limit entries in any or all regular classes, but nonregular classes will not be approved if the regular classes are limited. A club may limit entries in any or all regular classes to 64 in a Novice class, 56 in an Open class, or 48 in a Utility class.

Prominent announcement of such limits must appear on the title or cover page of the premium list for an obedience trial or immediately under the obedience heading in the premium list for a dog show, with a statement that entries in one or more specified classes or in the obedience trial will automatically close when a certain limit or limits have been reached, even though the official closing date for entries has not arrived.

Section 27. **Additional Judges, Reassignment, Split Classes.** If when the entries have closed, it is found that the entry under one or more judges exceeds the limit established in Section 25, the club shall immediately secure the approval of The American Kennel Club for the appointment of one or more additional judges, or for reassignment of its advertised judges, so that no judge will be required to exceed the limit.

If a judge with an excessive entry was advertised to judge more than one class, one or more of his classes shall be assigned to another judge. The class or classes selected for reassignment shall first be any nonregular classes for which he was advertised, and shall then be either the regular class or classes with the minimum number of entries, or those with the minimum scheduled time, which will bring the advertised judge's schedule within, and as close as possible to, the maximum limit. If a judge with an excessive entry was advertised to judge only one class, the Superintendent, Show Secretary, or Obedience Trial Secretary, shall divide the entry as evenly as possible between the advertised judge and the other judge by drawing lots.

The club shall promptly mail to the owner of each entry affected, a notification of any change of judge. The owner shall be permitted to withdraw such entry at any time prior to the day of the show, and the entry fee shall then be refunded. If the entry in any one class is split in this manner, the advertised judge shall judge the run-off of any tie scores that may develop between the two divisions of the class, after each judge has first run off any ties resulting from his own judging.

Section 28. **Split Classes in Premium List.** A club may choose to announce two or more judges for any class in its premium list. In such case the entries shall be divided by lots as provided above. The identification slips and judging program shall be made up so that the owner of each dog will know the division, and the judge of the division, in which his dog is entered, but no owner shall be entitled to a refund of entry fee. In such case the premium list shall also specify the judge for the run-off of any tie scores which may develop between the dogs in the different divisions, after each judge has first run off any ties resulting from his own judging.

Section 29. **Split Classes, Official Ribbons, Prizes.** A club which holds a split class, whether the split is announced in the premium list or made after entries close, shall not award American Kennel Club official ribbons in either division. The four dogs with the highest qualifying scores in the class, regardless of the division or divisions in which such scores were made, shall be called back into the ring and awarded the four American Kennel Club official ribbons by one of the judges of the class. This judge shall be responsible for recording the entry numbers of the four placed dogs in one of the judge's books.

If a split class is announced in the premium list, duplicate placement prizes may be offered in each division. If prizes have been offered for placements in a class that must be split after entries close, duplicate prizes or prizes of equal value may be offered in the additional division of the class.

Section 30. **Stewards.** The judge is in sole charge of his ring until his assignment is completed. Stewards are provided to assist him, but they may act only on the judge's instructions. Stewards shall not give information or instructions to owners and handlers except as specifically instructed by the judge, and then only in such a manner that it is clear that the instructions are those of the judge.

Section 31. **Ring Conditions.** If the judging takes place indoors the ring should be rectangular and should be about 35′ wide and 50′ long for all obedience classes. In no case shall the ring for a Utility class be less than 35′ by 50′, and in no case shall the ring for a Novice or Open class be less than 30′ by 40′. The floor shall have a surface or covering that provides firm footing for the largest dogs, and rubber or similar non-slip material must be laid for the take off and landing at all jumps unless the surface, in the judge's opinion, is such as not to require it. At an outdoor show or trial the rings shall be about 40′ wide and 50′ long. The ground shall be clean and level, and the grass, if any, shall be cut short. The Club and Superintendent are responsible for providing, for the Open classes, an appropriate place approved by the judge, for the handlers to go completely out of sight of their dogs. If inclement weather at an outdoor trial necessitates the judging of obedience under shelter, the requirements as to ring size may be waived.

Section 32. **Obedience Rings at Dog Shows.** At an outdoor dog show a separate ring or rings shall be provided for obedience, and a sign forbidding anyone to permit any dog to use the ring, except when being judged, shall be set up in each such ring by the Superintendent or Show Secretary. It shall be his duty as well as that of the Show Committee to enforce this regulation. At an indoor show where limited space does not permit the exclusive use of any ring for obedience, the same regulation will apply after the obedience rings have been set up. At a dog show the material used for enclosing the obedience rings shall be at least equal to the material used for enclosing the breed rings. The ring must be thoroughly cleaned before the obedience judging starts if it has previously been used for breed judging.

Section 33. **Judge's Report on Ring and Equipment.** The Superintendent and the officials of the club holding the obedience trial are responsible for providing rings and equipment which meet the requirements of these Regulations. However, the judge must check the ring and equipment provided for his use before starting to judge, and must report to The American Kennel Club after the trial any undesirable ring conditions or deficiencies that have not been promptly corrected at his request.

CHAPTER 2

Regulations for Performance and Judging

Section 1. **Standardized Judging.** Standardized judging is of paramount importance. Judges are not permitted to inject their own variations into the exercises, but must see that each handler and dog executes the various exercises exactly as described in these Regulations. A handler who is familiar with these Regulations should be able to enter the ring under any judge without having to inquire how the particular judge wishes to have any exercise performed, and without being confronted with some unexpected requirement.

Section 2. **Standard of Perfection.** The judge must carry a mental picture of the theoretically perfect performance in each exercise and score each dog and handler against this visualized standard which shall combine the utmost in willingness, enjoyment and precision on the part of the dog, and naturalness, gentleness, and smoothness in handling. Lack of willingness or enjoyment on the part of the dog must be penalized, as must lack of precision in the dog's performance, roughness in handling, military precision or peremptory commands by the handler. There shall be no penalty of less than ½ point or multiple of ½ point.

Section 3. **Qualifying Performance.** A judge's certification in his judge's book of a qualifying score for any particular dog constitutes his certification to The American Kennel Club that the dog on this particular occasion has performed all of the required exercises at least in accordance with the minimum standards and that its performance on this occasion would justify the awarding of the obedience title associated with the particular class. A qualifying score must never be awarded to a dog whose performance has not met the minimum requirements, nor to a dog that shows fear or resentment, or that relieves itself at any time while in an indoor ring for judging, or that relieves itself while performing any exercise in an outdoor ring, nor to a dog whose handler disciplines or abuses it in the ring, or carries or offers food in the ring.

In deciding whether a faulty performance of a particular exercise by a particular dog warrants a qualifying score, the judge shall consider whether the awarding of an obedience title would be justified if all dogs in the class performed the exercise in a similar manner. The judge must not give a qualifying score for the exercise if he decides that it would be contrary to the best interests of the sport if all dogs in the class were to perform in the same way.

Section 4. **Judge's Directions.** The judge's orders and signals should be given to the handlers in a clear and understandable manner, but in such a way that the work of the dog is not disturbed. Before starting each exercise, the judge shall ask "Are you ready?" At the end of each exercise the judge shall say "Exercise finished." Each contestant must be worked and judged separately except for the Group exercises, and in running off a tie.

Section 5. **No Added Requirements.** No judge shall require any dog or handler to do anything, nor penalize a dog or handler for failing to do anything, that is not required by these Regulations.

Section 6. **A and B Classes and Different Breeds.** The same methods and standards must be used for judging and scoring the A and B Classes, and in judging and scoring the work of dogs of different breeds.

Section 7. **Interference and Double Handling.** A judge who is aware of any assistance, interference, or attempts to control a dog from outside the ring, must act promptly to stop such double handling or interference, and shall penalize the dog substantially or, if in the judge's opinion the circumstances warrant, shall give the dog a score of zero for the exercise during which the aid was received.

Section 8. **Rejudging.** If a dog has failed in a particular part of an exercise, it shall not ordinarily be rejudged nor given a second chance; but if in the judge's opinion the dog's performance was prejudiced by peculiar and unusual conditions, the judge may at his own discretion rejudge the dog on the entire exercise.

Section 9. **Ties.** In case of a tie for any prize in a Novice or Open class, the dogs shall be tested again by having them perform at the same time all or some part of the Heel Free exercise. In the Utility class the dogs shall perform at the same time all or some part of the Signal exercise. The original scores shall not be changed.

Section 10. **Judge's Book and Score Sheets.** The judge must enter the scores and sub-total score of each dog in the official judge's book immediately after each dog has been judged on the individual exercises and before judging the next dog. Scores for the group exercises and total scores must be entered in the official judge's book immediately after each group of dogs has been judged. No score may be changed except to correct an arithmetical error or if a score has been entered in the wrong column. All final scores must be entered in the judge's book before prizes are awarded. No person other than the judge may make any entry in the judge's book. Judges may use separate score sheets for their own purposes, but shall not give out nor allow exhibitors to see such sheets, nor give out any other written scores, nor permit anyone else to distribute score sheets or cards prepared by the judge. Carbon copies of the sheets in the official judge's book shall be made available through the Superintendent or Show or Trial Secretary for examination by owners and handlers immediately after the prizes have been awarded in each class. If score cards are distributed by a club after the prizes are awarded they must contain no more information than is shown in the judge's book and must be marked "Unofficial score."

Section 11. **Announcement of Scores.** The judge shall not disclose any score or par-

tial score to contestants or spectators until he has completed the judging of the entire class or, in case of a split class, until he has completed the judging of his division; nor shall he permit anyone else to do so. After all the scores are recorded for the class, or for the division in case of a split class, the judge shall call for all available dogs that have won qualifying scores to be brought into the ring. Before awarding the prizes, the judge shall inform the spectators as to the maximum number of points for a perfect score, and shall then announce the score of each prize winner, and announce to the handler the score of each dog that has won a qualifying score.

Section 12. **Explanations and Errors.** The judge is not required to explain his scoring, and need not enter into any discussion with any contestant who appears to be dissatisfied. Any interested person who thinks that there may have been an arithmetical error or an error in identifying a dog may report the facts to one of the stewards or to the Superintendent or Show or Trial Secretary so that the matter may be checked.

Section 13. **Compliance with Regulations and Standards.** In accordance with the certification on the entry form, the handler of each dog and the person signing each entry form must be familiar with the Obedience Regulations applicable to the class in which the dog is entered.

Section 14. **Handicapped Handlers.** Judges may modify the specific requirements of these Regulations for handlers to the extent necessary to permit physically handicapped handlers to compete, provided such handlers can move about the ring without physical assistance or guidance from another person, except for guidance from the judge or from the handler of a competing dog in the ring for the Group exercises.

Dogs handled by such handlers shall be required to perform all parts of all exercises as described in these Regulations, and shall be penalized for failure to perform any part of an exercise.

Section 15. **Catalog Order.** Dogs should be judged in catalog order to the extent that it is practicable to do so without holding up the judging in any ring.

Judges are not required to wait for dogs for either the individual exercises or the group exercises. It is the responsibility of each handler to be ready with his dog at ringside when required, without being called. The judge's first consideration should be the convenience of those exhibitors who are at ringside with their dogs when scheduled, and who ask no favors.

A judge may agree, on request in advance of the scheduled starting time of the class, to judge a dog earlier or later than the time scheduled by catalog order. However, a judge should not hesitate to mark absent and to refuse to judge any dog and handler that are not at ringside ready to be judged in catalog order if no arrangement has been made in advance.

Section 16. **Use of Leash.** All dogs shall be kept on leash except when in the obedience ring or exercise ring. Dogs should be brought into the ring and taken out of the ring on leash. Dogs may be kept on leash in the ring when brought in to receive awards, and when waiting in the ring before and after the Group exercises. The leash shall be left on the judge's table or other designated place, between the individual exercises, and during all exercises except the Heel on Leash and Group exercises. The leash may be of fabric or leather and, in the Novice classes, need be only of sufficient length to provide adequate slack in the Heel on Leash exercise.

Section 17. **Collars.** Dogs in the obedience ring must wear well-fitting plain buckle or slip collars. Slip collars of an appropriate single length of leather, fabric or chain with two rings, one on each end are acceptable. Fancy collars, or special training collars, or collars that are either too tight or so large that they hang down unreasonably in front of the dogs, are not permitted. There shall not be anything hanging from the collars.

Section 18. **Heel Position.** The heel position as used in these Regulations, whether the dog is sitting, standing, or moving at heel, means that the dog shall be straight in line with the direction in which the handler is facing, at the handler's left side, and as close as practicable to the handler's left leg without crowding, permitting the handler freedom of motion at all times. The area from the dog's head to shoulder shall be in line with the handler's left hip.

Section 19. **Hands.** In all exercises in which the dog is required to come to or return to the handler and sit in front, the handler's arms and hands shall hang naturally at his sides while the dog is coming in and until the dog has sat in front. A substantial deduction shall be made if a handler's arms and hands are not hanging naturally at his sides.

Section 20. **Commands and Signals.** Whenever a command or signal is mentioned in these Regulations, a single command or signal only may be given by the handler, and any extra commands or signals must be penalized; except that whenever the Regulations specify "command and/or signal" the handler may give either one or the other or both command and signal simultaneously. When a signal is permitted and given, it must be a single gesture with one arm and hand only, and the arm must immediately be returned to a natural position. Delay in following a judge's order to give a command or signal must be penalized, unless the delay is directed by the judge because of some distraction or interference.

The signal for downing a dog may be given either with the arm raised or with a down swing of the arm, but any pause in holding the arm upright followed by a down swing of the arm will be considered an additional signal.

Signaling correction to a dog is forbidden and must be penalized. Signals must be inaudible and the handler must not touch the dog. Any unusual noise or motion may be considered to be a signal. Movements of the body that aid the dog shall be considered additional signals except that a handler may bend as far as necessary to bring his hand on a level with the dog's eyes in giving a signal to a dog in the heel position, and that in the Directed Retrieve exercise the body and knees may be bent to the extent necessary to give the direction to the dog. Whistling or the use of a whistle is prohibited.

The dog's name may be used once immediately before any verbal command or before a verbal command and signal when these Regulations permit command and/or signal. The name shall not be used with any signal not given simultaneously with a verbal command. The dog's name, when given immediately before a verbal command, shall not be considered as an additional command, but a dog that responds to its name without waiting for the verbal command shall be scored as having anticipated the command. The dog should never anticipate the handler's directions, but must wait for the appropriate commands and/or signals. Moving forward at the heel without any command or signal other than the natural movement of the handler's left leg, shall not be considered as anticipation.

Loud commands by handlers to their dogs create a poor impression of obedience and should be avoided. Shouting is not necessary even in a noisy place if the dog is properly trained to respond to a normal tone of voice. Commands which in the judge's opinion are excessively loud will be penalized.

Section 21. **Additional Commands or Signals.** If a handler gives an additional command or signal not permitted by these Regulations, either when no command or signal is permitted, or simultaneously with or following a permitted command or signal, or if he uses the dog's name with a permitted signal but without a permitted command, the dog shall be scored as though it had failed completely to perform that particular part of the exercise.

Section 22. **Praise.** Praise and petting are allowed between and after exercises, but points must be deducted from the total score for a dog that is not under reasonable control while being praised. A handler shall not carry or offer food in the ring. There shall be a substantial penalty for any dog that is picked up or carried at any time in the obedience ring.

Section 23. **Handling between Exercises.** In the Novice classes the dog may be guided gently by the collar between exercises and to get it into proper position for an exercise. No other physical guidance, such as placing the dog in position with the hands or straightening the dog with the knees or feet, is permitted and shall be substantially penalized even if occurring before or between the exercises.

In the Open and Utility classes there shall be a substantial penalty for any dog that is physically guided at any time or that is not readily controllable.

Posing for examination and holding for measurement are permitted. Imperfections in heeling between exercises will not be judged. Minor penalties shall be imposed for a dog that does not respond promptly to its handler's commands or signals before or between exercises in the Open and Utility classes.

Section 24. **Orders and Minimum Penalties.** The orders for the exercises and the standards for judging are set forth in the following chapters. The lists of faults are not intended to be complete but minimum penalties are specified for most of the more common and serious faults. There is no maximum limit on penalties. A dog which makes none of the errors listed may still fail to qualify or may be scored zero for other reasons.

Section 25. **Misbehavior.** Any disciplining by the handler in the ring, any display of fear or nervousness by the dog, or any uncontrolled behavior of the dog such as snapping, barking, relieving itself while in the ring for judging, or running away from its handler, whether it occurs during an exercise, between exercises, or before or after judging, must be penalized according to the seriousness of the misbehavior, and the judge may expel or excuse the dog from further competition in the class. If such behavior occurs during an exercise, the penalty must first be applied to the score for that exercise. Should the penalty be greater than the value of the exercise during which it is incurred, the additional points shall be deducted from the total score under Misbehavior. If such behavior occurs before or after the judging or between exercises, the entire penalty shall be deducted from the total score.

The judge must disqualify any dog that attempts to attack any person in the ring. He may excuse a dog that attacks another dog or that appears dangerous to other dogs in the ring.

Section 26. **Training on the Grounds.** There shall be no drilling nor intensive or abusive training of dogs on the grounds or premises at a licensed or member obedience trial or at a sanctioned match. No practice rings or areas shall be permitted at such events. All dogs shall be kept on leash except when in the obedience ring or exercise ring. Special training collars shall not be used on the grounds or premises at an obedience trial or match. These requirements shall not be interpreted as preventing a handler from moving normally about the grounds or premises with his dog at heel on leash, nor from giving such signals or such commands in a normal tone, as are necessary and usual in everyday life in heeling a dog or making it stay, but physical or verbal disciplining of dogs shall not be permitted except to a reasonable extent in the case of an attack on a person or another dog. The Superintendent, or Show or Trial Secretary, and the members of the Bench Show or Obedience Trial Committee, shall be responsible for compliance with this section, and shall investigate any reports of infractions.

Section 27. **Training and Disciplining in the Ring.** The judge shall not permit any handler to train his dog nor to practice any exercise in the ring either before or after he is judged, and shall deduct points from the total score of any dog whose handler does this. A dog whose handler disciplines it in the ring must not receive a qualifying score. The penalty shall be deducted from the points available for the exercise during which the disciplining may occur, and additional points may be deducted from the total score if necessary. If the disciplining does not occur during an exercise the penalty shall be deducted from the total score. Any abuse of a dog in the ring must be immediately reported by the judge to the Bench Show or Obedience Trial Committee for action under Chapter 2, Section 29.

Section 28. **Abuse of Dogs.** The Bench Show or Obedience Trial Committee shall investigate any reports of abuse of dogs or severe disciplining of dogs on the grounds or premises of a show, trial or match. Any person who, at a licensed or member obedience trial, conducts himself in such manner or in any other manner prejudicial to the best interests of the sport, or who fails to comply with the requirements of Chapter 2, Section 26, shall be dealt with promptly, during the trial if possible, after the offender has been notified of the specific charges against him, and has been given an opportunity to be heard in his own defense in accordance with Chapter 2, Section 29.

Any abuse of a dog in the ring must be immediately reported by the judge to the Bench Show or Obedience Trial Committee for action under Chapter 2, Section 29.

Article XII Section 2 of the Constitution and By-Laws of The American Kennel Club Provides:

Section 29. **Discipline.** The Bench Show, Obedience Trial or Field Trial Committee of a club or association shall have the right to suspend any person from the privileges of The American Kennel Club for conduct prejudicial to the best interests of pure-bred dogs, dog shows, obedience trials, field trials or The American Kennel Club, alleged to have occurred in connection with or during the progress of its show, obedience trial or field trial, after the alleged offender has been given an opportunity to be heard.

Notice in writing must be sent promptly by registered mail by the Bench Show, Obedience Trial or Field Trial Committee to the person suspended and a duplicate notice giving the name and address of the person suspended and full details as to the reasons for the suspension must be forwarded to The American Kennel Club within seven days.

An appeal may be taken from a decision of a Bench Show, Obedience Trial or Field Trial Committee. Notice in writing claiming such appeal together with a deposit of five ($5.00) dollars must be sent to The American Kennel Club within thirty days after the date of suspension. The Board of Directors may itself hear said appeal or may refer it to a committee of the Board, or to a Trial Board to be heard. The deposit shall become the property of The American Kennel Club if the decision is confirmed, or shall be returned to the appellant if the decision is not confirmed.

(See Guide for Bench Show and Obedience Trial Committees in Dealing with Misconduct at Dogs Shows and Obedience Trials for proper procedure at licensed or member obedience trials.)

(The Committee at a Sanctioned event does not have this power of suspension, but must investigate any allegation of such conduct and forward a complete and detailed report of any such incident to The American Kennel Club.)

CHAPTER 3
NOVICE

Section 1. **Novice A Class.** The Novice A class shall be for dogs not less than six months of age that have not won the title C.D. A dog that is owned or co-owned by a person who has previously handled or regularly trained a dog that has won a C.D. title may not be entered in the Novice A class, nor may a dog be handled in this class by such person.

Each dog in this class must have a different handler who shall be its owner or co-owner or a member of the immediate family of the owner or co-owner, provided that such member has not previously handled or regularly trained a C.D. dog. The same person must handle the same dog in all exercises. No person may handle more than one dog in the Novice A class.

Section 2. **Novice B Class.** The Novice B class shall be for dogs not less than six months of age that have not won the title C.D. Dogs in this class may be handled by the owner or any other person. A person may handle more than one dog in this class, but each dog must have a separate handler for the Long Sit and Long Down exercises when judged in the same group. No dog may be entered in both Novice A and Novice B classes at any one trial.

Section 3. **Novice Exercises and Scores.** The exercises and maximum scores in the Novice classes are:

1. Heel on Leash	40 points
2. Stand for Examination	30 points
3. Heel Free	40 points
4. Recall	30 points
5. Long Sit	30 points
6. Long Down	30 points
Maximum Total Score	200 points

Section 4. **C.D. Title.** The American Kennel Club will issue a Companion Dog certificate for each registered dog, and will permit the use of the letters "C.D." after the name of each dog that has been certified by three different judges to have received qualifying scores in Novice classes at three licensed or member obedience trials, provided the sum total of dogs that actually competed in the regular Novice classes at each trial is not less than six.

Section 5. **Heel on Leash & Figure Eight.** The principal feature of this exercise is the ability of the dog and handler to work as a team.

Orders for the exercise are "Forward," "Halt," "Right turn," "Left turn," "About turn," "Slow," "Normal"and "Fast." "Fast" signifies that the handler must run, handler and dog moving forward at noticeably accelerated speed. In excuting the About turn, the handler will always do a Right About turn.

The orders may be given in any sequence and may be repeated as necessary, but the judge shall attempt to standardize the heeling pattern for all dogs in any class.

The leash may be held in either hand or in both hands, providing the hands are in a natural position. However, any tightening or jerking of the leash or any act, signal or command which in the judge's opinion gives the dog assistance shall be penalized.

The handler shall enter the ring with his dog on a loose leash and stand with the dog sitting in the Heel Position. The judge shall ask if the handler is ready before giving the order, "Forward." The handler may give a command or signal to Heel, and shall walk briskly and in a natural manner with his dog on a loose leash. The dog shall walk close to the left side of the handler without swinging wide, lagging, forging or crowding. Whether heeling or sitting, the dog must not interfere with the handler's freedom of motion at any time. At each order to Halt, the handler will stop and his dog shall sit straight and promptly in the Heel Position without command or signal, and shall not move until the handler again moves forward on order from the judge. It is permissable after each Halt, before moving again, for the handler to give a command or signal to Heel. The judge shall say "Exercise finished" after this portion of the exercise.

Before starting the Figure Eight the judge shall ask if the handler is ready. Figure Eight signifies that on specific orders from the judge to Forward and Halt, the handler and dog, from a starting position midway between two stewards and facing the judge, shall walk briskly twice completely around and between the two stewards, who shall stand 8 feet apart. The Figure Eight in the Novice classes shall be done on leash. The handler may choose to go in either direction. There shall be no About turn or Fast or Slow in the Figure Eight, but the judge must order at least one Halt during and another Halt at the end of this portion of the exercise.

Section 6. **Heel on Leash & Figure Eight Scoring.** If a dog is unmanageable, or if its handler constantly controls its performance by tugging on the leash or adapts pace to that of the dog, the dog must be scored zero.

Substantial deductions shall be made for additional commands or signals to Heel and for failure of dog or handler to change pace noticeably for Slow and Fast.

Substantial or minor deductions shall be made for such things as lagging, heeling wide, poor sits, handler failing to walk at a brisk pace, occasional guidance with leash and other imperfections in heeling.

In scoring this exercise the judge shall accompany the handler at a discreet distance so that he can observe any signals or commands given by the handler to the dog. The judge must do so without interfering with either dog or handler.

Section 7. **Stand for Examination.** The principal features of this exercise are that the dog stand in position before and during the examination, and that the dog display neither shyness nor resentment.

Orders are "Stand your dog and leave when you are ready," "Back to your dog" and "Exercise finished." There will be no further command from the judge to the handler to leave the dog.

The handler shall take his dog on leash to a place indicated by the judge, where the handler shall remove the leash and give it to a steward who shall place it on the judge's table or other designated place.

On judge's order the handler will stand and/or pose his dog off leash by the method of his choice, taking any reasonable time if he chooses to pose the dog as in the show ring. When he is ready, the handler will give his command and/or signal to the dog to Stay, walk forward about six feet in front of the dog, turn around and stand facing the dog.

The judge shall approach the dog from the front, and shall touch only the dog's head, body and hindquarters, using the fingers and palm of one hand only. He shall then order,

"Back to your dog," whereupon the handler shall walk around behind his dog and return to the Heel Position. The dog must remain standing until after the judge has said "Exercise finished."

Section 8. **Stand for Examination, Scoring.** The scoring of this exercise will not start until the handler has given the command and/or signal to Stay, except for such things as rough treatment of the dog by its handler or active resistance by the dog to its handler's attempts to make it stand. Either of these shall be penalized substantially.

A dog that displays any shyness or resentment or growls or snaps at any time shall be scored zero, as shall a dog that sits before or during the examination or a dog that moves away before or during the examination from the place where it was left.

Minor or substantial deductions, depending on the circumstance, shall be made for a dog that moves its feet at any time or sits or moves away after the examination has been completed.

Section 9. **Heel Free, Performance and Scoring.** This exercise shall be executed in the same manner as Heel on Leash and Figure Eight except that the dog shall be off leash and that there shall be no Figure Eight. Orders and scoring shall also be the same.

Section 10. **Recall.** The principal features of this exercise are that the dog stay where left until called by its handler, and that the dog respond promptly to the handler's command or signal to "Come."

Orders are "Leave your dog," "Call your dog" and "Finish."

On order from the judge, the handler may give command and/or signal to the dog to Stay in the sit position while the handler walks forward about 35 feet to the other end of the ring, where he shall turn and stand in a natural manner facing his dog. On judge's order or signal, the handler will give command or signal for the dog to Come. The dog must come straight in at a brisk pace and sit straight, centered immediately in front of the handler's feet, close enough that the handler could readily touch its head without moving either foot or having to stretch forward. The dog must not touch the handler or sit between his feet.

On judge's order the handler will give command or signal to Finish and the dog must go smartly to the Heel Position and Sit. The manner in which the dog finishes shall be optional with the handler provided that it is prompt and that the dog sit straight at heel.

Section 11. **Recall, Scoring.** A dog must receive a score of zero for the following: not staying without additional command or signal, failure to come on the first command or signal, moving from the place where left before being called or signalled, not sitting close enough in front that the handler could readily touch its head without moving either foot or stretching forward.

Substantial deductions shall be made for a slow response to the Come, varying with the extent of the slowness; for extra command or signal to Stay if given before the handler leaves the dog; for the dog's standing or lying down instead of waiting in the sit position; for extra command or signal to Finish and for failure to Sit or Finish.

Minor deductions shall be made for slow or poor Sits or Finishes, for touching the handler on coming in or while finishing, and for sitting between the handler's feet.

Section 12. **Group Exercises.** The principal feature of these exercises is that the dog remain in the sitting or down position, whichever is required by the particualr exercise.

Orders are "Sit your dogs" or "Down your dogs," "Leave your dogs" and "Back to your dogs."

All the competing dogs in the class take these exercises together, except that if there are 12 or more dogs they shall, at the judge's option, be judged in groups of not less than 6 nor more than 15 dogs. When the same judge does both Novice A and Novice B, the two classes may be combined provided that there are not more than 15 dogs competing in the combined classes. The dogs that are in the ring shall be lined up in catalog order along one of the four sides of the ring. Handlers' armbands, weighted with leashes or other articles if necessary, shall be placed behind the dogs.

For the Long Sit the handlers shall, on order from the judge, command and/or signal their dogs to Sit if they are not already sitting. On further order from the judge to leave their dogs, the handlers shall give a command and/or signal to Stay and immediately leave their dogs. The handlers will go to the opposite side of the ring, turn and stand facing their respective dogs.

If a dog gets up and starts to roam or follows its handler, or if a dog moves so as to interfere with another dog, the judge shall promptly instruct the handler or one of the stewards to take the dog out of the ring or to keep it away from the other dogs.

After one minute from the time he has ordered the handlers to leave their dogs, the judge will give the order to return, whereupon the handlers must promptly go back to their dogs, each walking around and in back of his own dog to the Heel Position. The dogs must not move from the Sitting Position until after the judge has said, "Exercise finished." The judge shall not give the order "Exercise finished" until the handlers have returned to the Heel Position.

Before starting the Long Down the judge shall ask if the handlers are ready. The Long Down is done in the same manner as the Long Sit except that instead of sitting their dogs the handlers shall, on order from the judge, down their dogs without touching either the dogs or their collars, and except further that the judge will order the handlers to return after three minutes. The dogs must not move from the down position until after the judge has said, "Exercise finished."

The dogs shall not be required to sit at the end of the Down exercise.

Section 13. **Group Exercises, Scoring.** During these exercises the judge shall stand in such position that all of the dogs are in his line of vision, and where he can see all the handlers in the ring without having to turn around.

Scoring of the exercises will not start until after the judge has ordered the handlers to leave their dogs, except for such things as rough treatment of a dog by its handler or active resistance by a dog to its handler's attempts to make it Sit of lie Down. These shall be penalized substantially; in extreme cases the dog may be excused.

A score of zero is required for the following: the dog's moving at any time during either exercise a substantial distance away from the place where it was left, or going over to any other dog, or staying on the spot where it was left but not remaining in whichever position is required by the particular exercise until the handler has returned to the Heel Position, or repeatedly barking or whinning.

A substantial deduction shall be made for a dog that moves even a minor distance away from the place where it was left or that barks or whines only once or twice. Depending on the circumstance, a substantial or minor deduction shall be made for touching the dog or its collar in getting the dog into the Down position.

There shall be a minor deduction if a dog changes position after the handler has returned to the Heel Position but before the judge has said, "Exercise finished." The judge shall not give the order "Exercise finished" until the handlers have returned to the Heel Position.

CHAPTER 4
OPEN

Section 1. **Open A Class.** The Open A class shall be for dogs that have won the C.D. title but have not won the title C.D.X. Obedience judges may not enter or handle dogs in this class. Each dog must be handled by its owner or by a member of his immediate family. Owners may enter more than one dog in this class but the same person who handled each dog in the first five exercises must handle the same dog in the Long Sit and Long Down exercises, except that if a person has handled more than one dog in the first five exercises he must have an additional handler, who must be the owner or a member of his immediate family, for each additional dog, when more than one dog that he has handled in the first five exercises is judged in the same group for the Long Sit and Long Down.

Section 2. **Open B Class.** The Open B class will be for dogs that have won the title C.D. or C.D.X. A dog may continue to compete in this class after it has won the title U.D. Dogs in this class may be handled by the owner or any other person. Owners may enter more than one dog in this class but the same person who handled each dog in the first five exercises must handle each dog in the Long Sit and Long Down exercises, except that if a person has handled more than one dog in the first five exercises he must have an additional handler for each additional dog, when more than one dog that he has handled in the first five exercises is judged in the same group for the Long Sit and Long Down. No dog may be entered in both Open A and Open B classes at any one trial.

Section 3. **Open Exercises and Scores.** The exercises and maximum scores in the Open classes are:

1. Heel Free	40 points
2. Drop on Recall	30 points
3. Retrieve on Flat	20 points
4. Retrieve over High Jump	30 points
5. Broad Jump	20 points
6. Long Sit	30 points
7. Long Down	30 points
Maximum Total Score	200 points.

Section 4. **C.D.X. Title.** The American Kennel Club will issue a Companion Dog Excellent certificate for each registered dog, and will permit the use of the letters "C.D.X." after the name of each dog that has been certified by three different judges of obedience trials to have received qualifying scores in Open classes at three licensed or member obedience trials, provided the sum total of dogs that actually competed in the regular Open classes at each trial is not less than six.

Section 5. **Heel Free, Performance and Scoring.** This exercise shall be executed in the same manner as the Novice Heel on Leash and Figure Eight exercise, except that the dog is off leash. Orders and scoring are the same as in Heel on Leash and Figure Eight.

Section 6. **Drop on Recall.** The principal features of this exercise, in addition to those listed under the Novice Recall, are the dog's prompt response to the handler's command or signal to Drop, and the dog's remaining in the Down position until again called or signalled to Come. The dog will be judged on the promptness of its response to command or signal and not on its proximity to a designated point.

Orders for the exercise are "Leave your dog," "Call your dog," an order or signal to Drop the dog, another "Call your dog" and "Finish." The judge may designate in advance a point at which, as the dog is coming in, the handler shall give his command or signal to the dog to Drop. The judge's signal or designated point must be clear to the handler but not obvious or distracting to the dog.

On order from the judge, the handler may give command and/or signal for the dog to Stay in the sit position while the handler walks forward about 35 feet to the other end of the ring, where he shall turn and stand in a natural manner facing his dog. On judge's order or signal, the handler shall give command or signal to Come and the dog must start straight in at a brisk pace. On judge's order or signal, or at a point designated in advance by the judge, the handler shall give command or signal to Drop, and the dog must immediately drop completely to the down position, where he must remain until, on judge's order or signal, the handler again gives command or signal to Come. The dog must come straight in at a brisk pace and sit straight, centered immediately in front of the handler's feet, close enough that the handler could readily touch the dog's head without moving either foot or having to stretch forward. The dog must not touch the handler nor sit between his feet.

The Finish shall be executed as in the Novice Recall.

Section 7. **Drop on Recall, Scoring.** All applicable penalties listed under the Novice Recall as requiring a score of zero shall apply. In addition, a zero score is required for a dog that does not drop completely to the down position on a single command or signal, and for a dog that drops but does not remain down until called or signalled.

Substantial deductions, varying with the extent, shall be made for delayed or slow response to the handler's command or signal to Drop, for slow response to either of the Comes, for extra command or signal to Stay if given before the handler leaves the dog, for the dog's standing or lying down instead of waiting where left in a sit position, for extra command or signal to Finish and for failure to finish.

Minor deductions shall be made for slow or poor sits or finishes, for touching the handler on coming in or while finishing, or for sitting between the handler's feet.

Section 8. **Retrieve on the Flat.** The principal feature of this exercise is that the dog retrieve promptly.

Orders are "Throw it," "Send your dog," "Take it" and "Finish."

The handler shall stand with his dog sitting in the Heel Position in a place designated by the judge. On order, "Throw it," the handler shall give command and/or signal to Stay, which signal may not be given with the hand that is holding the dumbbell, and throw the dumbbell. On order to send his dog, the handler shall give command or signal to retrieve. The retrieve shall be executed at a fast trot or gallop, the dog going directly to the dumbbell and retrieving it without unnecessary mouthing or playing with the dumbbell. The dog must sit straight to deliver, centered immediately in front of the handler's feet, close enough that the handler can readily take the dumbbell without moving either foot or having to stretch forward. The dog must not touch the handler nor sit between his feet. On order from the judge to take it, the handler shall give command or signal and take the dumbbell.

The Finish shall be executed as in the Novice Recall.

The dumbbell, which must be approved by the judge, shall be made of one or more solid pieces of one of the heavy hardwoods, which shall not be hollowed out. It may be unfinished, or coated with a clear finish, or painted white. It shall have no decorations or attachments but may bear an inconspicuous mark for identification. The size of the dumbbell shall be proportionate to the size of the dog. The judge shall require the dumbbell to be thrown again before the dog is sent if, in his opinion, it is thrown too short a distance, or too far to one side, or too close to the ringside.

Section 9. **Retrieve on the Flat, Scoring.** A dog that fails to go out on the first command or signal, or goes to retrieve before the command or signal is given, or fails to retrieve, or does not return with the dumbbell sufficiently close that the handler can easily take the dumbbell as described above, must be scored zero.

Substantial deductions, depending on the extent, shall be made for slowness in going out or returning or in picking up the dumbbell, for not going directly to the dumbbell, for mouthing or playing with or dropping the dumbbell, for reluctance or refusal to release the dumbbell to the handler, for extra command or signal to finish and for failure to sit or finish.

Substantial or minor deductions shall be made for slow or poor sits or finishes, for touching the handler on coming in or while finishing, or for sitting between the handler's feet.

Section 10. **Retrieve over High Jump.** The principal features of this exercise are that the dog go out over the jump, pick up the dumbbell and promptly return with it over the jump.

Orders are "Throw it," "Send your dog," "Take it" and "Finish."

This exercise shall be executed in the same manner as the Retrieve on the Flat, except that the dog must clear the High Jump both going and coming. The handler must stand at least 8 feet, or any reasonable distance beyond 8 feet, from the jump but must remain in the same spot throughout the exercise.

The jump shall be as nearly as possible one and one-half times the height of the dog at the withers, as determined by the judge, with a minimum height of 8 inches and a maximum height of 36 inches. This applies to all breeds with the following exceptions:

The jump shall be once the height of the dog at the withers or 36 inches, whichever is less, for the following breeds—

Bloodhounds
Bullmastiffs
Great Danes
Great Pyrenees
Mastiffs
Newfoundlands
St. Bernards

The jump shall be once the height of the dog at the withers or 8 inches, whichever is greater, for the following breeds—

Spaniels (Clumber)
Spaniels (Sussex)
Basset Hounds
Dachshunds
Welsh Corgis (Cardigan)
Welsh Corgis (Pembroke)
Australian Terriers
Cairn Terriers
Dandie Dinmont Terriers
Norwich Terriers
Scottish Terriers
Sealyham Terriers
Skye Terriers
West Highland White Terriers
Maltese
Pekingese
Bulldogs
French Bulldogs

The jumps may be preset by the stewards based on the handler's advice as to the dog's height. The judge must make certain that the jump is set at the required height for each dog. He shall verify in the ring with an ordinary folding rule or steel tape to the nearest one-half inch, the height at the withers of each dog that jumps less than 36 inches. He shall not base his decision as to the height of the jump on the handler's advice.

The side posts of the High Jump shall be 4 feet high and the jump shall be 5 feet wide and shall be so constructed as to provide adjustment for each 2 inches from 8 inches to 36 inches. It is suggested that the jump have a bottom board 8 inches wide including the space from the bottom of the board to the ground or floor, together with three other 8 inch boards, one 4 inch board, and one 2 inch board. A 6 inch board may also be provided. The jump shall be painted a flat white. The width in inches, and nothing else, shall be painted on each side of each board in black 2 inch figures, the figure on the bottom board representing the distance from the ground or floor to the top of the board.

Section 11. **Retrieve over High Jump, Scoring.** Scoring of this exercise shall be as in Retrieve on the Flat. In addition, a dog that fails, either going or returning, to go over the jump, or that climbs or uses the jump for aid in going over, must be scored zero. Touching the jump in going over is added to the substantial and minor penalties listed under Retrieve on the Flat.

Section 12. **Broad Jump.** The principal features of this exercise are that the dog stay sitting until directed to jump and that the dog clear the jump on a single command or signal.

Orders are "Leave your dog," "Send your dog" and "Finish."

The handler will stand with his dog sitting in the Heel Position in front of and at least 8 feet from the jump. On order from the judge to "Leave your dog," the handler will give his dog the command and/or signal to Stay and go to a position facing the right side of the jump, with his toes about 2 feet from the jump, and anywhere between the lowest edge of the first hurdle and the highest edge of the last hurdle.

On order from the judge the handler shall give the command or signal to jump and the dog shall clear the entire distance of the Broad Jump without touching and, without further command or signal, return to a sitting position immediately in front of the handler as in the Recall. The handler shall change his position by executing a right angle turn while the dog is is mid-air, but shall remain in the same spot. The dog must sit and finish as in the Novice Recall.

The Broad Jump shall consist of four hurdles, built to telescope for convenience, made of boards about 8 inches wide, the largest measuring about 5 feet in length and 6 inches high at the highest point, all painted a flat white. When set up they shall be arranged in order of size and shall be evenly spaced so as to cover a distance equal to twice the height of the High Jump as set for the particular dog, with the low side of each hurdle and the lowest hurdle nearest the dog. The four hurdles shall be used for a jump of 52″ to 72″, three for a jump of 32″ to 48″, and two for a jump of 16″ to 28″. The highest hurdles shall be removed first. It is the judge's responsibility to see that the distance jumped is that required by these Regulations for the particular dog.

Section 13. **Broad Jump, Scoring.** A dog that fails to stay until directed to jump, or refuses the jump on the first command or signal, or walks over any part of the jump, or fails to clear the full distance, with its forelegs, must be scored zero. Minor or substantial deductions, depending on the specific circumstances in each case, shall be made for a dog that touches the jump in going over or that does not return directly to the handler. All other applicable penalites listed under the Recall shall apply.

Section 14. **Open Group Exercises, Performance and Scoring.** During the Long Sit and the Long Down exercises the judge shall stand in such a position that all of the dogs are in his line of vision, and where he can see all the handlers in the ring, or leaving and returning to the ring, without having to turn around.

These exercises in the Open classes are performed in the same manner as in the Novice classes except that after leaving their dogs the handlers must cross to the opposite side of the ring, and then leave the ring in single file as directed by the judge and go to a place designated by the judge, completely out of sight of their dogs, where they must remain until called by the judge after the expiration of the time limit of three minutes in the Long Sit and five minutes in the Long Down, from the time the judge gave the order to "Leave your dogs." On order from the judge the handlers shall return to the ring in single file in reverse order, lining up facing their dogs at the opposite side of the ring, and returning to their dogs on order from the judge.

Orders and scoring are the same as in the Novice Group exercises.

CHAPTER 5
UTILITY

Section 1. **Utility Class.** The Utility class shall be for dogs that have won the title C.D.X. Dogs that have won the title U.D. may continue to compete in this class. Dogs in this class may be handled by the owner or any other person. Owners may enter more than one dog in this class, but each dog must have a separate handler for the Group Examination when judged in the same group.

Section 2. **Division of Utility Class.** A club may choose to divide the Utility class into Utility A and Utility B classes, provided such division is approved by The American Kennel Club and is announced in the premium list. When this is done the Utility A class shall be for dogs which have won the title C.D.X. and have not won the title U.D. Obedience judges may not enter or handle dogs in this class. Owners may enter more than one dog in this class but the same person who handled each dog in the first five exercises must handle the same dog in the Group Examination, except that if a person has handled more than one dog in the first five exercises he must have an additional handler, who must be the owner or a member of his immediate family, for each additional dog, when more than one dog he has handled in the first five exercises is judged in the same group for the Group Examination. All other dogs that are eligible for the Utility class but not eligible for the Utility A class may be entered only in the Utility B class to which the conditions listed in Chapter 5, Section 1 shall apply. No dog may be entered in both Utility A and Utility B classes at any one trial.

Section 3. **Utility Exercises and Scores.** The exercises, maximum scores and order of judging in the Utility classes are:

1. Signal Exercise	40 points
2. Scent Discrimination Article No. 1	30 points
3. Scent Discrimination Article No. 2	30 points
4. Directed Retrieve	30 points
5. Directed Jumping	40 points
6. Group Examination	30 points
Maximum Total Score	200 points

Section 4. **U.D. Title.** The American Kennel Club will issue a Utility Dog certificate for each registered dog, and will permit the use of the letters "U.D." after the name of each dog that has been certified by three different judges of obedience trials to have received qualifying scores in Utility classes at three licensed or member obedience trials in each of which three or more dogs actually competed in the Utility class or classes.

Section 5. **Signal Exercise.** The principal features of this exercise are the ability of dog and handler to work as a team while heeling, and the dog's correct responses to the signals to Stand, Stay, Drop, Sit and Come.

Orders are the same as in Heel on Leash and Figure Eight, with the additions of "Stand your dog," which shall be given only when dog and handler are walking at normal pace, and "Leave your dog." The judge must use signals for directing the handler to signal the dog to Drop, to Sit and to Come, in that sequence, and to finish.

Heeling in the Signal Exercise shall be done in the same manner as in Heel Free, except that throughout the entire exercise the handler shall use signals only and must not speak to his dog at any time. On order from the judge, "Forward," the handler may signal his dog to walk at heel, and on specific order from the judge in each case, shall execute a "Left turn," "Right turn," "About turn," "Halt," "Slow," "Normal" and "Fast." These orders may be given in any sequence and may be repeated as necessary, but the judge shall attempt to standardize the heeling pattern for all dogs in the class.

On order from the judge, and while the dog is walking at heel, the handler shall signal his dog to Stand in the heel position near one end of the ring. On further order, "Leave your dog," the handler shall signal his dog to Stay, go to the other end of the ring and turn to face his dog. On separate and specific signals from the judge, the handler shall give his signals to Drop, to Sit, to Come and to Finish as in the Recall. During the heeling part of this exercise the handler may not give any signal except when a command or signal is permitted in the Heeling exercises.

Section 6. **Signal Exercise, Scoring.** A dog that fails, on a single signal from the handler, to stand or remain standing where left, or to drop, or to sit and stay, or to come, or that receives a command or audible signal from the handler to do any of these parts of the exercise, shall be scored zero.

Minor or substantial deductions depending on the specific circumstances in each case, shall be made for a dog that walks forward on the Stand, Drop or Sit portions of the exercise.

A substantial deduction shall be made for any audible command during the Heeling or Finish portions of the exercise.

All the penalties listed under the Heel on Leash and Figure Eight and the Recall exercises shall also apply.

Section 7. **Scent Discrimination.** The principal features of these exercises are the selection of the handler's article from among the other articles by scent alone, and the prompt delivery of the right article to the handler.

Orders are "Send your dog," "Take it" and "Finish."

In each of these two exercises the dog must select by scent alone and retrieve an article which has been handled by its handler. The articles shall be provided by the handler and shall consist of two sets, each comprised of five identical objects not more than six inches in length, which may be items of everyday use. One set shall be made entirely of rigid metal, and one of leather of such design that nothing but leather is visible except for the minimum amount of thread or metal necessary to hold the object together. The articles in each set must be legibly numbered, each with a different number and must be approved by the judge.

The handler shall present all 10 articles to the judge, who shall designate one from each set and make written note of the numbers of the two articles he has selected. These two handler's articles shall be placed on a table or chair within the ring until picked up by the handler, who shall hold in his hand only one article at a time. The judge or steward will handle each of the remaining 8 articles as he places them on the floor or ground about 15 feet in front of the handler and dog, at random about 6 inches apart. The judge must make sure that the articles are properly separated before the dog is sent, so that there may be no confusion of scent between the articles.

Handler and dog shall turn around after watching the judge or steward spread the articles, and shall remain facing away from those articles until the judge has taken the handler's scented article and given the order, "Send your dog."

The handler may use either article first, but must relinquish each one immediately when ordered by the judge. The judge shall make certain that the handler imparts his scent to each article only with his hands and that, between the time the handler picks up each article and the time he gives it to the judge, the article is held continuously in the handler's hands which must remain in plain sight.

On order from the judge, the handler will immediately place his article on the judge's book or work sheet. The judge, without touching the article with his hands, will place it among those on the ground or floor.

On order from the judge to "Send your dog," the handler may give the command to Heel before turning, and will execute a Right about Turn, stopping to face the articles, the dog in Heel Position. The handler shall then give the command or signal to retrieve. Handlers may at their discretion on order from the judge to "Send your dog," execute with their dog a Right about Turn to face the articles, simultaneously giving the command or signal to retrieve. In this instance the dog shall not assume a sitting position, but shall do directly to the articles. The handler may give his scent to the dog by gently touching the dog's nose with the palm of one open hand, but this may only be done while the dog and handler have their backs to the articles and the arm and hand must be returned to a natural position before handler and dog turn to face the articles.

The dog shall go at a brisk pace to the articles. It may take any reasonable time to select the right article, but only provided it works continuously. After picking up the right article the dog shall return at a brisk pace and complete the exercise as in the Retrieve on the Flat.

These procedures shall be followed for both articles. Should a dog retrieve a wrong article in the first exercise, that article shall be placed on the table or chair. The correct article must be removed, and the second exercise shall be conducted with one less article on the ground or floor.

Section 8. **Scent Discrimination, Scoring.** Deductions shall be the same as in the Retrieve on the Flat. In addition, a dog that fails to go out to the group of articles, or retrieves a wrong article, or fails to bring the right article to the handler, must be scored zero for the particular exercise.

Substantial deductions shall be made for a dog that picks up a wrong article, even though he puts it down again immediately, for any roughness by the handler in imparting his scent to the dog, and for any excessive motions by the handler in turning to face the articles.

Minor or substantial deductions, depending on the circumstances in each case, shall be made for a dog that is slow or inattentive, or that does not work continuously. There shall be no penalty for a dog that takes a reasonably long time examining the articles provided the dogs works smartly and continuously.

Section 9. **Directed Retrieve.** The principal features of the exercise are that the dog stay until directed to retrieve, that it go directly to the designated glove, and that it retrieve promptly. The orders for the exercise are "One," "Two" or "Three," "Take it" and "Finish." In this exercise the handler will provide three predominantly white, cotton work gloves, which must be open and must be approved by the judge. The handler will stand with his back to the unobstructed end of the ring with his dog sitting in the Heel Position mid-way between and in line with the two jumps. The judge or steward will then drop the three gloves across the end of the ring, while the handler and dog are facing the opposite direction, one glove in each corner and one in the center, about 3 feet from the end of the ring and for the corner gloves, about 3 feet from the side of the ring. All three gloves will be clearly visible to the dog and handler, when the handler turns to face the glove designated by the judge. There shall be no table or chair at this end of the ring.

The gloves shall be designated "One," "Two" or "Three" reading from left to right when the handler turns and faces the gloves. The judge will give the order "One," or "Two," or "Three." The handler then must give the command to Heel and turn in place, right or left to face the designated glove. The handler will come to a halt with the dog sitting in the Heel Position. The handler shall not touch the dog to get it in position. The handler will then give his dog the direction to the designated glove with a single motion of his left hand and arm along the right side of the dog, and will give the command to retrieve either simultaneously with or immediately following the giving of the direction. The dog shall then go directly to the glove at a brisk pace and retrieve it without unnecessary mouthing or playing with it, completing the exercise as in the Retrieve on the Flat.

The handler may bend his knees and body in giving the direction to the dog, after which the handler will stand erect in a natural position with his arms at his sides.

The exercise shall consist of a single retrieve, but the judge shall designate different glove numbers for successive dogs.

Section 10. **Directed Retrieve, Scoring.** A dog must receive a score of zero for the following: not going out on a single command, not going directly to the designated glove, not retrieving the glove, anticipating the handler's command to retrieve, not returning promptly and sufficiently close so that the handler can readily take the glove without moving either foot or stretching forward.

Depending on the extent, substantial or minor deductions shall be made for a handler who over-turns, or touches the dog or uses excessive motions to get the dog in position.

All other deductions listed under Retrieve on the Flat shall also apply.

Section 11. **Directed Jumping.** The principal features of this exercise are that the dog go away from the handler in the direction indicated, stop when commanded, jump as directed and return as in the Recall.

The orders are "Send your dog," the designation of which jump is to be taken, and "Finish."

The jumps shall be placed midway in the ring at right angles to the sides of the ring and 18 to 20 feet apart, the Bar Jump on one side, the High Jump on the other. The judge must make certain that the jumps are set at the required height for each dog by following the procedure described in Retrieve over the High Jump.

The handler, from a position on the center line of the ring and about 20 feet from the line of the jumps, shall stand with his dog sitting in the Heel Position and on order from the judge shall command and/or signal his dog to go forward at a brisk pace to a point about 20 feet beyond the jumps and in the approximate center. When the dog has reached this point the handler shall give a command to Sit; the dog must stop and sit with his attention on the handler but need not sit squarely.

The judge will designate which jump is to be taken first by the dog, and the handler shall command and/or signal the dog to return to him over the designated jump. While the dog is in mid-air the handler may turn so as to be facing the dog as it returns. The dog shall sit in front of the handler and, on order from the judge, finish as in the Recall. The judge will say "Exercise finished" after the dog has returned to the Heel Position.

When the dog is again sitting in the Heel Position the judge shall ask, "Are you ready?" before giving the order to send the dog for the second part of the exercise. The same procedure shall be followed for the second jump.

It is optional with the judge which jump is taken first, but both jumps must be taken to complete the exercise and the judge must not designate the jump until the dog is at the far end of the ring. The dog shall clear the jumps without touching them.

SUGGESTED CONSTRUCTION OF HIGH JUMP

FRONT VIEW OF HIGH JUMP

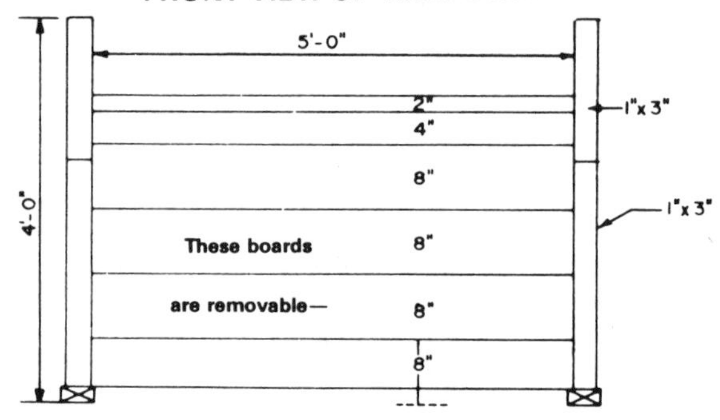

SIDE VIEW OF HIGH JUMP

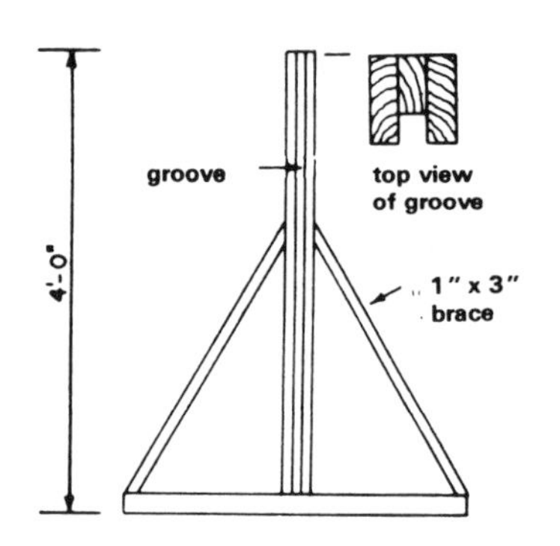

This upright consists of two pieces 1" x 3" and one piece 1" x 2", nailed together, with the 1" x 2" forming the groove for the boards to slide in.

The high jump must be painted a flat white.

SUGGESTED CONSTRUCTION OF BROAD JUMP

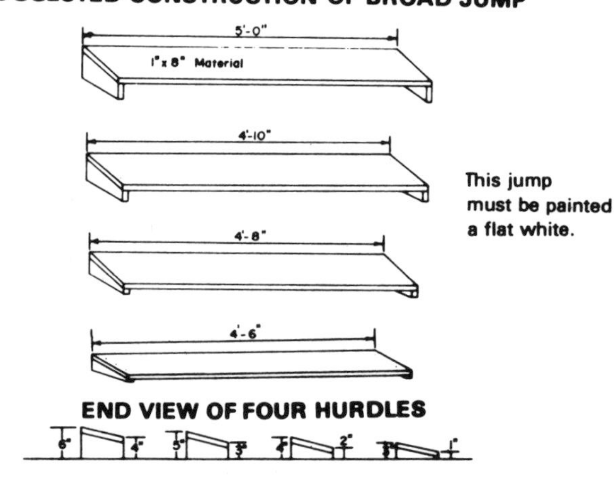

SUGGESTED CONSTRUCTION OF BAR JUMP

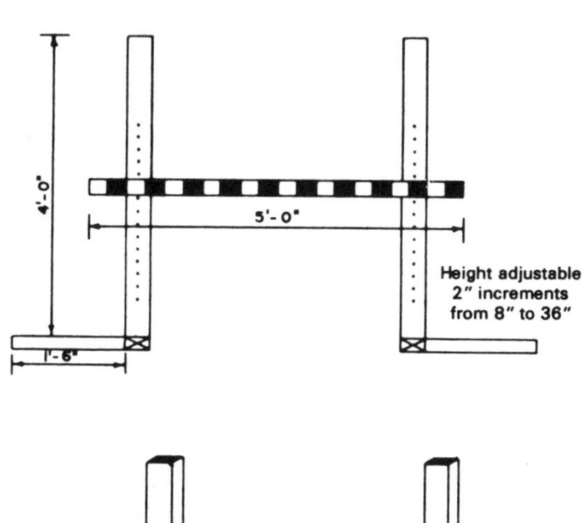

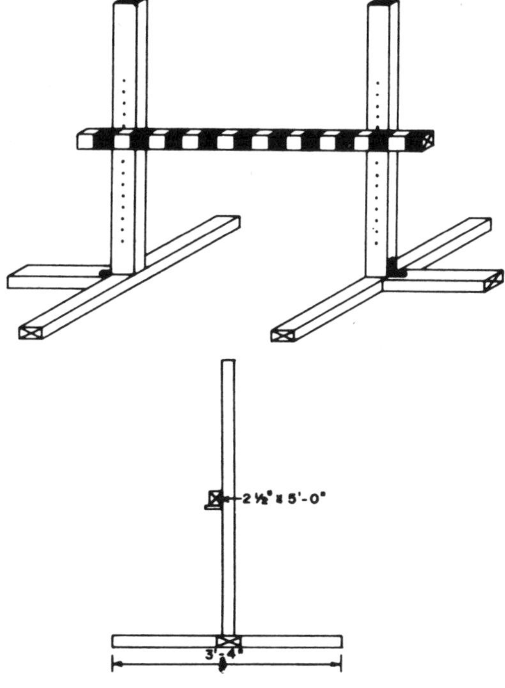

The height of the jumps shall be the same as required in the Open classes. The High Jump shall be the same as that used in the Open classes, and the Bar Jump shall consist of a bar between 2 and 2½ inches square with the four edges rounded sufficiently to remove any sharpness. The bar shall be painted a flat black and white in alternate sections of about 3 inches each. The bar shall be supported by two unconnected 4 foot upright posts about 5 feet apart. The bar shall be adjustable for each 2 inches of height from 8 inches to 36 inches, and the jump shall be so constructed and positioned that the bar can be knocked off without disturbing the uprights.

Section 12. **Directed Jumping, Scoring.** A dog must receive a score of zero for the following: anticipating the handler's command and/or signal to go out, not leaving the handler, not going out between the jumps, not going at least 10 feet beyond the jumps, not stopping on command, anticipating the handler's command and/or signal to jump, not jumping as directed, knocking the bar off the uprights, climbing or using the top of the High Jump for aid in going over.

Substantial deductions shall be made for a dog that does not stop in the approximate center of the ring; for a dog that turns, stops or sits before the handler's command to Sit, and for a dog that fails to sit.

Substantial or minor deductions, depending on the extent, shall be made for slowness in going out or for touching the jumps. All of the penalties listed under Recall shall also apply.

Section 13. **Group Examination.** The principal features of this exercise are that the dog stand and stay, and show no shyness or resentment.

All the competing dogs take this exercise together, except that if there are 12 or more dogs, they shall be judged in groups of not less than 6 nor more than 15 dogs, at the judge's option. The handlers and dogs that are in the ring shall line up in catalog order, side by side down the center of the ring, with the dogs sitting in the Heel Position. Each handler shall place his armband, weighted with leash or other article if necessary, behind his dog. The judge must instruct one or more stewards to watch the other dogs while he conducts the individual examination, and to call any faults to his attention.

On order from the judge, "Stand your dogs," all the handlers will stand or pose their dogs and on further order, "Leave your dogs," will give command and/or signal to Stay and walk forward to the side of the ring where they shall turn and stand facing their respective dogs. The judge will approach each dog in turn from the front and examine it, going over the dog with his hands as in dog show judging except that under no circumstance shall the examination include the dog's mouth or testicles.

When all dogs have been examined and after the handlers have been away from their dogs for at least three minutes, the judge will promptly order the handlers, "Back to your dogs," and the handlers will return, each walking around and in back of his own dog to the Heel Position, after which the judge will say, "Exercise Finished." Each dog must remain standing at its position in the line from the time its handler leaves it until the end of the exercise, and must show no shyness or resentment. The dogs are not required to sit at the end of this exercise.

Section 14. **Group Examination, Scoring.** There should be no attempt to judge the dogs or handlers on the manner in which the dogs are made to stand. The scoring will not start until after the judge has given the order to leave the dogs, except for such general things as rough treatment of a dog by its handler, or active resistance by a dog to its handler's attempts to make it stand. Immediately after examining each dog the judge must make a written record of any necessary deductions, subject to further deductions for subsequent faults.

A dog must be scored zero for the following: displaying shyness or resentment, moving a minor distance from the place where it was left, going over to any other dog, sitting or lying down before the handler has returned to the Heel Position, growling or snapping at any time during the exercise, repeatedly barking or whining.

Substantial or minor deductions, depending on the circumstance, must be made for a dog that moves its feet at any time during the exercise, or sits or lies down after the handler has returned to the Heel Position.

CHAPTER 6
OBEDIENCE TRIAL CHAMPIONSHIP

Section 1. **Dogs that May Compete.** Championship points will be recorded only for those dogs which have earned the Utility Dog Title. Any dog that has been awarded the Title of Obedience Trial Champion may continue to compete, and if such dog earns a First or Second place ribbon, that dog shall also earn the points.

Section 2. **Championship Points.** Championship points will be recorded for those dogs which have earned a First or Second place ribbon competing in the Open B or Utility Class (or Utility B, if divided), according to the schedule of points established by the Board of Directors of The American Kennel Club. In counting the number of eligible dogs in competition, a dog that is disqualified, or is dismissed, excused or expelled from the ring by the judge shall not be included.

Requirements for the Obedience Trial Champion are as follows:

1. Shall have won 100 points; and
2. shall have won a First place in Utility (or Utility B, if divided) provided there are at least three dogs in competition; and
3. shall have won a First place in Open B, provided there are at least six dogs in competition; and
4. shall have won a third First place under the conditions of 2 or 3 above; and
5. shall have won these three First places under three different judges.

Section 3. **O.T. Ch. Title Certificate.** The American Kennel Club will issue an Obedience Trial Championship Certificate for each registered dog and will permit the use of the letters O.T.Ch. preceding the name of each dog, that meets these requirements.

Section 4. **Ineligibility and Cancellation.** If an ineligible dog has been entered in any licensed or member obedience trial or dog show, or if the name of the owner given on the entry form is not that of the person or persons who actually owned the dog at the time entries closed, or if shown in a class for which it has not been entered, or if its entry form is deemed invalid or unacceptable by The American Kennel Club, all resulting awards shall be cancelled. In computing the championship points, such ineligible dogs, whether or not they have received awards, shall be counted as having competed.

Section 5. **Move Ups.** If an award in any of the regular classes is cancelled, the next highest scoring dog shall be moved up and the award to the dog moved up shall be counted the same as if it had been the original award. If there is no dog of record to move up, the award shall be void.

Section 6. **Return of Awards.** If the win of a dog shall be cancelled by The American Kennel Club, the owner of the dog shall return all ribbons and prizes to the show-giving club within ten days of receipt of the notice of cancellation from The American Kennel Club.

Section 7. **Point Schedule.**

OPEN B CLASS

NUMBER COMPETING	POINTS FOR FIRST PLACE	POINTS FOR SECOND PLACE
6-10	2	0
11-15	4	1
16-20	6	2
21-25	10	3
26-30	14	4
31-35	18	5

36-40	22	7
41-45	26	9
46-50	30	11
51-56	34	13

UTILITY CLASS

NUMBER COMPETING	POINTS FOR FIRST PLACE	POINTS FOR SECOND PLACE
3- 5	2	0
6- 9	4	1
10-14	6	2
15-19	10	3
20-24	14	4
25-29	18	5
30-34	22	7
35-39	26	9
40-44	30	11
45-48	34	13

CHAPTER 7
TRACKING

Section 1. **Tracking Test.** This test shall be for dogs not less than six months of age, and must be judged by two judges. A dog may continue to compete in this test after it has won the title "T. D." or "T. D. X." With each entry form for a licensed or member tracking test for a dog that has not passed an AKC tracking test there must be filed an original written statement, dated within six months of the date the test is to be held, signed by a person who has been approved by The American Kennel Club to judge tracking tests, certifying that the dog is considered by him to be ready for such a test. These original statements cannot be used again and must be submitted to The American Kennel Club with the entry forms. Written permission to waive or modify this requirement may be granted by The American Kennel Club in unusual circumstances. Tracking tests are open to all dogs that are otherwise eligible under these Regulations.

This test cannot be given at a dog show or obedience trial. The duration of this test may be one day or more within a 15 day period after the original date in the event of an unusually large entry or other unforeseen emergency, provided that the change of date is satisfactory to the exhibitors affected.

Section 2. **T.D. Title.** The American Kennel Club will issue a Tracking Dog certificate to a registered dog, and will permit the use of the letters "T.D." after the name of each dog which has been certified by the two judges to have passed a licensed or member tracking test in which at least three dogs actually participated.

The owner of a dog holding both the U.D. and T.D. titles may use the letters "U.D.T." after the name of the dog, signifying "Utility Dog Tracker."

Section 3. **Tracking.** The tracking test must be performed with the dog on leash, the length of the track to be not less than 440 yards nor more than 500 yards, the scent to be not less than one half hour nor more than two hours old and that of a stranger who will leave an inconspicuous glove or wallet, dark in color, at the end of the track where it must be found by the dog and picked up by the dog or handler. The article must be approved in advance by the judges. The tracklayer will follow the track which has been staked out with flags a day or more earlier, collecting all the flags on the way with the exception of one flag at the start of the track and one flag about 30 yards from the start of the track to indicate the direction of the track; then deposit the article at the end of the track and leave the course, proceeding straight ahead at least 50 feet. The tracklayer must wear his own shoes which, if not having leather soles, must have uppers of fabric or leather. The dog shall wear a harness to which is attached a leash between 20 and 40 feet in length. The handler shall follow the dog at a distance of not less than 20 feet, and the dog shall not be guided by the handler. The dog may be restrained by the handler, but any leading or guiding of the dog constitutes grounds for calling the handler off and marking the dog "Failed." A dog may, at the handler's option, be given one, and only one, second chance to take the scent between the two flags, provided it has not passed the second flag.

Section 4. **Tracking Tests.** A person who is qualified to judge Obedience Trials is not necessarily capable of judging a tracking test. Tracking judges must be familiar with the various conditions that may exist when a dog is required to work a scent trail. Scent conditions, weather, lay of the land, ground cover, and wind, must be taken into consideration, and a thorough knowledge of this work is necessary.

One or both of the judges must personally lay out each track, a day or so before the test, so as to be completely familiar with the location of the track, landmarks and ground conditions. At least two of the right angle turns shall be well out in the open where there are no fences or other boundaries to guide the dog. No part of any track shall follow along any fence or boundary within 15 yards of such boundary. The track shall include at least two right angle turns and should include more than two such turns so that the dog may be observed working in different wind directions. Acute angle turns should be avoided whenever possible. No conflicting tracks shall be laid. No track shall cross any body of water. No part of any track shall be laid within 75 yards of any other track. In the case of two tracks going in opposite directions, however, the first flags of these tracks may be as close as 50 yards from each other. The judges shall make sure that the track is no less than 440 yards nor more than 500 yards and that the tracklayer is a stranger to the dog in each case. It is the judges' responsibility to instruct the tracklayer to insure that each track is properly laid and that each tracklayer carries a copy of the chart with him in laying the track. The judges must approve the article to be left at the end of each track, must make sure that it is thoroughly impregnated with the tracklayer's scent, and must see that the tracklayer's shoes meet the requirements of these regulations.

There is no time limit provided the dog is working, but a dog that is off the track and is clearly not working should not be given any minimum time, but should be marked Failed. The handler may not be given any assistance by the judges or anyone else. If a dog is not tracking it shall not be marked Passed even though it may have found the article. In case of unforseen circumstances, the judges may in rare cases, at their own discretion, give a handler and his dog a second chance on a new track. A track for each dog entered shall be plotted on the ground by one or both judges not less than one day before the test, the track being marked by flags which the tracklayer can follow readily on the day of the test. A chart of each track shall be made up in duplicate, showing the approximate length in yards of each leg, and major landmarks and boundaries, if any. Both of these charts shall be marked at the time the dog is tracking, one by each of the judges, so as to show the approximate course followed by the dog. The judges shall sign their charts and show on each whether the dog "Passed" or "Failed," the time the tracklayer started, the time the dog started and finished tracking, a brief description of ground, wind and weather conditions, the wind direction, and a note of any steep hills or valleys.

The Club or Tracking Test Secretary, after a licensed or member tracking test, shall forward the two copies of the judges' marked charts, the entry forms with certifications attached, and a marked and certified copy of the catalog pages or sheets listing the dogs entered in the tracking test, to The American Kennel Club so as to reach its office within seven days after the close of the test.

CHAPTER 7A

Section 1. **Tracking Dog Excellent Test.** This test shall be for dogs that have earned the title T.D., and must be judged by two judges. The maximum number of dogs two judges may be asked to test in one day is five. Dogs that have earned this title T.D.X. may continue to compete. This test cannot be given at a dog show or obedience trial. In the event of an unforeseen emergency, the duration of this test may be more than one day but within a 15 day period after the original date provided that the extension of the test is satisfactory to the exhibitors affected.

Section 2. **T.D.X.** The American Kennel Club will issue a Tracking Dog Excellent certificate to a registered dog, and will permit the use of the letters "T.D.X." after the name of each dog that has been certified by the two judges to have passed a licensed or member club. Tracking Dog Excellent Test in which at least two dogs actually participated.

The owner of the dog holding the "U.D." and "T.D.X." titles may use the letters "U.T.D.X." after the name ofthe dog, signifying "Utility Dog Tracker Excellent."

Section 3. **The T.D.X. Track.** The Tracking Dog Excellent Test must be performed with dog on leash. The length of the track shall not be less than 800 yards nor more than 1000 yards. The scent shall be not less than three hours nor more than four hours old and must be that of a stranger. The actual track, laid earlier, shall be crossed at two widely separated places by more recent tracks.

Four personal dissimilar articles, well impregnated with the tracklayer's scent, will be dropped by the tracklayer at designated points directly on the track. The articles must be approved in advance by the judges.

At a point more than 75 yards from the start of the track the tracklayer will be given a map of the track. He will place one article at the starting flag then follow the track which has been staked out with flags, a day or more earlier. Along the way of the actual track he will collect all but the first flag. He will drop the remaining three articles directly on the track at points designated on the map. The articles shall not be dropped within 30 yards of a turn or cross track. After dropping the last article the tracklayer will proceed straight ahead for at least 30 yards and then leave the field.

One hour to one hour and a half after the actual tracklaying has been completed the judges will instruct two people, strangers to the dog, to start from a given point, walking side by side about four feet apart, and follow each of the two cross tracks which have been staked out with flags a day or more earlier, collecting all of the flags along the way.

While tracking the dog shall wear a harness to which is attached a leash 20 feet to 40 feet in length. To avoid entanglement the leash may be dropped during the tracking but must be retrieved. The dog must be under the handler's control at all times. At the start of the track the dog will be given ample time to take the scent and begin tracking. No guidance of any kind is to be employed by the handler while starting the dog on the track. Since there is no second flag in this test, the handler must wait for the dog to commit itself before he leaves the starting flag. Once the handler has left the starting flag the test has begun and shall not be restarted. The handler may pick up the article at the starting flag and may use it, as well as subsequent articles, to give the scent to the dog while on the track. Where obstacles, barriers or terrain demand, a handler may aid the dog, but any leading or guiding of the dog shall constitute grounds for calling the handler off and marking the dog "Failed."

Should the dog follow one of the cross tracks for distance of more than 50 yards, the dog is to be marked "Failed." The dog must follow the track and either indicate or retrieve the second, third and fourth articles. In order for the dog to be marked "Passed," these articles must be presented to the judge, when the track is completed.

Section 4. **Essentials for a T.D.X. Test,** AKC tracking judges may be approved to judge this test. Such judges must have experience with advanced tracking and be familiar with conditions that present themselves when a dog is reguired to work a scent trail. Scent conditions such as weather, age, terrain, ground cover changes, natural as well as man-made obstacles, cross tracks, streams and roads must be taken into consideration when judging advanced tracking.

Both judges must personally lay out each track a day or so before the test in order to be completely familiar with the location of the track, landmarks and ground conditions. The track shall be not less than 800 yards nor more than 1000 yards and shall contain at least three turns and two widely separated double cross tracks. The cross tracks shall intersect the actual track at right angles. All types of terrain and cover, including gulleys, plowed land, woods and vegetation of any density may be used. Natural obstacles such as streams or man-made obstacles such as hedgerows fences, bridges, or lightly traveled roads may also be used. No portion of any track, including the tracklayer's escape route or the escape route of the cross tracklayers, may be within 75 yards of any other track.

It is the judges' responsibility to instruct the tracklayer and the cross tracklayers so as to insure that each track is properly laid and that they each carry a copy of the chart with them while laying track.

For each dog entered a track shall be plotted on the grounds by both of the judges, not less than one day before the test, the track being marked by flags which the tracklayer can readily follow on the day of the test. A chart of each track shall be made up in duplicate, showing the approximate length in yards of each leg, major landmarks and boundaries, and clearly defined points for dropping the three remaining articles. Both of these charts shall be marked at the time the dog is tracking, one by each of the judges, to show the approximate course followed by the dog. The judges shall sign their charts and show on each whether the dog "Passed" or "Failed." The judges shall also mark the time the tracklayer started, the time the cross tracklayers started, the times the dog started and finished tracking, a brief description of ground, weather conditions and wind direction.

Four personal dissimilar articles shall be dropped on the track. Only the last article may be a glove or wallet. The first article shall be placed at the starting flag and shall be clearly visible to the handler. The 2nd, 3rd, and 4th articles shall be dropped directly on the track at wide intervals and should not be visible to the handler from a distance of 20 feet. The drops shall be clearly marked on the chart and shall not be within 30 yards of a turn or a cross track. Articles must be small enough to be easily carried by the handler while completing the track. The judges must approve the four articles to be used making sure that they have been thoroughly impregnated with the tracklayer's scent. The tracklayer must wear his own shoes which may be of any material. Particular attention should be paid to instructing cross tracklayers and to keeping them away from the start of the actual track.

There is no time limit provided the dog is working. A dog that clearly is not working should not be given any minimum time, but should be marked "Failed." The handler may not be given any assistance by the judges or anyone else. If the dog is not tracking, it shall not be marked "Passed," even though it may find the articles.

In the event of peculiar or unusual circumstances, the judges may, at their own discretion, in rare cases, give a handler and dog a second chance on a new track.

Upon the completion of a licensed or member Tracking Dog Excellent Test, the secretary of the club shall forward to The American Kennel Club, so as to reach the AKC office within seven days after the close of the test, the following:

a. Two copies of the judges' marked charts.

b. Entry forms.

c. Marked and certified copy of the catalog pages or sheets listing dogs entered in this test.

CHAPTER 8

NONREGULAR CLASSES

Section 1. Graduate Novice Class. The Graduate Novice class shall be for C.D. dogs that have not been certified by a judge to have received a qualifying score toward a C.D.X. title prior to the closing of entries. Dogs in this class may be handled by the owner or any other person. A person may handle more than one dog in this class, but each dog must have a separate handler for the Long Sit and Long Down exercises when judged in the same group. Dogs entered in Graduate Novice may also be entered in one of the Open classes.

Performances and judging shall be as in the Regular classes, except that the Figure 8 is omitted from the Heel on Leash exercise. The exercises, maximum scores and order of judging in the Graduate Novice class are:

1. Heel on Leash (no Figure 8)	30
2. Stand for Examination	30
3. Open Heel Free	40
4. Open Drop on Recall	40
5. Open Long Sit	30
6. Open Long Down	30
Maximum Total Score	200

Section 2. **Brace Class.** The Brace class shall be for braces of dogs of the same breed that are eligible under these Regulations and capable of performing the Novice exercises. The dogs need not be owned by the same person, but must be handled by one handler. Dogs may be shown unattached or coupled, the coupling device to be not less than six inches over-all length; whichever method is used must be continued througout all exercises. A separate Official Entry Form must be completed in full for each dog entered.

Exercises, performances and judging shall be as in the Novice class. The brace should work in unison at all times. Either or both dogs in a brace may be entered in another class or classes at the same trial.

Section 3. **Veterans Class.** The Veterans class shall be for dogs that have an obedience title and are eight or more years old prior to the closing of entries. The exercises shall be performed and judged as in the Novice class. Dogs entered in the Veterans class may not be entered in any Regular class.

Section 4. **Versatility Class.** The Versatility class shall be for dogs that are eligible under these Regulations and capable of performing the Utility exercises. Owners may enter more than one dog. Dogs in this class may be handled by the owner or any other person, and may be entered in another class or classes at the same trial.

Six exercises will be performed, two each from the Novice, Open and Utility classes, except that there will be no Group exercises. The exercises will be performed and judged as in the Regular classes. For the purpose of this class, Scent Discrimination articles number 1 and number 2 shall be considered as a single Utility exercise. The exercises to be performed by each dog will be determined by the handlers drawing one of a set of cards listing combinations of the six exercises totaling 200 points. These cards will be furnished by the trial-giving clubs. Each handler shall provide a dumbbell, Scent Discrimination articles and Directed Retrieve gloves.

Novice exercise No. 1	25
Novice exercise No. 2	25
Open exercise No. 1	35
Open exercise No. 2	35
Utility exercise No. 1	40
Utility exercise No. 2	40
Maximum Total Score	200

Section 5. **Team Class.** The Team class shall be for teams of any four dogs that are eligible under these Regulations. Five dogs may be entered, one to be considered an alternate for which no entry fee shall be required. However, the same four dogs must perform all exercises. Dogs need not be owner-handled, need not be entered in another class at the same trial, and need not have obedience titles. A separate Official Entry Form must be completed in full for each dog entered.

There shall be two judges, one of whom will call commands while the other scores the teams' performances. The teams will be judged one at a time, except for the Long Sit and Long Down exercises which shall be done with no more than four teams (16 dogs) in the ring.

The dogs on a team will perform the exercises simultaneously and will be judged as specified for the Novice class, except that a Drop on Recall will be used in place of the Recall exercise. In all exercises except the Drop on Recall, the teams have the option of executing the judge's commands on the team captain's repeat of the command.

In the Figure Eight portion of the Heel on Leash exercise, five stewards will be used. The stewards shall stand 8 feet apart in a straight line. One dog and his handler shall stand between two stewards, all members of the team facing in the same direction. On orders from the judge, the team shall perform the Figure Eight, each handler starting around the steward on his left and circling only the two stewards between whom he had been standing.

In the Drop on Recall exercise, the handlers will leave their dogs simultaneously on command of the judge. The dogs shall be called or signalled in, one at a time, on a separate command from the judge to each handler. The handler shall, without any additional command from the judge, command or signal his dog to drop at a spot mid-way between the line of dogs and the handlers. Each dog shall remain in the Down position until all four have been called and dropped, whereupon the judge shall give the command to call the dogs, which shall be called or signalled simultaneously. The finish shall be done in unison on command from the judge.

Section 6. **Team Class, Scoring.** Scoring of the Team class shall be based on the performance of the dogs and handlers individually plus team precision and coordination. Each dog and handler will be scored against the customary maximum, for a team total of 800 maximum available points. Individual dog's scores need not be recorded. The exercises and maximum scores are:

1. Heel on Leash	160
2. Stand for Examination	120
3. Heel Free	160
4. Drop on Recall	120
5. Long Sit	120
6. Long Down	120
Maximum Total Score	800

BIBLIOGRAPHY

ALL OWNERS of pure-bred dogs will benefit themselves and their dogs by enriching th knowledge of breeds and of canine care, training, breeding, psychology and other important aspe of dog management. The following list of books covers further reading recommended by judg veterinarians, breeders, trainers and other authorities. Books may be obtained at the finer bo stores and pet shops, or through Howell Book House Inc., publishers, New York.

Breed Books

- AFGHAN HOUND, Complete *Miller & Gilbert*
- AIREDALE, New Complete *Edwards*
- AKITA, Complete *Linderman & Funk*
- ALASKAN MALAMUTE, Complete *Riddle & Seeley*
- BASSET HOUND, Complete *Braun*
- BEAGLE, New Complete *Noted Authorities*
- BLOODHOUND, Complete *Brey & Reed*
- BOXER, Complete *Denlinger*
- BRITTANY SPANIEL, Complete *Riddle*
- BULLDOG, New Complete *Hanes*
- BULL TERRIER, New Complete *Eberhard*
- CAIRN TERRIER, Complete *Marvin*
- CHESAPEAKE BAY RETRIEVER, Complete *Cherry*
- CHIHUAHUA, Complete *Noted Authorities*
- COCKER SPANIEL, New *Kraeuchi*
- COLLIE, New *Official Publication of the Collie Club of America*
- DACHSHUND, The New *Meistrell*
- DALMATIAN, The *Treen*
- DOBERMAN PINSCHER, New *Walker*
- ENGLISH SETTER, New Complete *Tuck, Howell & Graef*
- ENGLISH SPRINGER SPANIEL, New *Goodall & Gasow*
- FOX TERRIER, New Complete *Silvernail*
- GERMAN SHEPHERD DOG, New Complete *Bennett*
- GERMAN SHORTHAIRED POINTER, New *Maxwell*
- GOLDEN RETRIEVER, New Complete *Fischer*
- GORDON SETTER, Complete *Look*
- GREAT DANE, New Complete *Noted Authorities*
- GREAT DANE, The—Dogdom's Apollo *Draper*
- GREAT PYRENEES, Complete *Strang & Giffin*
- IRISH SETTER, New Complete *Eldredge & Vanacore*
- IRISH WOLFHOUND, Complete *Starbuck*
- JACK RUSSEL TERRIER, Complete *Plummer*
- KEESHOND, Complete *Peterson*
- LABRADOR RETRIEVER, Complete *Warwick*
- LHASA APSO, Complete *Herbel*
- MINIATURE SCHNAUZER, Complete *Eskrigge*
- NEWFOUNDLAND, New Complete *Chern*
- NORWEGIAN ELKHOUND, New Complete *Wallo*
- OLD ENGLISH SHEEPDOG, Complete *Mandeville*
- PEKINGESE, Quigley Book of *Quigley*
- PEMBROKE WELSH CORGI, Complete *Sargent & Harper*
- POODLE, New Complete *Hopkins & Irick*
- POODLE CLIPPING AND GROOMING BOOK, Complete *Kalstone*
- ROTTWEILER, Complete *Freeman*
- SAMOYED, Complete *Ward*
- SCHIPPERKE, Official Book of *Root, Martin, Kent*
- SCOTTISH TERRIER, New Complete *Marvin*
- SHETLAND SHEEPDOG, The New *Riddle*
- SHIH TZU, Joy of Owning *Seranne*
- SHIH TZU, The (English) *Dadds*
- SIBERIAN HUSKY, Complete *Demidoff*
- TERRIERS, The Book of All *Marvin*
- WEST HIGHLAND WHITE TERRIER, Complete *Marvin*
- WHIPPET, Complete *Pegram*
- YORKSHIRE TERRIER, Complete *Gordon & Bennett*

Breeding

- ART OF BREEDING BETTER DOGS, New *Onstott*
- BREEDING YOUR OWN SHOW DOG *Seranne*
- HOW TO BREED DOGS *Whitney*
- HOW PUPPIES ARE BORN *Prine*
- INHERITANCE OF COAT COLOR IN DOGS *Little*

Care and Training

- COUNSELING DOG OWNERS, Evans Guide for *Eva*
- DOG OBEDIENCE, Complete Book of *Saunde*
- NOVICE, OPEN AND UTILITY COURSES *Saunde*
- DOG CARE AND TRAINING FOR BOYS AND GIRLS *Saunde*
- DOG NUTRITION, Collins Guide to *Colli*
- DOG TRAINING FOR KIDS *Benjam*
- DOG TRAINING, Koehler Method of *Koeh*
- DOG TRAINING Made Easy *Tuck*
- GO FIND! Training Your Dog to Track *Da*
- GUARD DOG TRAINING, Koehler Method of *Koeh*
- MOTHER KNOWS BEST—The Natural Way to Train Your Dog *Benjam*
- OPEN OBEDIENCE FOR RING, HOME AND FIELD, Koehler Method of *Koeh*
- STONE GUIDE TO DOG GROOMING FOR ALL BREEDS *Sto*
- SUCCESSFUL DOG TRAINING, The Pearsall Guide to *Pears*
- TOY DOGS, Kalstone Guide to Grooming All *Kalsto*
- TRAINING THE RETRIEVER *Kers*
- TRAINING TRACKING DOGS, Koehler Method of *Koeh*
- TRAINING YOUR DOG—Step by Step Manual *Volhard & Fis*
- TRAINING YOUR DOG TO WIN OBEDIENCE TITLES *Mors*
- TRAIN YOUR OWN GUN DOG, How to *Gooc*
- UTILITY DOG TRAINING, Koehler Method of *Koeh*
- VETERINARY HANDBOOK, Dog Owner's Home *Carlson & Gi*

General

- AKC'S WORLD OF THE PURE-BRED DOG *American Kennel C*
- CANINE TERMINOLOGY *Sp*
- COMPLETE DOG BOOK, The *Official Publication American Kennel Cl*
- DOG IN ACTION, The *Ly*
- DOG BEHAVIOR, New Knowledge of *Pfaffenber*
- DOG JUDGE'S HANDBOOK *Tiet*
- DOG JUDGING, Nicholas Guide to *Nicho*
- DOG PEOPLE ARE CRAZY *Rid*
- DOG PSYCHOLOGY *Whitr*
- DOGSTEPS, Illustrated Gait at a Glance *Ell*
- DOG TRICKS *Haggerty & Benjan*
- ENCYCLOPEDIA OF DOGS, International *Dangerfield, Howell & Rid*
- EYES THAT LEAD—Story of Guide Dogs for the Blind *Tuc*
- FRIEND TO FRIEND—Dogs That Help Mankind *Schwa*
- FROM RICHES TO BITCHES *Shattu*
- HAPPY DOG/HAPPY OWNER *Sie*
- IN STITCHES OVER BITCHES *Shattu*
- JUNIOR SHOWMANSHIP HANDBOOK *Brown & Mas*
- MY TIMES WITH DOGS *Fletc*
- OUR PUPPY'S BABY BOOK (blue or pink)
- SUCCESSFUL DOG SHOWING, Forsyth Guide to *Fors*
- TRIM, GROOM & SHOW YOUR DOG, How to *Saund*
- WHY DOES YOUR DOG DO THAT? *Bergm*
- WILD DOGS in Life and Legend *Rid*
- WORLD OF SLED DOGS, From Siberia to Sport Racin *Coppin*